LEE AT APPOMATTOX

AND OTHER PAPERS

LEE AT APPOMATTOX

AND OTHER PAPERS

BY

CHARLES FRANCIS ADAMS

SECOND EDITION, ENLARGED.

Essay Index Reprint Series

 BOOKS FOR LIBRARIES PRESS
FREEPORT, NEW YORK

First Published 1902
Reprinted 1970

INTERNATIONAL STANDARD BOOK NUMBER:
0-8369-1901-7

LIBRARY OF CONGRESS CATALOG CARD NUMBER:
77-134047

PRINTED IN THE UNITED STATES OF AMERICA

PREFACE TO SECOND EDITION

THE last paper included in the present volume —
that entitled "Shall Cromwell have a Statue?" — was
not in the first edition of it. The obvious sequel to
the paper entitled "Lee at Appomattox," the occasion
for it had not arisen at the time the material for
the earlier edition was brought together. Read at
Worcester in October, 1901, the "Lee at Appomattox" was designed to influence, if possible, the course
of events then taking place in South Africa, calling attention to the example of Lee, thirty-six years before,
under not dissimilar circumstances. Republished in
England, it excited no inconsiderable notice, and was
referred to by Mr. Chamberlain in the House of Commons. Subsequently, and during the final stages of
the South African war, the capitulation of Lee was
always in the minds of influential members of the
British Cabinet, and official instructions were sent to
Lord Milner to take it as an example.

The future of South Africa is hereafter to develop
itself. As bearing upon its possibilities, it was of
interest to ascertain the existing state of feeling in
the United States, now that a generation had passed
away since Appomattox. An invitation to deliver the
annual oration before the Phi Beta Kappa Society of

the University of Chicago seemed to offer a fitting
place, as well as a favorable opportunity, for eliciting
an expression. The paper entitled "Shall Cromwell have a Statue?" was prepared with this end
in view. The result was undeniably instructive. A
very general response followed from all sections of
the country, though more especially from the South.
The character of that response varied. The response
from the North was, as a rule, couched in terms of general dissent from the proposition; but this dissent,
whether uttered through the press or by letter, was in no
single case couched in the declamatory, patriotic strain,
at once injured, indignant, and denunciatory or vitu-
perative, which would no less assuredly than naturally
have marked it thirty years ago. On the contrary, the
objections urged were invariably rational, and, in many
cases, well reasoned. Great personal respect for Lee,
and even admiration of him, were expressed; but the
noticeable feature was that, almost without exception,
the writers reverted to the days of slavery, and the
issues and events of the Civil War. The ground upon
which recognition was urged in the address seemed to
escape notice, though emphasized in its closing lines.

The essential and distinctive feature of the American Civil War, as contrasted with all previous struggles of a similar character, was the acceptance of
results by the defeated party at its close, and the subsequent rebuilding of an entire geographical community, socially and industrially, upon a new and,

in certain aspects, odious basis imposed on it by external force. The course thus instinctively pursued was indicative of much political sound sense; for it was due to a statesmanlike confidence in time, and the consciousness of an inherent race-capacity for leadership.

It was with this outcome of the war, and not with its anterior causes or its vicissitudes, that the name of Robert E. Lee should hereafter be commemorated. As is well known, after the total collapse of the Confederacy Jefferson Davis, accepting the position in which he found himself placed, lived and died, not without dignity, a disfranchised Confederate. To make use of the ordinary expression, he was never " reconstructed." Lee, on the other hand, in a way at once more marked and more dignified than any other character prominently connected with the Confederacy, contributed to the acceptance and rebuilding above referred to. He went home ; and, thenceforward, silently minded his own business. The Confederate, as well as the Unionist, enters as an essential factor into the Nation that now is, and, in future, is to be. It is this, the statue of Lee in Washington would typify, and preserve in perpetual memory.

C. F. A.

Lincoln, Mass., August 8, 1902.

CONTENTS

LEE AT APPOMATTOX
AND OTHER PAPERS

I

LEE AT APPOMATTOX [1]

THE present seems a sufficiently proper occasion, and this an appropriate place, to call attention to a matter perhaps only germane to the purpose of this Society, because as yet hardly antiquarian. None the less, historical in character, it conveys a lesson of grave present import.

One of the most unhappy, and, to those concerned in it, disastrous wars since the fall of Napoleon, is, in South Africa, now working itself to a close apparently still remote, and in every way unsatisfactory. There is reason to think that the conflict was unnecessary in its inception; that by timely and judicious action it might long since have been brought to a close; and that it now continues simply because the parties to it cannot be brought together to discuss and arrive at a sensible basis of adjustment, — a basis upon which both in reality would be not unwilling to agree. Nevertheless, as the cable despatches daily

[1] A paper read before the American Antiquarian Society at its annual meeting in Worcester, Mass., Wednesday, October 30, 1901.

show, the contest drags wearily along, to the probable destruction of one of the combatants, to the great loss of the other, and, so far as can be seen, in utter disregard of the best interests of both.

My immediate purpose, however, is to draw attention to the hairbreadth escape we ourselves had from a similar experience, now thirty-six years ago, and to assign to whom it belongs the credit for that escape. In one word, in the strong light of passing events, I think it now opportune to set forth the debt of gratitude this reunited country of ours — Union and Confederate, North and South — owes to Robert E. Lee, of Virginia.

Most of those here — for this is not a body of young men — remember the state of affairs which existed in the United States, especially in what was then known as the Confederate States, or the rebellious portion of the United States, in April, 1865. Such as are not yet as mature as that memory implies have read and heard thereof. It was in every respect almost the identical state of affairs which existed in South Africa at the time of the capture of Pretoria by General Roberts, in June a year ago.

On the 2d of April, 1865, the Confederate army found itself compelled to abandon the lines in front of Petersburg; and the same day — a very famous Sabbath — Jefferson Davis, hastily called from the church services he was attending, left Richmond to find, if he might, a new seat of government, at Danville. The following morning our forces at last entered the rebel capital. This was on a Monday; and, two days later, the Confederate President issued from Danville his manifesto. In it he said to the

people of the South, — " We have now entered upon
a new phase of the struggle. Relieved from the necessity of guarding particular points, our army will
be free to move from point to point, to strike the
enemy in detail far from his base. If, by the stress
of numbers, we should be compelled to a temporary
withdrawal from her [Virginia's] limits, or those of
any other border State, we will return until the baffled
and exhausted enemy shall abandon in despair his
endless and impossible task of making slaves of a
people resolved to be free." The policy, and line of
military action, thus indicated were precisely those laid
down and pursued by the Boer leaders during the last
sixteen months.

It is unnecessary for me even to refer to the series
of events which followed our occupation of Richmond,
and preceded the surrender of Appomattox. It is
sufficient to say that on the Friday which followed
the momentous Sunday, the capitulation of the Army
of Northern Virginia had become inevitable. Not
the less for that, the course thereafter to be pursued
as concerned further resistance on the part of the
Confederacy was still to be decided. As his Danville
proclamation showed, Jefferson Davis, though face to
face with grave disaster, had not for an instant given
up the thought of continuing the struggle. To do so
was certainly practicable, — far more practicable than
now in South Africa, both as respects forces in the
field and the area of country to be covered by the
invader. Foreign opinion, for instance, was on this
point settled; it was in Europe assumed as a certainty of the future that the conquest of the Confederacy was "impossible." The English journals had

always maintained, and still did maintain, that the defeat of Lee in the field, or even the surrender of all the Confederate armies, would be but the close of one phase of the war and the opening of another, — the final phase being a long, fruitless effort to subdue a people, at once united and resolved, occupying a region so vast that it would be impossible to penetrate every portion of it, much less to hold it in peaceful subjection. As an historical fact, on this point the scales, on the 9th of April, 1865, hung wavering in the balance; a mere turn of the hand would decide which way they were to incline. Thus, on the morning of that momentous day, it was an absolutely open question, an even chance, whether the course which subsequently was pursued should be pursued, or whether the leaders of the Confederacy would adopt the policy which President Krüger and Generals Botha and De Wet have in South Africa more recently adopted, and are now pursuing.

The decision rested in the hands of one man, the commander of the Army of Northern Virginia. Fairly reliable and very graphic accounts of interviews with General Lee during those trying days and in the morning hours of April 9th have either appeared in print or been told in conversation, and to two of these accounts I propose to call attention. The first I find in a book, entitled *The End of an Era*, recently published by John Sargent Wise, a son of Henry A. Wise, once prominent in our national politics. Though in 1865 but a youth of nineteen, John S. Wise was a hot Confederate, and had already been wounded in battle. At the time now in question he chanced, according to his own account, to have been sent by Jefferson Davis, then on his way to Danville, with despatches to Lee. At length, after many hair-breadth escapes from capture, he reached the Confederate headquarters late in the night following the disastrous battle of Sailor's Creek. By it the line of march of the Confederate army towards Danville had been intercepted, and it had been forced to seek a more circuitous route in the direction of Lynchburg. "It was past midnight," writes Mr. Wise, "when I found General Lee. He was in an open field north of Rice's Station and east of the High Bridge. A camp-fire of rails was burning low. Colonel Charles Marshall sat in an ambulance with a lantern and a lap-desk. He was preparing orders at the dictation of General Lee, who stood near, with one hand resting on a wheel and one foot upon the end of a log, watching intently the dying embers, as he spoke in a low tone to his amanuensis."

Explaining his mission to the Confederate leader, Mr. Wise passed the remaining hours of the night in bivouac near by; and early in the morning, the headquarters having moved, he again set out on his quest. It was now Friday, the 7th. He had not gone far when he stumbled across his father, in bivouac with his brigade. Henry A. Wise was then nearly sixty years of age; but the son found him wrapped in a blanket, stretched on the ground like a common soldier, and asleep among his men. Essentially a Virginian, and in many respects typically a Southerner and "fire-eater," Henry A. Wise was governor at the time of the John Brown Harper's Ferry raid, in October, 1859, his term expiring shortly after Brown's execution. A member of the Virginia Convention which, immediately after the fall of Sumter, passed the ordinance of secession, Wise, though an extreme States-rights man, had been in favor of "fighting it out in the Union," as the phrase then went; but when Virginia became plainly bent on secession, he unhesitatingly "went with his State." Commissioned as a brigadier-general almost at once, he had served in the Confederate army throughout the war, and was in the thick of the fight at Sailor's Creek. Now, on the morning after that engagement, aroused from an uneasy sleep by the unexpected appearance of his son, almost the first wish he expressed was to see General Lee, and he asked impetuously of his whereabouts. The two started together to go to him. John S. Wise has described vividly the aspect of affairs as they passed along : — "The roads and fields were filled with stragglers. They moved looking behind them, as if they expected to be attacked and harried by a pursuing foe. Demoralization, panic, abandonment of all hope, appeared on every hand. Wagons were rolling along without any order or system. Caissons and limber-chests, without commanding officers, seemed to be floating aimlessly upon a tide of disorganization. Rising to his full height, casting a glance around him like that of an eagle, and sweeping the horizon with his long arm and bony forefinger, my father exclaimed : ' This is the end ! ' It is impossible to convey an idea of the agony and the bitterness of his words and gestures." Then follows this description of the interview which ensued : —

" We found General Lee on the rear portico of the house that I have mentioned. He had washed his face in a tin basin, and stood drying his beard with a coarse

towel as we approached. 'General Lee,' exclaimed
my father, ' my poor, brave men are lying on yonder
hill more dead than alive. For more than a week they
have been fighting day and night, without food, and,
by God, sir, they shall not move another step until
somebody gives them something to eat!'

" ' Come in, general,' said General Lee soothingly.
' They deserve something to eat, and shall have it ; and
meanwhile you shall share my breakfast.' He disarmed
everything like defiance by his kindness.

" It was but a few moments, however, before my
father launched forth in a fresh denunciation of the
conduct of General Bushrod Johnson [1] in the engagement of the sixth. I am satisfied that General Lee
felt as he did ; but, assuming an air of mock severity,
he said, ' General, are you aware that you are liable to
court-martial and execution for insubordination and
disrespect toward your commanding officer?'

" My father looked at him with lifted eyebrows and
flashing eyes, and exclaimed : ' Shot ! You can't afford to shoot the men who fight for cursing those who
run away. Shot ! I wish you would shoot me. If
you don't, some Yankee probably will within the next
twenty-four hours.'

" Growing more serious, General Lee inquired what
he thought of the situation.

" ' Situation ? ' said the bold old man. ' There is
no situation ! Nothing remains, General Lee, but to
put your poor men on your poor mules and send them
home in time for spring ploughing. This army is

---

[1] Elsewhere in his book (pp. 358, 359), and in another connection,
J. S. Wise is equally severe in his characterization of Bushrod Johnson.

hopelessly whipped, and is fast becoming demoralized. These men have already endured more than I believed flesh and blood could stand, and I say to you, sir, emphatically, that to prolong the struggle is murder, and the blood of every man who is killed from this time forth is on your head, General Lee.'

"This last expression seemed to cause General Lee great pain. With a gesture of remonstrance, and even of impatience, he protested: 'Oh, general, do not talk so wildly. My burdens are heavy enough. What would the country think of me, if I did what you suggest?'

"'Country be d——d!' was the quick reply. 'There is no country. There has been no country, general, for a year or more. You are the country to these men. They have fought for you. They have shivered through a long winter for you. Without pay or clothes, or care of any sort, their devotion to you and faith in you have been the only things which have held this army together. If you demand the sacrifice, there are still left thousands of us who will die for you. You know the game is desperate beyond redemption, and that, if you so announce, no man or government or people will gainsay your decision. That is why I repeat that the blood of any man killed hereafter is upon your head.'

"General Lee stood for some time at an open window, looking out at the throng now surging by upon the roads and in the fields, and made no response." [1]

It will be remembered that John Sargent Wise was individually present at this conversation, a youth of nineteen. I have as little respect as any one well can

[1] *The End of an Era*, pp. 433-435.

h ive for the recollection of thirty years since as a basis
of history. Nevertheless, it would seem quite out of
the question that a youth of only nineteen could have
been present at such a scene as is here described, and
that the words which then passed, and the incidents
which occurred, should not have been indelibly im-
printed upon his memory. I am disposed, therefore,
to consider this reliable historical material. Meanwhile, it so chances that I am able to supplement it by
similar testimony from another quarter.

Some years ago I was, for a considerable period,
closely associated with General E. P. Alexander, who,
in its time, had been chief of artillery in Longstreet's famous corps ; and it was General Alexander
who, on the morning of July 3, 1863, opened on the
Union line at Gettysburg what Hancock described as
" a most terrific and appalling cannonade," intended
to prepare the way for the advance of Pickett's division. In April, 1865, General Alexander was, if my
recollection serves me right, in command of the artillery of the Army of Northern Virginia. In many
connections I had found occasion to notice the singular tenacity of his memory. He seemed to forget
nothing ; nor was he less accurate in matters of detail
than in generalities. He delighted in reminiscence
of the great war, and he recalled its incidents with
the particularity of a trained officer of the general
staff. He thus many times, always with the same
precision, repeated to me, or in my hearing, the details
of interviews with Lee during the retreat from Petersburg, and more especially of one, on the morning of
April 9th. Of what he said I have since retained
a vivid memory. During Friday, April 7th, the

day Wise found his way to Lee's headquarters, the weary Confederate army pressed forward, vainly trying to elude the hot pursuit of the Union advance, led by Sheridan. On Saturday, the 8th, according to General Alexander, the leading Confederate officers became so demoralized that one of them, General Pendleton, was authorized by a sort of informal council to wait on Lee, and to tell him that, a surrender seeming inevitable, they were prepared to take the responsibility of advising it. Recognizing his military obligations, and not yet convinced that his command was hopelessly involved, Lee distinctly resented the advice. He told General Pendleton that there were too many men yet remaining in the ranks to think of laying down arms, and his air and manner conveyed a rebuke.

Twenty-four additional hours of fasting, marching, and fighting put a new face on the situation. Two days before, on the 7th, shortly after the Wise interview, General Alexander had met Lee at Farmville, and a consultation over the maps took place. Alexander had then pointed out Appomattox as " the danger point," the roads to Lynchburg there intersecting, and the enemy having the shortest line. Sheridan did not lose his advantage, and, on Sunday, the 9th of April, Lee found his further progress blocked. That morning General Alexander again met Lee. Both realized the situation fully. Moreover, as chief of artillery, Alexander was well aware that the limber-chests were running low ; his arm of the service was in no condition to go into another engagement. Yet the idea of an abandonment of the cause had never occurred to him as among the probabilities.

All night he had lain awake, thinking as to what was next to be done. Finally he had come to the conclusion that there was but one course to pursue. The Confederate army, while nominally capitulating, must in reality disperse, and those composing it should be instructed, whether individually or as part of detachments, to get each man to his own State in the most direct way and shortest possible time, and report to the governor thereof, with a view to a further and continuous resistance.

Thus, exactly what is now taking place in South Africa was to take place in the Confederacy. General Alexander told me that, as he passed his batteries on his way to headquarters, the men called out to him, in cheery tones, that there were still some rounds remaining in the caissons, and that they were ready to renew the fight. He found Lee seated on the trunk of a fallen tree before a dying camp-fire. He was dressed in uniform, and invited Alexander to take a seat beside him. He then asked his opinion of the situation, and of the course proper to be pursued. Full of the idea which dominated his mind, Alexander proceeded at once to propound his plan, for it seemed to him the only plan worthy of consideration. As he went on, General Lee, looking steadily into the fire with an abstracted air, listened patiently. Alexander said his full say. A brief pause ensued, which Lee finally broke in somewhat these words: " No ! General Alexander, that will not do. You must remember we are a Christian people. We have fought this fight as long as, and as well as, we knew how. We have been defeated. For us, as a Christian people, there is now but one course to pursue. We

must accept the situation ; these men must go home
and plant a crop, and we must proceed to build up
our country on a new basis. We cannot have recourse to the methods you suggest." I remember
being deeply impressed with Alexander's comment, as
he repeated these words of Lee. They had evidently
burned themselves into his memory. He said : " I
had nothing to urge in reply. I felt that the man
had soared way up above me, — he dominated me completely. I rose from beside him ; silently mounted
my horse ; rode back to my command ; and waited
for the order to surrender."

Then and there, Lee decided its course for the Confederacy. And I take it there is not one solitary man
in the United States to-day, North or South, who does
not feel that he decided right.

The Army of Northern Virginia, it will be remembered, laid down its arms on the 9th of April. But
General Joseph Johnston was in command of another
Confederate army then confronting Sherman, in
North Carolina, and it was still an open question what
course he would pursue. His force numbered over
40,000 combatants ; more than the entire muster of
the Boers in their best estate. Lee's course decided
Johnston's. S. R. Mallory, who was present on the
occasion, has left a striking account of a species of
council held at Greensboro, North Carolina, on the
evening of the 10th of April, by Jefferson Davis and
the members of his cabinet, with General Johnston.
Davis, stubborn in temper, and bent on a policy of continuous irregular resistance, expressed the belief that
the disasters recently sustained, though "terrible,"
should not be regarded as "fatal." " I think," he

added, " we can whip the enemy yet, if our people
will turn out." When he ceased speaking, a pause
ensued. Davis at last said, " We should like to hear
your views, General Johnston." Whereupon Johnston, without preface or introduction, and with a tone
and manner almost spiteful, remarked in his terse,
concise, demonstrative way, as if seeking to condense
thoughts that were crowding for utterance : " My
views are, sir, that our people are tired of the war,
feel themselves whipped, and will not fight." [1]

We all know what followed. Lee's great military
prestige and moral ascendency made it easy for some
of the remaining Confederate commanders, like Johnston, to follow the precedent he set ; while others of
them, like Kirby Smith, found it imposed upon them.
A firm direction had been given to the course of
events ; an intelligible policy was indicated.

I have in my possession a copy of the *Index*, the
weekly journal published in London during our civil
war. The official organ of the Confederate agents
in Europe, it was intended for the better enlighten-
ment of foreign opinion, more especially the English
press. The surrender of Lee was commented upon
editorially in the issue of that paper for April 27th.
" The war is far from concluded," it declared. " A
strenuous resistance and not surrender was the unalterable determination of the Confederate authorities,
. . . and if the worst comes to the worst there is the
trans-Mississippi department, where the remnant of
[Johnston's] army can find a shelter, and a new and
safe starting-point." [2] On the 11th of May follow-

---

[1] Alfriend: *Life of Jefferson Davis*, pp. 622–626.

[2] Captain Raphael Semmes, of *Alabama* fame, wrote as follows, in

ing, the surrender of Johnston's army was announced on the same terms as that of Lee; but in summing up the situation, the *Index* still found "the elements of a successful, or, at least, a protracted resistance." On the 25th of May, it had an article entitled "Southern Resistance in Texas," in which it announced that, "Such a war will be fierce, ferocious, and of long duration," — in a word, such an expiring struggle as we are to-day witnessing in South Africa. In its issue of June 1st, the *Index* commented on "The capture of President Davis;" and then, and not until then, forestalling the trans-Mississippi surrender of Kirby Smith, brought to it by the following mail, it raised the wailing cry, "*Fuit Ilium*. . . . The South has fallen."

Comparing the situation which then existed in the Confederacy with that now in South Africa, it must also be remembered that General Lee assumed the responsibility he did assume, and decided the policy to be pursued in the way it was decided, under no

a private letter to an English friend, published in the London *Morning Herald*, during March, 1865: "The State of Texas alone has within her limits all the materials, and is fast getting the appliances, for equipping and maintaining armies, and when you reflect that she has three times as much territory as France, and that countless herds of horses and beef cattle wander over her boundless prairies, you can well imagine with what contempt this warlike people regard the insane threat of subjugation. If our armies were driven to-morrow across the Mississippi River, we could still fight the enemy for a century to come in Texas alone. So dismiss all your fears, my friend, our independence is an accomplished fact, let the war continue as long as the Yankee pleases, and with what varying results it may." In its issue of March 15, 1865, the London *Times* editorially said: "These territories are too vast to be occupied, and the elements of rebellion they contain are too rife to be left to themselves. They may be penetrated in every direction, but we do not see how they are to be held or subdued."

ameliorating conditions. Politically, unconditional surrender was insisted upon ; and Lee's surrender was, politically, unconditional. Even more so was Johnston's ; for, in Johnston's case, the modifying terms of capitulation agreed on in the first place between him and Sherman were roughly disallowed at Washington, and the truce, by an order coming thence, abruptly terminated. Then Johnston did what Lee had already done ; ignoring Davis, he surrendered his army.

In the case of the Confederacy, also, an absolutely unconditional political surrender implied much. The Emancipation Proclamation of January, 1863, which confiscated the most valuable chattel property of the Confederacy, remained the irreversible law of the land. The inhabitants of the South were, moreover, as one man disfranchised. When they laid down their arms they had before them, first, a military government ; and, after that, the supremacy of their former slaves. A harder fate for a proud people to accept could not well be imagined. The bitterness of feeling, the hatred, was, too, extreme. It may possibly be argued that the conditions in this country then were different from those now in South Africa, inasmuch as here it was a civil war, — a conflict between communities of the same race and speech involving the vital question of the supremacy of law. This argument, however, seems to imply that, in case of strife of this description, a general severity may fairly be resorted to in excess of that permissible between nations ; in other words, that we are justified in treating our brethren with greater harshness than we would treat aliens in blood and speech. Obviously, this is a questionable contention.

It might possibly also be claimed that the bitterness of civil war is not so insurmountable as that of one involving a question of race dominance. Yet it is difficult to conceive bitterness of greater intensity than existed between the sections at the close of our civil war. There is striking evidence of this in the book of Mr. Wise, from which I have already quoted. Toward its close he speaks of the death of Lincoln. He then adds the following: —

" Perhaps I ought to chronicle that the announcement was received with demonstrations of sorrow. If I did, I should be lying for sentiment's sake. Among the higher officers and the most intelligent and conservative men, the assassination caused a shudder of horror at the heinousness of the act, and at the thought of its possible consequences; but among the thoughtless, the desperate, and the ignorant, it was hailed as a sort of retributive justice. In maturer years I have been ashamed of what I felt and said when I heard of that awful calamity. However, men ought to be judged for their feelings and their speech by the circumstances of their surroundings. For four years we had been fighting. In that struggle, all we loved had been lost. Lincoln incarnated to us the idea of oppression and conquest. We had seen his face over the coffins of our brothers and relatives and friends, in the flames of Richmond, in the disaster at Appomattox. In blood and flame and torture the temples of our lives were tumbling about our heads. We were desperate and vindictive, and whosoever denies it forgets or is false. We greeted his death in a spirit of reckless hate, and hailed it as bringing agony and bitterness to those who were the cause of our own agony and bitterness. To us, Lincoln was an inhuman monster, Grant a butcher, and Sherman a fiend."

Indeed, recalling the circumstances of that time, it is fairly appalling to consider what in 1865 must have occurred, had Robert E. Lee then been of the same turn of mind as was Jefferson Davis, or as implacable and unyielding in disposition as Krüger or Botha have more recently proved. The national government had in arms a million men, inured to the hardships and accustomed to the brutalities of war; Lincoln had been freshly assassinated; the temper of the North was thoroughly aroused, while its patience was exhausted. An irregular warfare would inevitably have resulted, a warfare without quarter.[1] The Confederacy would have been reduced to a smouldering wilderness, — to what South Africa to-day is. In such a death grapple, the North, both in morale and in means, would have suffered only less than the South. From both sections that fate was averted.

It is not my purpose to enter into any criticism of the course of events in South Africa, or of the policy there on either side pursued. It will be for the future to decide whether the prolonged, irregular resistance we are witnessing is justifiable, or, if justifiable, whether it is wise. Neither of these questions do I propose to discuss. My purpose simply is to call attention, in view of what is now taking place elsewhere,

---

[1] Commenting on the "Suddenness of the Collapse," the *Index* said, editorially, in its issue of June 8, 1865: "The loss of the armies left no alternative but private war, which never yet redeemed a country without foreign help, and which is as much directed against society as against a public foe. Such a course was inconsistent with the genius of the Southern people, which is eminently law-abiding and orderly. Brave men know how to accept defeat, and the Southerners have accepted theirs, bitter though it is, as only brave men can."

to the narrow escape we ourselves, thirty-six years ago, had from a similar awful catastrophe. And I again say that, as we look to-day upon Krüger and Botha and De Wet, and the situation existing in the Transvaal and the Orange Free State, I doubt if one single man in the United States, North or South, — whether he participated in the civil war or was born since that war ended, — would fail to acknowledge an infinite debt of gratitude to the Confederate leader, who on the 9th of April, 1865, decided, as he did decide, that the United States, whether Confederate or Union, was a Christian community, and that his duty was to accept the responsibility which the fate of war had imposed upon him, — to decide in favor of a new national life, even if slowly and painfully to be built up by his own people under conditions arbitrarily and by force imposed on them.

In one of the Confederate accounts of the great war [1] is to be found the following description of Lee's return to his Richmond home immediately after he had at Appomattox sealed the fate of the Confederacy. With it I will conclude this paper. On the afternoon of the previous day, the first of those paroled from the surrendered Army of Northern Virginia had straggled back to Richmond. The writer thus goes on : " Next morning a small group of horsemen appeared on the further side of the pontoons. By some strange intuition it was known that General Lee was among them, and a crowd collected all along the route he would take, silent and bareheaded. There was no excitement, no hurrahing; but as the great chief passed, a deep, loving murmur, greater than these,

---

[1] De Leon: *Four Years in Rebel Capitals*, p. 367.

rose from the very hearts of the crowd. Taking off his hat and simply bowing his head, the man great in adversity passed silently to his own door ; it closed upon him, and his people had seen him for the last time in his battle harness."

AFTER preparing the foregoing paper, I wrote to General Alexander, asking him to verify my recollection of the account of what passed at his meeting with General Lee at Appomattox. His reply did not reach me in time for the meeting of the American Antiquarian Society, at which the paper was read. He wrote in part as follows : " I am greatly interested in what you wish, having often thought and spoken of the contrast between Lee's views of the duty of the leaders of a people, and those held at the time by President Davis, and now held by Krüger and the Boer leaders ; and I have written of it, too, in my own war recollections, which I am writing out for my children.

" *Essentially*, your recollections are entirely correct ; though some of the details are not exact. Two days before, I had talked with General Lee over his map, and noted Appomattox Courthouse as the ' danger point.' When I came up on the 9th to where he had halted on the road, he called me to him, and began by referring to previous talk, and then he asked me, — ' What shall we do to-day ? ' For an account of our conversation I will cut out of a scrap-book two pages which contain a clipping from the Philadelphia *Press* of a letter I wrote twenty years ago."

In the course of his letter, General Alexander further said, — " The gist of my argument to General Lee was that the governors of the Southern States might make some sort of ' Terms,' which would bar trials for treason, etc. ; and it was based on the assumption that Grant would demand 'unconditional surrender.' And I certainly think, too, that Grant deserves equal praise and gratitude for *his* high-mindedness in his liberal treatment of his foe — more absolutely at his mercy than was Buckner at Fort Donelson, or Pemberton at Vicksburg." . . .

"I particularly remember, too, his (Lee's) dwelling on the fact that the men were already, as it were, 'demoralized' by four years of war, and would but too easily become mere bushwhackers."

The clipping referred to was from an issue of the *Press* of July, 1881. The narrative contained in it, now not easily accessible, is of such interest and obvious historical value, as throwing light on what was passing in Lee's mind at one of the most critical moments in the national history, that I here reproduce it in full : —

"The morning of the 9th of April, 1865, found the Confederate army in a position in which its inevitable fate was apparent to every man in it. The skirmishing which had begun in its front as its advance guard reached Appomattox Courthouse the night before had developed into a sharp fight, in which the continuous firing of the artillery and the steady increase of the musketry told to all that a heavy force had been thrown across our line of march, and that reinforcements to it were steadily arriving. The long trains of wagons and artillery were at first halted in the road and then parked in the adjoining fields, allowing the rear of the column to close up and additional troops to pass to the front to reinforce the advanced guard and to form a reserve line of battle in their rear,

under cover of which they might retire when necessary. While these dispositions were taking place,
General Lee, who had dismounted and was standing
near a fire on a hill about two miles from the Courthouse, called the writer to him, and, inviting him to a
seat on a log near by, referred to the situation and
asked : ' What shall we do this morning ? ' Although
this opportunity of expressing my views was unexpected, the situation itself was not, for two days
before, while near Farmville, in a consultation with
General Lee over his map, the fact of the enemy's
having the shortest road to the Appomattox Courthouse had been noted and the probability of serious
difficulty there anticipated, and in the mean time
there had been ample opportunity for reflection on all
of the emergencies that might arise. Without replying directly to the question, however, I answered first
that it was due to my command (of artillery) that I
should tell him that they were in as good spirits,
though short of ammunition and with poor teams, as
they had ever been, and had begged, if it came to a
surrender, to be allowed to expend first every round
of ammunition on the enemy, and surrender only the
empty ammunition chests. To this General Lee replied that there were remaining only two divisions of
infantry sufficiently well organized and strong to be
fully relied upon (Field's and Mahone's), and that
they did not number eight thousand muskets together ;
and that that force was not sufficient to warrant him
in undertaking a pitched battle. ' Then,' I answered,
' general, there are but two alternatives, to surrender
or to order the army to abandon its trains and disperse in the woods and bushes, every man for himself,

and each to make his best way, with his arms, either
to the army of General Johnston, in North Carolina,
or home to the governor of his State. We have all
foreseen the probability of such an alternative for two
days, and I am sure I speak the sentiments of many
others besides my own in urging that rather than surrender the army you should allow us to disperse in
the woods and go, every man for himself.'

" ' What would you hope to accomplish by this ? '

" I answered : ' If there is any hope at all for the
Confederacy or for the separate States to make terms
with the United States or for any foreign assistance,
this course stands the chances, whatever they may be ;
while if this army surrenders this morning, the Confederacy is dead from that moment. Grant will turn
150,000 fresh men against Johnston, and with the
moral effect of our surrender he will go, and Dick
Taylor and Kirby Smith will have to follow like a row
of bricks, while if we all take to dispersing in the
woods, we inaugurate a new phase of the war, which
may be indefinitely prolonged, and it will at least
have great moral effect in showing that in our pledges
to fight it out to the last we meant what we said. And
even, general, if there is no hope at all in this course
or in any other, and if the fate of the Confederacy is
sealed whatever we do, there is one other consideration which your soldiers have a right to urge on you,
and that is your own military reputation, in which
every man in this army, officer or private, feels the
utmost personal pride and has a personal property
that his children will prize after him. The Yankees
brought Grant here from the West, after the failure
of all their other generals, as one who had whipped

everybody he had ever fought against, and they call him " Unconditional Surrender " Grant, and have been bragging in advance that you would have to surrender too. Now, general, I think you ought to spare us all the mortification of having you to ask Grant for terms, and have him answer that he had no terms to offer you.'

" I still remember most vividly the emotion with which I made this appeal, increasing as I went on, until my whole heart was in it; and it seemed to me at the moment one which no soldier could resist and against which no consideration whatever could be urged; and when I closed, after urging my suggestions at greater length than it is necessary to repeat, looking him in the face and speaking with more boldness than I usually found in his presence, I had not a doubt that he must adopt some such course as I had urged.

" He heard me entirely through, however, very calmly, and then asked : ' How many men do you estimate would escape if I were to order the army to disperse ? '

" I replied : ' I suppose two thirds of us could get away, for the enemy could not disperse to follow us through the woods.'

" He said : ' We have here only about sixteen thousand men with arms, and not all of those who could get away would join General Johnston, but most of them would try and make their way to their homes and families, and their numbers would be too small to be of any material service either to General Johnston or to the governors of the States. I recognize fully that the surrender of this army is the end of the Confederacy, but no course we can take can prevent or even delay that result. I have never believed that we would receive foreign assistance, or get our liberty otherwise than by our own arms. The end is now upon us, and it only remains to decide how we shall close the struggle. But in deciding this question we are to approach it not only as soldiers but as Christian men, deciding on matters which involve a great deal else besides their own feelings. If I should order this army to disperse, the men with their arms, but without organization or control, and without provisions or money, would soon be wandering through every State in the Confederacy, some seeking to get to their homes, and some with no homes to go to. Many would be compelled to rob and plunder as they went to save themselves from starvation, and the enemy's cavalry would pursue in small detachments, particularly in efforts to catch the general officers, and raid and burn over large districts which they will otherwise never reach, and the result would be the inauguration of lawlessness and terror and of organized bands of robbers all over the South. Now, as Christian men, we have not the right to bring this state of affairs upon the country, whatever the sacrifice of personal pride involved. And as for myself, you young men might go to bushwhacking, but I am too old ; and even if it were right for me to disperse the army, I should surrender myself to General Grant as the only proper course for one of my years and position. But I am glad to be able to tell you one thing for your comfort: General Grant will not demand an unconditional surrender, but offers us most liberal terms — the paroling of the whole army not to fight until

exchanged.' He then went on to speak of the probable details of the terms of surrender, and to say that
about 10 A. M. he was to meet General Grant in the
rear of the army, and would then accept the terms
offered.

"Sanguine as I had been when he commenced that
'he *must* acquiesce in my views,' I had not one word
to reply when he had finished. He spoke slowly and
deliberately, and with some feeling ; and the completeness of the considerations he advanced, and which he
dwelt upon with more detail than I can now fully recall, speaking particularly of the women and children,
as the greatest sufferers in the state of anarchy which
a dispersion of the army would bring about, and his reference to what would be his personal course if he did
order such dispersion, all indicated that the question
was not then presented to his mind for the first time.

"A short time after this conversation General Lee
rode to the rear of the army to meet General Grant
and arrange the details of the surrender. He had
started about a half hour when General Fitz Lee sent
word to General Longstreet that he had broken through
a portion of the enemy's line, and that the whole army
might make its way through. General Longstreet, on
learning this, directed Colonel Haskell of the artillery,[1]

---

[1] Colonel J. C. Haskell, of South Carolina; "a born and a resource-
ful artilleryman, [who] knew no such thing as fear." General Longstreet evidently used General Alexander's paper in the Philadelphia
Press in preparing the account, contained in his *Manassas to Appomattox*, of what occurred on the day of Lee's surrender. A further re-
ferehce to Colonel Haskell may be found in Wise : *The End of an Era*
(p. 360). Longstreet says that, at Appomattox, "there were 'surrendered or paroled' 28,356 officers and men." A week previous to the
capitulation, Lee's and Johnston's combined forces numbered consid-
erably over 100,000 combatants. [C. F. A.]

who was very finely mounted, to ride after General Lee at utmost speed, killing his horse, if necessary, and recall him before he could reach General Grant. Colonel Haskell rode as directed, and a short distance in rear of the army found General Lee and some of his staff dismounted by the roadside. As he with difficulty checked his horse, General Lee came up quickly, asking what was the matter; but, without waiting for a reply, said: 'Oh! I'm afraid you have killed your beautiful mare. What did you ride her so hard for?' On hearing General Longstreet's message, he asked some questions about the situation, and sent word to General Longstreet to use his own discretion in making any movements; but he did not himself return, and in a short while another message was received that the success of the cavalry under General Fitz Lee was but temporary, and that there was no such gap in the enemy's line as had been supposed. Soon afterward a message was brought from the enemy's picket that General Grant had passed around to the front and would meet General Lee at Appomattox Courthouse, and General Lee accordingly returned.

" Meanwhile, as the Confederate line under General Gordon was slowly falling back from Appomattox Courthouse after as gallant a fight against overwhelming odds as it had ever made, capturing and bringing safely off with it an entire battery of the enemy's, General Custer, commanding a division of Federal cavalry, rode forward with a flag of truce, and, the firing having ceased on both sides, was conducted to General Longstreet as commanding temporarily in General Lee's absence. Custer demanded the surrender of the army to himself and General Sheridan, to which Gen-

eral Longstreet replied that General Lee was in communication with General Grant upon that subject, and
that the issue would be determined between them.
Custer replied that he and Sheridan were independent
of Grant, and unless the surrender was made to them
they would ' pitch in ' at once.   Longstreet's answer
was a peremptory order [to Custer] at once [to return]
to his own lines, and ' try it if he liked.'   Custer was
accordingly escorted back; but fire was not reopened,
and both lines remained halted, the Confederate about
a half mile east of the Courthouse.

" General Lee, returning from the rear shortly afterward, halted in a small field adjoining Sweeney's house,
a little in rear of his skirmish line, and, seated on
some rails under an apple-tree, awaited a message from
General Grant.   This apple-tree was not only entirely
cut up for mementos within two days afterward, but
its very roots were dug up and carried away under
the false impression that the surrender took place
under it.[1]

" About noon a Federal staff officer rode up and announced that General Grant was at the Courthouse,
and General Lee with one of his staff accompanied
him back.   As he left the apple-tree General Longstreet's last words were : ' Unless he offers you liberal
terms, general, let us fight it out.'

" It would be a difficult task to convey to one who

---

[1] The surrender took place in the house of a Mr. McLean, a gentleman who, by a strange coincidence, owned a farm on Bull Run at the
beginning of the war. General Beauregard's headquarters were at
McLean's house, just in the rear of Blackburn's ford, during the first
battle fought by the army, July 18, 1861. McLean moved from Bull
Run to get himself out of the theatre of war. The last battle took
place on his new farm, and the surrender in his new residence.

was not present an idea of the feeling of the Confederate army during the few hours which so suddenly, and so unexpectedly to it, terminated its existence, and with it all hopes of the Confederacy. Having been sharply engaged that very morning, and its movements arrested by the flag of truce, while one portion of it was actually fighting and nearly all the rest, infantry and artillery, had just been formed in line of battle in sight and range of the enemy, and with guns unlimbered, it was impossible to realize fully that the war, with all its hopes, its ambitions, and its hardships, was thus ended. There was comparatively very little conversation, and men stood in groups looking over the scene ; but the groups were unusually silent. It was not at first generally known that a surrender was inevitable, but there was a remarkable pre-acquiescence in whatever General Lee should determine, and the warmest expressions of confidence in his judgment. Ranks and discipline were maintained as usual, and there is little doubt that, had General Lee decided to fight that afternoon, the troops would not have disappointed him. About 4 P. M. he returned from the Courthouse, and, after informing the principal officers of the terms of the surrender, started to ride back to his camp.

" The universal desire to express to him the unabated love and confidence of the army had led to the formation of the gunners of a few battalions of artillery along the roadside, with orders to take off their hats in silence as he rode by. When he approached, however, the men could not be restrained, but burst into the wildest cheering, which the adjacent infantry lines took up ; and, breaking ranks, they all crowded around him, cheering at the tops of their voices. General Lee stopped his horse, and, after gaining silence, made the only speech to his men that he ever made. He was very brief, and gave no excuses or apologies for his surrender, but said he had done all in his power for his men, and urged them to go as quickly and quietly to their homes as possible, to resume peaceful avocations, and to be as good citizens as they had been soldiers ; and this advice marked the course which he himself pursued so faithfully to the end."

BOSTON, November 6, 1901.

NOTE. — While the foregoing was passing through the press, there appeared in the *Century* magazine for April, 1902 (volume lxiii. pp. 921–944), a series of papers relating to the surrender of Appomattox. One of these papers, entitled "Personal Recollections of the Break-up of the Confederacy," was by General Alexander. Another was by Colonel Charles Marshall, the military secretary to General Lee, referred to by Mr. John Sargent Wise. (*Supra*, page 5.) In the *Century* paper General Alexander recounts the circumstances of his interview with General Lee more in detail, and with greater exactness, than in his contribution to the Philadelphia *Press* of twenty years before ; but the two narratives differ in no material respect.

II

THE TREATY OF WASHINGTON : BEFORE AND AFTER [1]

NEGOTIATED during the spring of 1871, and signed on the 8th of May of that year, the Treaty of Washington not only put to rest questions of difference of long standing, big with danger, between the two leading maritime nations of the world, but it incorporated new principles of the first importance into the body of accepted International Law. The degree, moreover, to which that treaty has influenced, and is now influencing, the course of human affairs and historical evolution in both hemispheres is, I think, little appreciated. To that subject I propose this evening to address myself.

The time to make use of unpublished material bearing on this period — material not found in newspapers, public archives, or memoirs, which have already seen the light — has, moreover, come. So far as any considerable political or diplomatic result can be said to be the work of one man, the Treaty of Washington

[1] This paper was originally prepared as an address, to be delivered before the New York Historical Society on its ninety-seventh anniversary, on the evening of Tuesday, November 19, 1901. Owing to the length to which it grew in preparation, it was on that occasion so compressed in delivery as to occupy but one hour. Subsequently revised, it supplied the material for a course of four lectures before the Lowell Institute in Boston, on the 3d, 6th, 10th, and 13th of the following December.

was the work of Hamilton Fish.   Mr. Fish died in
September, 1893 — now over eight years ago.   When
the treaty was negotiated, General Grant was President; and General Grant has been dead more than
sixteen years.   In speaking of this treaty, and describ-
ing the complications which led up to it, and to which
it incidentally gave rise, frequent reference must be
made to Charles Sumner and John Lothrop Motley;
and, while Mr. Sumner died nearly twenty-eight years
ago, Mr. Motley followed him by a little more than
three years only.   Thus, between the 11th of March,
1874, and the 7th of September, 1893, all those I have
named — prominent actors in the drama I am to describe — passed from the stage.   They belonged to a
generation that is gone.   Other public characters have
since come forward; new issues have presented themselves.   The once famous Alabama claims are now
" ancient history," and the average man of to-day
hardly knows what is referred to when allusion is
made to " Consequential Damages," or " National
Injuries," in connection therewith; indeed, why should
he? — for when, in June, 1872, that issue was at Geneva
finally put to rest, he who is now (1901) President of
the United States was a boy in his fourteenth year.
None the less, as the Treaty of Washington was a very
memorable historical event, so President Grant, Secretary Fish, Senator Sumner, and Minister Motley are
great historic figures.   Their achievements and dissen-
sions have already been much discussed, and will be
more discussed hereafter; and to that discussion I
propose now to contribute something.   My theme in-
cludes the closing scene of a great drama; a scene in
the development of which the striking play of individual character will long retain an interest.

History aside, moreover, the Treaty of Washington itself is a living, and it may even be said a controlling, factor in the international situation of to-day : —

> " And enterprises of great pith and moment
> With this regard their currents turn awry,
> And lose the name of action."

That treaty was signed at Washington on the 8th of May, 1871; the battle of Majuba Hill took place in South Africa nine years from the following 27th of February. Separated in time, and occurring on different sides of both the equator and the Atlantic, the two events had little apparent bearing on each other; yet the settlement effected through the American treaty forestalled the outcome of the African war.

I

Between 1861 and 1865 the United States was engaged in a struggle which called for the exertion of all the force at its command ; as, to a lesser extent, Great Britain is now. The similarity between the war in South Africa and the Confederate war in this country early attracted the attention of English writers, and one of the most thoughtful of their civil and military critics has put on record a detailed comparison of the two.[1] " Each of these conflicts," this authority asserts, " had its origin in conditions of long and gradual growth, rendering an ultimate explosion inevitable. Each of them deeply affected the whole existence of the communities which found themselves in antagonism. In each case, therefore, the energy and the duration of the fighting far exceeded the expectations of most of those who might have seemed

[1] Spenser Wilkinson : *War and Policy* (1900), pp. 422–439.

to be in a position to judge." To the same effect, another author [1] refers to the " striking resemblance " between the two struggles. " The analogy," he says, " like any other historical analogy, must not be pressed too far, but there is a remarkable parallelism in the general character of the political issues, in the course of negotiations preceding war, and in the actual conduct of the campaigns, a parallelism which sometimes comes out in the most insignificant details." This analogy the writer might advantageously have carried into his discussion of the effect of both wars on foreign opinion at the time of each. He correctly enough admits that, during the struggle in South Africa, — " The whole of Europe almost was against us, not so much from any consideration of the merits of the case, as from the dislike and jealousy of England which have developed so enormously in the last decade ; " but he significantly adds, — " In the United States sympathies were much divided." In fact, during our Civil War the entire sympathies and hearty good-will of the great body of those composing what are known as the governing and influential classes throughout Europe, west of the Vistula, were enlisted on the side of the Confederacy. In these classes would be included all those of rank, members of the learned professions, the commercial, financial and banking circles, and officers of the two services — the army and the navy. And then also, as in the case of the South African war, this instructive accord arose, not " from any consideration of the merits of the case," but from " dislike and jealousy ; " — the dislike and jealousy of American democracy, which " had developed so enor-

[1] The Times : *History of the War in South Africa.*

mously in the course " of the decade or two immediately preceding the outbreak of 1861. This was no-
ticeably the case in England; there " sympathies were
much divided," but the line of cleavage was horizontal.
Speaking largely, and allowing, of course, for numerous
exceptional cases, the more conscientious and thinking among the poor and lowly, especially of the non-
conformists, instinctively sympathized with the Union
and the North; while of the privileged and the monied,
the commercial and manufacturing classes, it may
safely be asserted that nine out of ten were heart
and soul on the side of the rebel and slaveholder. It
is only necessary for me further to premise that as
respects foreign governments, and the principles of
international law and amity relating to the concession
of belligerent rights, — the recognition of nationality,
neutrality, and participation of neutrals, direct and
indirect, in the operations of war, — the position of
the Confederacy and the two South African republics
were in essentials the same. The latter, it is true,
were not maritime countries, so that no questions of
blockade, and comparatively few of contraband, arose;
but, on the other hand, while the Confederates were,
as respects foreign nations, insurgents, pure and simple,
the South African republics had governments *de jure*
as well as *de facto*. Great Britain claimed over them
a species of suzerainty only, undefined at best, and
plainly questionable by any power disinclined to recognize it. This the British authorities[1] deplore, and
try to explain away; but the fact is not denied.

So far, therefore, as the status of those in arms
against a government claiming sovereignty is of mo-

[1] The Times: *History*, vol. i. chap. iv.

ment, the position of the South African republics was, in 1900, far stronger with all nations on terms of amity with Great Britain than was the position of the Confederacy in 1861–62 with nations then at amity with the United States. It consequently followed that any precedent created, or rule laid down, by a neutral for its own guidance in international relations during the first struggle was applicable in the second, except in so far as such rule or precedent had been modified or set aside by mutual agreement of the parties concerned during the intervening years. What, then, were these rules and precedents established by Great Britain in its dealings with the United States in 1861–65, which, unless altered by mutual consent during the intervening time, would have been applicable by the United States to Great Britain in 1899–1901?

In the opening pages of his account of the doings of the agents of the Confederacy in Europe during our Civil War, Captain James D. Bulloch, of the Confederate States Navy, the most trusted and efficient of those agents, says that "the Confederate government made great efforts to organize a naval force abroad;" and he adds, truly enough, that "the naval operations of the Confederate States which were [thus] organized abroad possess an importance and attraction greater than their relative effect upon the issue of the struggle." Captain Bulloch might well have gone further. He might have added that, in connection with those operations, the public men, high officials, courts of law, and colonial authorities of Great Britain more especially, supported by the press and general public opinion of that country, labored conjointly and strenuously, blindly and successfully, to build up a structure of rules and precedents, not less complete and solid than well calculated, whenever the turn of Great Britain might come, — as come in time it surely would, — to work the downfall of the empire. As that record carries in it a lesson of deep significance to all intrusted with the temporary administration of national affairs, it should neither be forgotten nor ignored. It is well that statesmen, also, should occasionally be reminded that, with nations as with individuals, there is a to-morrow, and the whirligig of time ever brings on its revenges. " All things come to him who waits; " and the motto of the house of Ravenswood was, " I bide my time."

When hostilities broke out in April, 1861, the so-called Confederate States of America did not have within their own limits any of the essentials to a maritime warfare. With a long coast line and numerous harbors, in itself and by itself, so far as aggressive action was concerned, the Confederacy could not be, or be made, a base of naval operations. It had no machine shops nor yards; no shipwrights, and no collection of material for shipbuilding or the equipment of ships. In the days when rebellion was as yet only incipient, it was correctly deemed of prime importance to get cruisers; but a diligent search throughout the ports of the seceding States disclosed but one small steamer at all adapted for a cruising service. Under these circumstances, the minds of those composing the as yet embryonic government at Montgomery turned naturally to Europe; and, in the early days of May, 1861, immediately after the reduction of Fort Sumter, a scheme was matured for making Great Britain the base

of Confederate naval operations against the United
States.   The nature and scope of the British statutes
had already been looked into ; the probability of the
early issuance of a proclamation of neutrality by the
government of Great Britain was considered, and the
officials of the Confederate Navy Department were
confident that the Montgomery government would be
recognized by European powers as a *de facto* organization.   If belligerent rights were then conceded to it,
the maritime shelter and privileges common to belligerents under the amity of nations must, it was assumed,
be granted to its regularly commissioned cruisers.

The officials in question next looked about for some
competent Confederate sympathizer, who might be
despatched to Europe, and there be a species of secretary *in partibus*.   They decided upon James D.
Bulloch, at the time a lieutenant in the United States
Navy, detailed by the government for the command
of the *Bienville*, a privately owned mail steamer running between New York and New Orleans.   A Geor-
gian by birth and appointment, Lieutenant Bulloch,
according to the form of speech then much in vogue,
went with his State, and at once, after Georgia seceded,
put his services at the disposal of the Confederate government.   He was requested forthwith to report at
Montgomery ; and there, on the 8th and 9th of May,
he received from S. R. Mallory, the Confederate naval
secretary, verbal instructions covering all essential
points of procedure.   On the night of the 9th of May,
Bulloch left Montgomery for Liverpool, his duly designated seat of operations.   Arriving there on the 4th
of June, Secretary Mallory's assistant at once entered
on his duties, not only purchasing naval supplies, but,

before the close of the month, he had contracted with
a Liverpool shipbuilder for the construction of a
cruiser, and it was already partly in frame. The
Queen's proclamation of neutrality had then been
issued some six weeks. The vessel now on the stocks
was at first called the *Oreto ;* afterwards it attained
an international celebrity as the *Florida.* Acting
with an energy which fully justified his selection for
the work of the Confederacy then in hand to be done,
Captain Bulloch, on the 1st of the following August,
entered into another contract, this time with the
Messrs. Laird, under which the keel of a second
cruiser was immediately afterwards laid in the yards of
that firm at Birkenhead. The purpose of the Confederate government was well defined. In the words
of Captain Bulloch, it was " not merely to buy or
build a single ship, but it was to maintain a permanent representative of the Navy Department [in
Great Britain], and to get ships and naval supplies
without hindrance as long as the war lasted." The
ports of the Mersey, the Clyde, and the Thames were
to be the arsenals, and furnish the shipyards, of the
Confederacy. Nor did the scheme stop here. A cor-
responding branch of the Confederate Treasury Department had already been established in Liverpool,
officially designated the " Depositories " of that organization ; [1] and, regardless of any pretence of concealment, the naval representative of the Confederacy had
an office in the premises hired by its fiscal agents.[2]

[1] Bulloch: *Secret Service of the Confederate States in Europe,* vol.
i. p. 65 ; also vol. ii. pp. 216, 416.

[2] Geneva Arbitration : *Correspondence concerning Claims against
Great Britain,* vol. vi. p. 185. The papers officially published in connection with the Geneva Arbitration are voluminous and confusing.

No hindrance to the operations of the combined branch bureaus was anticipated. In other words, Great Britain was to be made the base of an organized maritime warfare against the United States, the Confederacy itself being confessedly unable to conduct such a warfare from within its own limits. The single question was, — Would Great Britain permit itself to be thus utilized for the construction, equipment, and despatch of commerce-destroyers and battleships intended to operate, in a domestic insurrection, against a nation with which it was at peace?

Excepting only the good faith, friendly purpose, and apparently obvious self-interest of a civilized government in the last half of the nineteenth century, the provisions of the British Foreign Enlistment Act of 1819 constituted the only barrier in the way of the consummation of this extraordinary project, — a project which all will now agree was tantamount to a proposal that, so far as commerce-destroyers were concerned, the first maritime nation of the world should become an accomplice before the fact in what bore a close family resemblance to piracy. As the date of its enactment (1819) implies, the British Foreign Enlistment Act was passed at the time of the troubles incident to the separation of its American dependencies from Spain, and was designed to prevent the fitting out in British ports of piratical expeditions

The references under the title "Geneva Arbitration," in the notes to this volume, are to the original editions presented to the tribunal at Geneva. These papers were printed between 1869 and 1872 in Washington, London, Paris, and Geneva, as the exigencies of the case required. To supersede them in part, Congress (as Cong. Doc., Serial Nos. 1553 1556) caused four volumes to be printed, here cited as *Papers relating to Treaty of Washington* (1872).

against Spanish commerce, under cover of letters of marque, etc., issued by South American insurrectionary governments. Owing to the long peace which ensued on its passage, the act had slept innocuously on the statute-book, no case involving a forfeiture ever having been brought to trial under it. It was an instance of desuetude, covering more than forty years.

" Labored and cumbrous in the extreme," [1] the Foreign Enlistment Act was, after the manner of English Acts of Parliament, " overloaded with a mass of phrases, alike unprecise and confused, with so much of tedious superfluity of immaterial circumstances " as to suggest a suspicion that it must have been " specially designed to give scope to bar chicanery, to facilitate the escape of offenders, and to embarrass and confound the officers of the government charged with the administration of law." [2] It was, in short, one of those statutes in which the British parliamentary draughtsman has prescriptively revelled, and through the clauses of which judge and barrister love, as the phrase goes, to drive a coach-and-six. But it so chanced that, in the present case, the coach-and-six had, as passengers, the whole British Ministry ; and in it they were doomed to flounder pitifully along " in the flat morass of [a] meaningless verbosity and confused circumlocution." [3] Upon the proper construction of this notable act, the Confederate representatives at once sought the opinion of counsel ; and they were presently advised that, under its provisions, it would be an offence for a British subject to build,

[1] Montague Bernard : *Historical Account of the Neutrality of Great Britain during the American Civil War* (London, 1870), p. 404.
[2] Geneva Arbitration : *Argument of the United States*, pp. 52, 61.
[3] *Ib.*, p. 52.

arm, *and* equip a vessel to cruise against the commerce of a friendly state ; but the mere building of a ship, though with the full intent of so using her, was no offence ; nor was it an offence to equip a vessel so built, if it was without the intent so to use her. To constitute an offence, the two acts of building a ship with intent of hostile use, and equipping the same, must be combined ; and both must be done in British waters.[1] It hence followed that, under the act, it was lawful for an English firm to build a ship in a British shipyard designed purposely to prey on American commerce ; it was also lawful to sell or buy, of this same English firm if more convenient, the articles of necessary equipment for such vessel from cordage to arms and ammunition ; but the articles of war equipment must not go into the vessel, thus making of her a complete cruiser, within British maritime jurisdiction. The final act of conjunction must be effected at some distance greater than one league from where a British writ ran. Assuming this construction of the Foreign Enlistment Act to be correct, its evasion was simple. It could be enforced practically only with a government strong enough to decline to allow its international obligations to be trifled with. If, however, officials evinced the slightest indifference respecting the enforcement of those obligations, and much more if the government was infected by any spirit of connivance, the act at once became a statute mockery.

In any large view of policy Great Britain then was, as it now is, under strong inducement to insist on the highest standard of international maritime observance. As the foremost ocean-carrier of the world, it ill be-

[1] Bulloch, vol. i. pp. 65–67.

came her to connive at commerce-destroying. But, in 1861, Great Britain had a divided interest; and British money-making instincts are well developed. She was the arsenal and shipbuilder of the world, as well as its ocean-carrier. Her artisans could launch from private dockyards vessels of any size, designed for any purpose, thoroughly equipped whether for peace or war; and all at the shortest possible notice. Under ordinary circumstances, this was a legitimate branch of industry. It admitted, however, of easy perversion; and the question in 1861 was whether the first of commercial nations would permit its laws to be so construed as to establish the principle that, in case of war, any neutral might convert its ports into nurseries of corsairs for the use or injury of either belligerent, or of both.

It is now necessary briefly to recall a once familiar record showing the extent to which Great Britain lent itself to the scheme of the Confederacy, and the precedents it created while so doing. All through the later summer of 1861, — the months following the disgrace of Bull Run and the incident of the *Trent*, — the work of Confederate naval construction was pushed vigorously along in the Liverpool and Birkenhead shipyards. Hardly any concealment was attempted of the purpose for which the *Oreto* and the " 290 " — as the two vessels were called or designated — were designed. As the work on them progressed, it was openly supervised by agents known to be in the Confederate employ, while British government officials, having free access to the yards, looked to it that the empty letter of the law was observed. Never was a solemn mockery more carefully enacted; never was there a more insulting

pretence at the observance of international obligations ; never a more perfect instance of connivance at
a contemplated crime, though not so nominated in the
bond.

The *Oreto*, or *Florida*, we are told by Captain Bulloch, was the first regularly built war vessel of the
Confederate States Navy. " She has," he wrote at
the time, " been twice inspected by the Custom House
authorities, in compliance with specific orders from the
Foreign Office. . . . The hammock-nettings, ports,
and general appearance of the ship sufficiently indicate
the ultimate object of her construction, but . . . regis-
tered as an English ship, in the name of an Englishman, commanded by an Englishman, with a regular
official number under the direction of the Board of
Trade, she seems to be perfectly secure against capture or interference, until an attempt is made to arm
her." Another vessel, carrying the armament of this
contemplated commerce-destroyer, left England at so
nearly the same time as the *Oreto* that those in
charge of the latter increased her speed, being apprehensive that their consort would arrive first at the
point of rendezvous. Making Nassau, an English
port, the last pretence at concealment as to character
and destination disappeared, in consequence of the
heedless talk of a Confederate officer there to join
her. A portion of her crew, also, immediately reported to the British naval commander at the station
that the vessel's destination could not be ascertained.
She was seized ; but, after some legal forms and a
pretence of a hearing, a decree of restoration was
entered. Subsequently, before being herself destroyed,
she captured, and burnt or bonded, some forty ves-

sels carrying the United States flag. A precedent complete at every point had been created.

Relying on the advice of counsel and the experience gained in the case of the *Florida*, there was absolutely no concealment of purpose even attempted as respects the *Alabama*. Built under a contract entered into with the avowed agent of the Confederacy, that the " 290 " was designed as a Confederate commerce-destroyer was town talk in Liverpool, — " quite notorious," as the American consul expressed it. She was launched on the 15th of May, 1862, as the *Enrica*, with " no attempt," as Captain Bulloch testifies, " to deceive any one by any pretence whatever." Everything was done in the " ordinary commonplace way ; " and, as Bulloch afterwards wrote, he " always attributed the success of getting the *Alabama* finished as a sea-going ship, and then despatched, to the fact that no mystery or disguise was attempted." [1] John Laird, Sons & Co., of Birkenhead, the contracting shipwrights, knew perfectly well that they were building a cruiser for the Confederate government, specially constructed as a commerce-destroyer ; and they carefully observed what their counsel advised them was the law of the land. They simply built a vessel designed to do certain work in a war then in progress ; the equipment of that vessel, including its armament, was in course of preparation elsewhere. Of that they knew nothing. They were not informed ; nor, naturally, did they care to ask. The vessel and her equipment would come together outside of British jurisdiction. Such was the law ; Great Britain lived under a government of law ; and " to strain the law "

[1] Bulloch, vol. i. p. 229.

the government was then in no way inclined. The agents of the Confederacy, moreover, " had the means of knowing with well-nigh absolute certainty what was the state of the negotiations between the United States Minister and Her Majesty's Government." [1] The work of completion was, however, pressed forward with significant energy after the launching of the vessel; so that, by the middle of June, she went out on a trial trip. An Englishman, having a Board of Trade certificate, was then engaged " merely to take the ship to an appointed place without the United Kingdom," [2] where she was to meet a consort bearing her armament.

This was in Liverpool; meanwhile the proposed commerce-destroyer's armament was in course of preparation at London, and included " everything required for the complete equipment of a man-of-war." The goods, when ready, were " packed, marked, and held for shipping orders." The *Agrippina*, a suitable barque of 400 tons measurement, was then purchased, and quietly loaded. Between the two vessels — the one building on the Mersey, the other taking on board a cargo in the Thames — there was no apparent connection. Every arrangement for the destruction of the commerce of a nation at peace with Great Britain was being made under the eyes of the customs officials, but with scrupulous regard to the provisions of the Foreign Enlistment Act.

A single word from the British Foreign Office would then have sufficed to put a stop to the whole scheme. That office was fully advised by the American Minister

---

[1] Bulloch, vol. i. pp. 229, 260, 261.
[2] *Ib.*, vol. i. p. 231.

of what was common town talk at Liverpool. The
Confederate agent there in charge of operations was
as well known as the Collector of the Port; probably
much more frequently pointed out, and curiously observed. Had those then officially responsible for Great
Britain's honor and interests been in earnest, public
notice would have been given to all concerned, including belligerents, — under the designation of evil-dis-
posed persons, — that Her Majesty's Government did
not propose to have Great Britain's neutrality trifled
with, or the laws evaded. Her ports were not to be
made, by either belligerent, directly or through evasion, a basis of naval operations against the other.
Any ship constructed for warlike purposes, upon the
builders of which notice had been served at the application of either belligerent, would be held affected by
such notice ; and thereafter, in case of evasion, would
not be entitled to the rights of hospitality in any British waters. Whether, under the principles of international law, such vessel could be held so tainted by
evasion after notice as to be subject to seizure and
detention whenever and wherever found within British
jurisdiction, would be matter of further consideration.
This course was one authorized by international law,
and well understood at the time. At a later day, the
Attorney-General, for instance, in debate declared, —
" I have not the least doubt that we have a right, if
we thought fit, to exclude from our own ports any particular ship or class of ships, if we consider that they
have violated our neutrality." [1] And, three months before the first law adviser of the Crown thus expressed

[1] House of Commons, May 13, 1864. Geneva Arbitration : *Correspondence,* etc., vol. v. p. 583 ; see, also, *Ib.,* p. 571. The situation was

himself, Mr. William Vernon Harcourt, then first
coming into notice as a writer on questions of international law under the pseudonym of " Historicus," had
said in a letter published in the *Times*, — " It is a sound
and salutary rule of international practice, established
by the Americans themselves in 1794, that vessels
which have been equipped in violation of the laws of
a neutral state shall be excluded from that hospitality
which is extended to other belligerent cruisers, on
whose origin there is no such taint. . . . I think that
to deny to the *Florida* and the *Alabama* access to
our ports would be the legitimate and dignified manner of expressing our disapproval of the fraud which
has been practised on our neutrality. If we abstain
from taking such a course, I fear we may justly lie
under the imputation of having done less to vindicate
our good faith than the American government consented at our instance, on former occasions, to do."[1]

novel, and the solution of the difficulty through " notice " does not
seem to have suggested itself to the government. Writing long after
the event, Lord Selborne, who, as Sir Roundell Palmer, was, during
the Rebellion, the chief law adviser of the Crown, thus expressed
himself : — " [The neutral] might, indeed, by previous notice, exclude
all or any particular ships of war of either belligerent from his ports ;
and it might be a reasonable opinion, that an exclusion of a particular
ship on the ground that she had been equipped within his territory,
contrary to his neutrality laws, would be justifiable." (*Memorials,
Part II., Personal and Political,* 1865–95, vol. i. p. 268.) Viscount
D'Itajuba, in his opinion at Geneva, formulated the rule in its full
extent : — " This principle of seizure, of detention, or at any rate of
preliminary notice that a vessel, under such circumstances, will not
be received in the ports of the neutral whose neutrality she has violated, is fair and salutary. . . . The commission with which such a
vessel is provided is insufficient to protect her as against the neutral
whose neutrality she has violated." *Papers Relating to Treaty of
Washington* (1872), vol. iv. pp. 97, 98.

[1] London *Times*, February 17, 1864. Geneva Arbitration : *Correspondence*, etc., vol. iv. pp. 203, 204. This point was vigorously insisted

Finally, England's Chief Justice laid down the rule in the following broad terms, — " A sovereign has absolute dominion in and over his own ports and waters. He can permit the entrance into them to the ships of other nations, or refuse it; he can grant it to some, can deny it to others ; he can subject it to such restrictions, conditions, or regulations as he pleases. But, by the universal comity of nations, in the absence of such restrictions or prohibition, the ports and waters of every nation are open to all comers." [1]

Unless, therefore, the British Ministry was willing to stand forward as openly conniving at proceedings calculated to bring into contempt the law and the Queen's proclamation, the course to be pursued was plain ; and the mere declaration of a purpose to pursue that course, while it would not in the slightest have interfered with legitimate ship construction, would have put an instant and effectual stop to the building and equipment of commerce-destroyers. The law, even as it then stood, was sufficient, had the government only declared a purpose. Had the will been there, a way had not been far to seek.

No such notice was conveyed. In vain the American Minister protested. No evidence as to the character of the proposed cruiser, or the purpose for which

upon by Mr. Cobden in his speech in the House of Commons, April 24, 1863. "Why," he said, "do you not forbid the reëntry of those vessels into your ports, that left them, manned by a majority of English sailors, in violation of the Foreign Enlistment Act ? Would any person have a right to complain of that ? Proclaim the vessels that thus steal away from your ports, outlaws, so far as your ports are concerned." Speeches (London, 1870), vol. ii. p. 97.

[1] *Papers relating to Treaty of Washington* (1872), vol. iv. pp. 416–418. Supplement to the London *Gazette*, September 24, 1872, pp. 4263, 4264.

she was designed, possible for him to adduce, was adjudged satisfactory ; and, finally, when the case became so flagrant that action could not in decency be delayed, a timely intimation reached the Confederate agent through some unknown channel, and, on the 29th of July, 1862, the *Alabama* went out on a trial trip at the mouth of the Mersey, from which she did not return.[1] With British papers, and flying the British flag, she two days later got under weigh for the Azores. At almost the some hour, moving under orders from the Confederate European naval bureau at Liverpool, her consort, the *Agrippina*, loaded with munitions and equipment, cleared from London. The two met at the place designated ; and there, outside of British jurisdiction, the stores, arms, and equipment were duly transferred. A few days later, the forms of transfer having been gone through with, the British master turned the ship over to the Confederate commander, his commission was read, and the Confederate

---

[1] Much has been written, and more said, as to the particular person upon whom rested responsibility for the evasion of the *Alabama*. Collusion on the part of officers has been charged, and it was at one time even alleged that Mr. S. Price Edwards, then collector of the port of Liverpool, had been the recipient of a bribe. This is emphatically denied by Captain Bulloch (vol. i. pp. 258–264), and no evidence has ever come to light upon which to rest such an improbable imputation. Under these circumstances, the following intensely characteristic avowal of Earl Russell, in his volume of *Recollections and Suggestions*, published in 1875, has a refreshing sound. Such curt frankness causes a feeling of respect for the individual man to predominate over any, or all, other sentiments. The passage referred to (p. 407) is as follows : — " I assent entirely to the opinions of the Lord Chief Justice of England [in his award in the Geneva Arbitration] that the *Alabama* ought to have been detained during the four days in which I was waiting for the opinion of the Law Officers. But I think that the fault was not that of the Commissioners of the Customs [as asserted by Lord Cockburn] ; it was my fault, as Secretary of State for Foreign Affairs."

flag run up. Upon which somewhat empty ceremonies, the " 290," now the *Alabama*, stood purified of any evasion of English law, and, as a duly commissioned foreign man-of-war, was thereafter entitled to all belligerent rights and hospitalities within British jurisdiction. Incredible as it now must seem to Englishmen as well as to us, a British Ministry, of which Lord Palmerston was the head, then professed itself impotent to assert the majesty, or even the dignity, of the law. It had been made the dupe of what Lord Cockburn afterwards not inaptly termed " contrivances," — " the artifices and tricks, to which the unscrupulous cunning of the Confederate agents did not hesitate to resort in violation of British neutrality; "[1] and yet the poor victim of these " artifices and tricks " professed itself utterly unable to make itself respected, much less to vindicate its authority. At a later day Earl Russell recovered the use of his faculties and his command of language. He then, though the law had not in the mean time been changed, found means to let the Confederate agents understand that " such shifts and stratagems " were " totally unjustifiable and manifestly offensive to the British Crown."[2]

Such are the simple facts in the case. And now, looking back through the perspective of forty years, and speaking with all moderation, is it unfair to ask, — Was any great nation ever guilty of a more wanton, a more obtuse, or a more criminal dereliction? The world's great ocean-carrier permitted a belliger-

[1] Supplement to the London *Gazette*, September 24, 1872, p. 4231. *Papers relating to Treaty of Washington* (1872), vol. iv. p. 377.

[2] Earl Russell to Messrs. Mason, Slidell, and Mann, February 13, 1865. Geneva Arbitration : *Correspondence*, etc., vol. i. p. 631.

ent of its own creation to sail a commerce-destroyer
through its statutes; and then, because of an empty
formality observed in a desert mid-ocean rendezvous,
which chanced to be under Portuguese jurisdiction,[1]
set up a pretence, which can only be adequately characterized as both brazen and sneaking, that in afford-
ing protection and hospitality to the vessel thus existing through a contemptuous evasion of its own law,
Great Britain did not stand an accomplice in commerce-destroying.[2] " Shall the blessed sun of heaven
prove a micher and eat blackberries ? — a question not
to be asked.   Shall the son of England prove a thief,
and take purses ? — a question to be asked."

[1] Bulloch, vol. i. p. 117.

[2] Something bearing a close family resemblance to this plea of
impotency to resent a fraud practised on itself in contempt of law,
or to vindicate the majesty of the Crown, was advanced by Dr. Bernard, in defence of the Palmerston-Russell Ministry, even as late as
1870.   The rule of international law he first laid down correctly : —
" Every Sovereign has a general right to exclude from his ports
either all ships-of-war, or any particular ship, or to impose on admission any conditions he may think fit; although the exclusion of a
particular ship would be unjust and offensive, unless reasonable
grounds could be shown for it." (*Historical Account*, p. 413.)   He
then admits (*Ib.*, p. 437) that : — " The various contrivances by which
[the Confederate commerce-destroyers] were procured and sent to
sea were discreditable to the Confederate Government, and offensive
and injurious to Great Britain.   Such enterprises were, and were
known to be, calculated to embroil the country with the United States ;
they were carried into effect by artifices which must be accounted
unworthy of any body of persons calling themselves a Government
— of any community making pretensions to the rank of an independent people.   Every transaction was veiled in secrecy, and masked
under a fictitious purchase, or a false destination.   By such devices it
was intended to blind the eyes of the government of Great Britain."
Moreover, — " It would be erroneous, I conceive, to contend that the
taint of illegality, if any, adhering to the *Alabama*, was ever 'deposited,'
as the phrase is, by the termination of her original cruise.   She never
made but one cruise." (*Ib.*, p. 414 n.)   All this, it might naturally be

It is not necessary further to follow the law of Great Britain as then laid down, or to enumerate the precedents created under it. One thing led to another. In the autumn of 1861 Captain Bulloch ran the blockade, and, visiting Richmond, conferred with his chief, the Secretary of the Confederate Navy. He then learned that the designs of the Richmond government, as respects naval operations from a British base, had "assumed a broader range."[1] Secretary Mallory now contemplated the construction in Great Britain of "the best type of armored vessels for operations on the coast . . . to open and protect the blockaded ports. . . . It was impossible to build them in the Confederate States — neither the materials nor the mechanics were there; and besides, even if iron

inferred, would constitute, if anything could constitute, "reasonable grounds" for the exclusion of the vessel in question from the ports of the country so outraged. Instead, however, of reaching that obvious conclusion, the learned publicist concluded that to exclude the ship so offending would have been "a measure likely to be embarrassed by some difficulties;" and that for the losses occasioned by failure to resent an outrage on itself, "the British nation is not justly responsible."

In justice to Earl Russell it should be said that, on the suggestion of the Duke of Argyll, he did propose to the Cabinet that the colonial authorities should be instructed to detain the "290," or the *Alabama*, if she should come within their power, and he even drew up a despatch to that effect. All the other members of the Cabinet were, however, against this course, and the despatch was not sent. Lord Westbury, the Chancellor, was "vehement" against it. (Spencer Walpole: *Lord John Russell*, vol. ii. p. 355. See, also, Sir Roundell Palmer: *Memorials*, 1766–1865, vol. ii. p. 431.) In this case it does not appear that the order of detention was intended to apply to the vessel after its transfer in other waters to the Confederate authorities. Presumably, it was limited to the "290," or *Enrica*, in case she followed the course of the *Oreto*, going direct from the port of evasion to some other port within British jurisdiction. This the "290" did not do.

[1] Bulloch, vol. i. p. 377.

and skilled artisans had been within reach, there was
not a mill in the country to roll the plates, nor fur-
naces and machinery to forge them, nor shops to make
the engines." [1]   This was a distinct step in advance ;
also a long one.   It might almost be called a stride.
Earl Russell had declared that one great object of the
British government was to preserve "for the nation
the legitimate and lucrative trade of shipbuilding ; "
and if it was " legitimate" to construct a single commerce-destroyer to take part in hostilities then going
on, why was it not legitimate to construct a squadron
of turreted iron-clads ?   It certainly was more " lucrative."   In the words of Mr. Gladstone, then Chancellor of the Exchequer, the Confederate leaders, having made an army, " are making, it appears, a navy ; "
and the " lucrative trade " of constructing that navy
naturally fell to the shipwrights of the Mersey.   The
Prime Minister of Great Britain now, also, boldly
took the ground in parliamentary debate — speaking, of course, for the Government — that of this no
belligerent had any cause to complain.   " As a mercantile transaction," British merchants and manu-
facturers were at liberty to supply, and had a right
to supply, one or both of " the belligerents, not only
with arms and cannon, but also with ships destined
for warlike purposes." [2]   To the same effect the

---

[1] Bulloch, vol. i. p. 380.

[2] House of Commons, July 23, 1863. Geneva Arbitration : *Correspondence*, etc., vol. v. p. 695. " It is quite as much within the International Law to sell ships of war to another nation as it is to sell any
munitions of war." (Lord Robert Cecil, now (1902) Marquis of Salis-
bury, House of Commons, May 13, 1864.) *Per contra*, in April, 1863,
Mr. Cobden drew the distinction forcibly. He declared the two
questions totally distinct. "There is no law in this country that
prohibits the buying and selling or manufacturing or exporting

Secretary for Foreign Affairs informed the United States Minister that, " except on the ground of any proved violation of the Foreign Enlistment Act . . . Her Majesty's Government cannot interfere with commercial dealings between British subjects and the so-styled Confederate States, whether the subject of those dealings be money or contraband goods, or even ships adapted for warlike purposes." "The cabinet," he moreover on another occasion stated, " were of opinion that the law [thus set forth] was sufficient; but that legal evidence could not always be procured." [1] Of the sufficiency of that evidence, the Government, acting through its legal advisers, was the sole judge. As such, it demanded legal proof of a character sufficient not only to justify a criminal indictment, but to furnish reasonable grounds for securing a conviction thereon. The imputation and strong circumstances which led directly to the door of proof gave, in this case, no satisfaction. Facts of unquestioned notoriety could not be adduced, — " notoriety " was not evidence.[2] A petty jury in an English criminal court became thus the final arbiter of Britain's international obligations. If that august

arms and munitions of war. . . . I am astonished," he went on, in terms peculiarly Cobdenesque, " that Mr. Adams and Mr. Seward should have mixed that question up in their correspondence with that of equipments for war. I will not say that I was astonished at Mr. Seward, because he writes so much that he is in danger of writing on every subject, and on every side of a subject; but I am astonished that Mr. Adams should have mixed this question up with what is really a vital question — that of furnishing and equipping ships of war." Speeches (London, 1870), vol. ii. pp. 84, 85.

[1] Russell to Lyons, March 27, 1863. Geneva Arbitration: *Correspondence*, etc., vol. i. p. 585.

[2] Geneva Arbitration: *Treaty of Washington Papers* (1872), vol. iv. pp. 377, 479 ; see, also, *Correspondence*, etc., vol. iv. p. 530.

tribunal pronounced a case not proven, though the real facts were common town talk, the law was not violated, and, whatever acts of maritime wrong and ocean outrage followed, foreign nations had no grounds for reclamation. And this was gravely pronounced law; " Ay, marry; crowner's quest law !"

Here, indeed, was the inherent, fundamental defect of the British position, — what was afterwards described as the " insularity " of the British contentions. Unable to rise above the conception of a municipal rule of conduct, the governmental vision was bounded on the one side by a jury box, and on the other by the benches of the House of Commons. Uncertainty, closely bordering on vacillation, naturally resulted; for Earl Russell had a firm grasp neither on the principles of international law involved, nor on the questions of policy. On the one hand, he wished to preserve for the shipwrights of the Mersey and the Clyde that " trade of shipbuilding, in which our people excel, and which is to great numbers of them a source of honest livelihood ; " [1] but, on the other, in an apparently unguarded moment, he admitted that it was " the duty of nations in amity with each other not to suffer their good faith to be violated by ill-disposed persons within their borders, merely from the inefficiency of their prohibitory policy." One day he would write to Mr. Adams that the government found itself " unable to go beyond the law, municipal and international," — a proposition which few would be disposed to controvert ; and then, twelve days later, he went through a similar form of reply, assigning " the letter

---

[1] Russell to Adams, October 20, 1863. Geneva Arbitration : *Correspondence*, etc., vol. iii. p. 201.

of the existing [meaning, apparently, the municipal] law " [1] as the extreme of interference.[2]

At last, on full reflection and at a subsequent day, he settled on a defence of his action which was almost humorously illustrative of " insularity." He triumphantly declared, in complete and final justification thereof, that the object of the Palmerston-Russell Ministry throughout was "to preserve for the subject the security of trial by jury, and for the nation the legitimate and lucrative trade of shipbuilding " ! [3] British Shipyards and Trial by Jury ! — here, indeed, was a hustings cry.   When he formulated it, no trial was impending ; no general election was imminent ; he was himself permanently retired from official life. Yet instinctively, and in obedience to a lifelong parliamentary habit, his mind reverted to time-honored political catch-words.   Invoking them, a British ministry could face with confidence either the benches of the Opposition or the ordeal of the constituencies.   The

[1] Earl Russell to Mr. Adams, October 4 and 16, 1862.   Geneva Arbitration : *Correspondence*, etc., vol. vi. pp. 426–429.

[2] Subsequently Lord Selborne expressed himself on this point, as follows : — " It is unnecessary to say that no one in this country contended for a proposition so plainly untenable as that municipal law is a proper and sufficient measure of the neutral rights and obligations of nations." (*Memorials, Part I.*, 1766–1865, vol. ii. p. 413.) This was written subsequent to the Geneva Arbitration ; the converse was certainly assumed at Geneva (*Treaty of Washington Papers*, etc. (1872), vol. iii. pp. 19–24), and it is difficult in reading the Alabama correspondence to avoid the conclusion that Earl Russell was not clear in thought and expression, and his difficulty arose from his inability to grasp the fact that Great Britain was under an obligation beyond any established by act of Parliament. He did not really attain to a clear perception of this principle until actually confronted with the issue presented by the case of the Laird rams. It seems to have been an instance of education in the elements of international law, so gradual as to be suggestive of extreme reluctance under instruction.

[3] *Speeches and Despatches* (1870), vol. ii. p. 266.

cry was epigrammatic ; any one could understand it ; it did not admit of an answer, — at least, not at West-minster nor at the polling-booths.

But to those of other nations, called on to stand impassively by while their merchant-marine vanished in smoke, this sturdy British appeal carried in it a somewhat empty, not to say mocking, sound. Trial by jury might be the palladium of the British consti-tution ; shipbuilding was unquestionably a lucrative craft : but when the last became an instrument for utilizing Great Britain as a base of naval warfare in the hands of one belligerent against another, between whom, being at peace with each, Great Britain pro-fessed to maintain a perfect and even-handed neutral-ity ; and when trial by jury, through pre-ordained verdicts of " not proven," was perverted into an accom-plice before the fact in piracy, — when these things came about, foreign nations would not improbably find themselves compelled to have recourse to such other means of self-preservation as the law of nations might afford. The hustings and jury box were not the final arbiters between warring States.

Those tribunals, moreover, highly respectable, no doubt, as well as ancient, were distinctly insular. They had no place in the code. On the contrary, the principle of international law controlling the situation was plain. As laid down by the leading English pub-licist of that day, it read as follows :—" Each State has a right to expect from another the observance of inter-national obligations, without regard to what may be the municipal means which it possesses for enforcing this observance." [1] But, with one eye always fixed on the

---

[1] Phillimore : *International Law*, vol. i., preface to second edition, p. 21, cited in Geneva Arbitration : *Argument of United States*, p. 35.

Opposition benches at Westminster, and the other wandering in the direction of the Lancashire jury box, Earl Russell instinctively contended that the international obligations of Great Britain were coterminous with its parliamentary enactments. If the law of England did not provide adequate protection for the rights of foreign nations, it might indeed be changed; but, until changed, it was most unreasonable for the representatives of those nations to present claims and complaints to Her Majesty's Government. The government, responsible to Parliament and the jury, had done its best. Against it no charge of inefficiency would lie. The fact that Great Britain was being made the base of naval warfare was ignored, — although notorious, " not proven," — and the trade in ships was pronounced no more contraband than that in guns. It is almost unnecessary to say that this rule also is one which, in its converse operation, might not infrequently lead to inopportune results.

The Foreign Enlistment Act of 1819 was then passed in review. It was pronounced " effectual for all reasonable purposes, and to the full extent to which international law or comity can require." [1] In the opinion of the Government, there was no occasion for its amendment or strengthening. No move was made to that end; no recommendation submitted to Parliament. On the contrary, when in March, 1863, the neutrality laws were in debate, Lord Palmerston did not hesitate to declare from the ministerial benches, if the cry that those laws were manifestly defective was raised " for the purpose of driving Her Majesty's Gov-

---

[1] Mr. Hammond to Messrs. Lamport and others, July 6, 1863. Geneva Arbitration: *Correspondence*, etc., vol. i. p. 673.

ernment to do something . . . which may be derogatory to the dignity of the country, in the way of altering our laws for the purpose of pleasing another government, then all I can say is that such a course is not likely to accomplish its purpose ; . . . but the people and Government of the United States . . . must not imagine that any cry which may be raised will induce us to come down to this House with a proposal to alter the law." [1] Thus another door of future possible escape was on this occasion closed, so to speak with a slam, by the British Premier. The law, however manifestly defective, was not to be changed to please any one.

Meanwhile, as if to make the record at all points complete, and to show how very defective this immutable law was, the courts passed upon the much discussed Act. Under the pressure brought to bear by the United States Minister a test case had been arranged. It was tried before a jury in the Court of Exchequer on the 22d of June, 1863, the Laird iron-clads being then still on the ways, but in an advanced stage of construction. The vessel thus seized and proceeded against, in order to obtain a construction of the forty-four years old statute, was the *Alexandra*. This vessel was being built with a view to warlike equipment. Of that no denial was possible. That she was intended for use in the Confederate service was a moral certainty. The *Alabama* was at that time in its full career of destruction, — carrying out the declared purpose of its commander, to "burn, sink, and destroy." Before her ravages the merchant marine of the United States was fast disappearing, — the ships

[1] Debate of March 27, 1863. Geneva Arbitration: *Correspondence*, etc., vol. iv. pp. 530, 531. See, also, Russell to Adams, September 25, 1863. *Ib.*, vol. i. p. 674.

composing it either going up in smoke, or being transferred to other flags. With all these facts admitted, or of common knowledge, the Lord Chief Baron presiding at the *Alexandra* trial proceeded to instruct the jury on the law. The Foreign Enlistment Act was, he told them, not designed for the protection of belligerent powers, or to prevent Great Britain being made the base of naval operations directed against nations with which that country was at peace. The purpose of the Act was solely to prevent hostile naval encounters within British waters; and, to that end, it forbade such equipment of the completed ship as would make possible immediate hostile operations, it might be, " before they left the port." Such things had happened; " and that has been the occasion of this statute." He closed with these words:—"If you think the object was to build a ship in obedience to an order, and in compliance with a contract, leaving those who bought it to make what use they thought fit of it, then it appears to me the Foreign Enlistment Act has not been in any degree broken."

Under such an interpretation of the statute, the jury, of course, rendered a verdict for the defendants; and that verdict the audience in the court-room received with an outburst of applause. This outburst of applause was significant; more significant than even the charge of the judge. Expressive of the feelings of the British people, it pointed directly to the root of the trouble. The trial took place towards the close of June, 1863, — a few days only before Gettysburg; and, at that time, England, so far as the United States was concerned, had reached a state of mind Elizabethan rather than Victorian. The buccaneering blood — the blood of Drake, of Cavendish, and of Frobisher — was stirring in British veins. The *Alabama* then stood high in public admiration, — a British built ship, manned by a British crew, armed with British guns, it was successfully eluding the " Yankee " ships of war, and destroying a rival commercial marine. Wherever the British jurisdiction extended, the *Alabama* was a welcome sojourner from the weary sea.[1] The company on the decks of British mail steamers cheered her to the echo as they passed.

Speaking in the House of Commons on the 24th of April, 1863, Mr. Cobden dryly observed of the English people, — " We generally sympathize with everybody's rebels but our own ; " and passing utterances in both Europe and this country relating to operations now in progress, whether in South Africa or on the islands of the Pacific, point distinctly to the general truth of the remark. The sympathy, and the lack of sympathy, referred to are in no way peculiar to the people of Great Britain. But, in accordance with the principle of human nature thus alluded to, so strong among the influential classes of Great Britain was the feeling of sympathy for the South in 1863, and so intense was the enmity to the Union, mixed with a contempt as outspoken as it was ill-advised, that those sentiments were well-nigh all-pervasive. Speaking shortly after, Mr. Cobden again said : — " I declare to you that, looking at what is called in a cant phrase in London, ' society ; ' looking at society — and society, I must tell you, means the upper ten thousand, with whom members of Parliament are liable to como in

[1] Geneva Arbitration : Correspondence, etc., vol. vi. pp. 494–501.

contact at the clubs and elsewhere in London ; looking at what is called 'society'—looking at the ruling class, if we may use the phrase, that meet in the
purlieus of London, nineteen-twentieths of them were
firmly convinced from the first that the Civil War in
America could only end in separation." [1]   Captain
Bulloch asserted twenty years later that, being thrown
while in England a good deal among army and navy
men, " I never met one of either service who did not
warmly sympathize with the South ; " [2] and he further expressed his belief that this was the feeling of
" at least five out of every seven in the middle and
upper classes." [3]   To the like effect, Mr. G. W. P.
Bentinck—a member of Parliament—declared in a
speech at Kings Lynn, October 31, 1862, that, as far
as his experience went, " throughout the length and
breadth of the land, wherever I have travelled, I never
yet have met the man who has not at once said, —
' My wishes are with the Southerners ; ' " and he went
on to add that this feeling was mainly due to the fact
that the Southerner was " fighting against one of the
most grinding, one of the most galling, one of the most
irritating attempts to establish tyrannical government
that ever disgraced the history of the world." [4]   Mr.

[1] At Rochdale, November 24, 1863. Speeches (London, 1870), vol.
ii. p. 103.

[2] Bulloch, vol. ii. p. 303.

[3] *Ib.*, vol. i. p. 294.

[4] Mr. G. W. P. Bentinck was a member of Parliament in his day,
and doubtless esteemed by others, as by himself, a man not wholly
devoid of intelligence, nor, perhaps, of judgment even. In the light
of comments now frequently heard throughout continental Europe,
and also in America, on the methods of warfare pursued by the English in South Africa, the following extract from the closing sentences
of Mr. Bentinck's speech on the occasion referred to is suggestive.
Every struggle seems, in the opinion of observers in sympathy with

Gladstone's unfortunate utterance at about the same time passed into history; from which it failed not afterwards to return sorely to plague him. " We may anticipate with certainty the success of the Southern States so far as regards their separation from the North. . . . That event is as certain as any event yet future and contingent can be; " [1] and again, ten months later, he said in Parliament, — " We do not believe that the restoration of the American Union by force is attainable. I believe that the public opinion of this country is unanimous upon that subject. . . . I do not think there is any real or serious ground for doubt as to the issue of this contest." [2]   Four months previous, Mr. Gladstone's associate in the cabinet, Earl Russell,

the worsted combatant, to be marked by atrocities theretofore unprecedented in civilized warfare. Mr. Bentinck thus delivered himself : — " So long, I say, as such acts, in open defiance of all humanity and all civilization, are performed and are avowed by the government of the Northern States, they cease to have a claim to be ranked among civilized nations. I am not asserting that there are not hundreds and thousands of men in the Northern States who are men of education, of right, and of Christian feeling, of civilized habits and ideas. Far be it from me to make so unfounded an assertion. But there is a further lesson to be learned. The result of these much vaunted institutions, which we have heard praised before, and which we shall again hear praised by the hired spouters of associations, is this, that the nation becomes so brutalized that the civilized man disappears; he is afraid to put himself forward; he is ashamed of his country; he has no voice in the conduct of her affairs; and the whole nation is turned over to the control of men such as Lincoln and Butler, whom I do not hesitate to denounce, after their conduct in the last few months, as men who are a disgrace to civilization."

The whole of this interesting, and extremely suggestive, speech can be found in the columns of the London *Morning Post*, of November 4, 1862.

[1] Speech at Newcastle, October 7, 1862. *London Times*, October 9, 1862.

[2] House of Commons, June 30, 1863. Geneva Arbitration : *Correspondence*, etc., vol. v. p. 666.

had lent emphasis to this opinion by declaring in the House of Lords, — "There may be one end of the war that would prove a calamity to the United States and to the world, and especially calamitous to the negro race in those countries, and that would be the subjugation of the South by the North." [1] With this idea that there could be but one outcome of the struggle firmly established in their minds, influential members of the Cabinet did not urge recognition simply because, in view of the certainty of the result, they deemed such action unnecessary and impolitic.[2] The whole British policy during the Civil War was shaped with a view to this future state of affairs, and the creation of bad precedents was ignored accordingly. The Union was to be divided into two republics, unfriendly to each other. There was to be one democratic, free-labor republic, or more probably two such, lying between the British possessions on the north, and a slave-labor, cotton-growing republic on the south; the latter, almost of necessity, acting in close harmony of interest, commercial and political, with Great Britain. For Great Britain, eternity itself had thus no day of reckoning.

Relying on this simple faith in a certain future, — this absolute confidence that the expected only could occur, — utterances like the following appeared in the editorial columns of the *Morning Post*, the London journal understood most closely to reflect the opinions of the Prime Minister: — "From the ruling of the judge [in the case of the *Alexandra*] it appeared that the Confederate government might with ease obtain

[1] House of Lords, February 5, 1863. Geneva Arbitration: *Correspondence*, etc., vol. iv. p. 535.

[2] Bulloch, vol. ii. p. 5.

as many vessels in this country as they pleased without in any manner violating our laws.   It may be a great hardship to the Federals that their opponents should be enabled to create a navy in foreign ports, but, like many other hardships entailed on belligerents, it must be submitted to ; " while, five months before, this same organ of " society " and the " influential classes " had reached the comfortable conclusion that, so far as the *Alabama* was concerned, the fact " she sails upon the ocean is one of those chances of war to which the government of the United States ought with dignity and resignation to submit." [1]

II

Fortunately for maritime law, fortunately for itself, the British government paused at this point.   The " Laird rams," as they were now known, presented a test case.   London " society " and the irresponsible press of Great Britain might, like the audience in the Court of Exchequer, applaud the charge of the Lord Chief Baron, and gladly accept the law he laid down that it was legal for a belligerent to create a navy in a neutral port ; but, none the less, in the words of one of the dissenting Barons, by the rulings of the Court "the spirit of international law [had been] violated, and the spirit and letter of the statute evaded." [2]   There

[1] *Morning Post*, March 14, August 10, 1863.

[2] " A very learned judge has said that we might drive, not a coach-and-six, but a whole fleet of ships through that [Foreign Enlistment] Act of Parliament.   If that be a correct description of our law, then I say we ought to have the law made more clear and intelligible."   Earl Russell in the House of Lords, February 10, 1804. Geneva Arbitration : *Correspondence*, etc., vol. v. p. 528.

was no longer any danger, scarcely any inconvenience, in a belligerent fitting out a vessel of war in a British port, and sailing directly thence to begin a hostile cruise.[1] This, indeed, was at that very time actually in preparation. Theretofore the cases had been those of individual commerce-destroyers only. Now, an armament was in course of construction in a British port, intended for a naval operation of magnitude against a foreign belligerent with which Great Britain was at peace. The vessels composing it were, moreover, equipped with weapons of offensive warfare — their beaks. Their purpose and destination could not be proven in any legal proceedings ; but, known of all men, they were hardly concealed by fraudulent bills of sale. The law as laid down by the Lord Chief Baron in the case of the *Alexandra* might, therefore, as " crowner's quest law," be of the very first class ; but for Her Majesty's Government, such a construc-

---

[1] The construction of such cruisers was, moreover, for the shipwright, an uncommonly safe, as well as profitable, business ; and under the practical working of the law as it then stood, the more the interference, the greater the profit. This was curiously illustrated in the case of the Laird iron-clads. The original contract price for the two vessels was £187,500. (Bulloch, vol. i. p. 386.) Owing to fear of a seizure by the Government, the contract was transferred to a French banker named Bravay, who professed to represent the Pacha of Egypt. A gratuity of £5000 was paid to the Messrs. Laird as a consideration for their consent to this transfer. (*Ib.*, p. 404.) It then became apparent that the transfer was a mere cover for fraud, and the vessels were seized. In the existing state of public opinion, the Government was unwilling to go to a jury, — in fact, after the ruling of the Chief Baron in the *Alexandra* trial, it could not have done so with any chance of a condemnation, — and accordingly it proceeded to negotiate for the purchase of the vessels on its own account. The Messrs. Laird now asked for them £300,000, and in the end actually got £220,000. (Lord Selborne : *Memorials, Part I.,* 1766–1865, vol. ii. p. 450.) Thus, contrary to the usual experience, the more their business was interfered with, the richer they became.

tion of the law — an act in the statute-book of Great Britain — obviously involved serious consequences. Were they prepared to go to the journey's end on the road thus pointed out? To what might it lead? To what might it not lead?

Into the causes of the change of policy which now took place it is not necessary here to enter. The law was expounded in the *Alexandra* case on the 24th of June, 1863; the battle of Gettysburg was fought, and Vicksburg surrendered, on the 3d and 4th of the following July; three months later, on the 9th of October, the detention of the Laird iron-clads was ordered. After the rulings of the court in the *Alexandra* case, there can be no question that in this instance the law was "strained." In due time the proceeding was made the ground of attack on the government in both Houses of Parliament, on the ground that the detention was in violation of law, and without sufficient proofs. In these debates the spokesmen of the government at last took the proper ground. They admitted that Great Britain was under an obligation to give to the United States its rights under the law of nations, whether acts of Parliament furnished the means of so doing or not. The position thus at last assumed was approved by a comparatively small majority. A surprise to the American Minister then representing the country in London, the detention of the iron-clads thus marked a radical change in the policy pursued by the Palmerston-Russell Ministry. Earl Russell apparently now first realized the fact he afterwards announced in Parliament, "that in this conflict the Confederate States have no ports, except those of the Mersey and the Clyde, from which to fit

out ships to cruise against the Federals; " [1] and it
seems to have dawned upon him that, in the case of
future hostilities, other nations besides Great Britain
had ports, and, in certain not impossible contingencies,
those ports might become bases — perhaps inconvenient bases — of maritime warfare, as were now those
of the Mersey and the Clyde.   It was a thing much to
be deplored that rules did work both ways, and that
curses, like chickens, would come home to roost; but,
this being so, it behooved prudent statesmen to give
a certain degree of consideration to the precedents
they were creating.

Whether Earl Russell reasoned in this wise or not,
certain it is that after September, 1863, Great Britain
ceased to be available as a base of Confederate naval
operations.   The moment it felt so disposed, Her
Majesty's Government found means to cause the neutrality of Great Britain to be respected.   My own belief, derived from a tolerably thorough study of the
period, is that numerous causes contributed to that
change.   Among the more potent of these I should
enumerate the stirring of the British conscience which
followed the Emancipation Proclamation of September,
1862; the conviction, already referred to, that any
decisive action on the part of Great Britain was unnecessary as well as impolitic, the ultimate success of the
Confederacy being a foregone conclusion; the troubled
state of affairs on the Continent as respects both Po-
land and Denmark; and, above all, the honest anger
of Earl Russell at the consequences which had ensued
from the evasion of the *Alabama*.   The precedent he

---

[1] House of Lords, April 26, 1864.   Geneva Arbitration: *Correspondence*, etc., vol. v. p. 535.

had himself helped to create startled him, — he recoiled in presence of its logical consequences; and, in view of the complications then existing on the Continent, or there in obvious process of development, the great financial and commercial interests of Great Britain showed signs of awakening. Awkward questions were shortly in order; and, on the evening of the 13th of May, 1864, the head of the great commercial house of Barings fairly startled the country by rising in the House of Commons, and suggesting certain queries to the Government, — queries, now, thirty-seven years later, of much significance in connection with events in South Africa. "I am," Mr. Baring said, "desirous of inviting the attention of the House to the situation in which this country will be if the precedents now established are acted upon in the event of our being involved in war, while other States are neutral. Under the present construction of our municipal law there is no necessity that a belligerent should have a port or even a seashore. Provided she has money, or that money is supplied to her by a neutral, she may fit out vessels, and those vessels need not go to the country to which they are said to belong, but may go about the seas dealing destruction to British shipping and property. Take the case, which I hope we shall avoid, of our being at war with Germany. There would, as things now stand, be nothing to prevent the Diet of Frankfort from having a fleet. A number of the small States of Germany might unite together, and become a great naval power. Money is all that is required for the purpose; and Saxony, without a seashore, might have a First Lord of the Admiralty, without any docks, who might have a large fleet at his disposal.

The only answer we could make under those circumstances to France and the United States, who as neutrals might fit out vessels against us on the pretence that they were German cruisers, was that we would go to war with them; so that by the course of policy which we are pursuing we render ourselves liable to the alternative of having our property completely destroyed, or entering into a contest with every neutral Power in the world. We ought, under these circumstances, to ask ourselves what we have at stake. I will not trouble the House with statistics on the point, but we all know that our commerce is to be found extending itself to every sea, that our vessels float in the waters of every clime, that even with our cruisers afloat it would not be easy to pick up an *Alabama*, and that the destruction of our property might go on despite all our powers and resources. What would be the result? That we must submit to the destruction of our property, or that our shipping interests must withdraw their ships from the ocean. That is a danger, the apprehension of which is not confined to myself, but is shared by many who are far better able to form a judgment than I am. Recollect that your shipping is nearly twice as large as that of the United States. If you follow the principle you are now adopting as regards the United States, you must be prepared to stand the consequences; so strongly was this felt by ship-owners that memorials have already been addressed to the Government upon the subject. . . . Last night the honorable Member for Liverpool presented a petition, signed by almost all the great ship-owners of that place, enforcing the same view and expressing the same anxiety. I am a little surprised at this manifestation, because what is happening around us is a source of great profit to our ship-owners ; but it is a proof that they are sensible that the future danger will far preponderate over the present benefit and advantages." [1]

When too late, it thus dawned even on the ship-builders of the Mersey that, for a great commercial people, confederacy with corsairs might be a dangerous, even if not, in their own eyes, a discreditable vocation. Firms openly dealing in burglars' tools are not regarded as reputable.

But one way of escape from their own precedents might yet remain. It was always the contention of Mr. Charles Sumner that a neutral-built ship-of-war could not be commissioned by a belligerent on the high seas. It was and remained a pirate, — the common enemy of mankind, — until its arrival at a port of the belligerent to which it belonged, where alone, after " depositing its taint," it could be fitted out and commissioned as a ship-of-war.[2] As any port will do in a storm, and drowning men proverbially clutch at straws, it is possible to imagine a British ship-owner, as he foresaw in vision the Transvaal and the Orange Free State involved in a war with Great Britain, appropriating this contention, and trying to incorporate it into the International Code. He would then have proceeded to argue somewhat as follows : — " Mr. Baring was a banker, not a publicist. As a publicist he was wrong. A non-maritime nation cannot be a maritime belligerent," etc., etc. But, during the course of our Civil War, the British authorities, legal and political,

---

[1] Geneva Arbitration : *Correspondence*, etc., vol. v. p. 579.
[2] *Works*, vol. vii. pp. 358, 452-460 ; vol. xiii. p. 68. Pierce : *Sumner*, vol. iv. p. 394.

seemed to take pleasure in shutting against themselves every possible outlet of future escape. So, in this case, referring to the contention of Mr. Sumner, the Attorney-General, speaking after Mr. Baring, expressed himself as follows: — " To say that a country whose ports are blockaded is not at liberty to avail herself of all the resources which may be at her command in other parts of the world, that she may not buy ships in neutral territory and commission them as ships of war without bringing them to her own country first, is a doctrine which is quite preposterous, and all the arguments founded upon such a doctrine only tend to throw dust into men's eyes, and to mislead them." [1]

The morning following this significant debate the tone of Lord Palmerston's London organ underwent a notable change. Grant and Lee were that day confronting each other in the Wilderness, resting for a brief space after the fearful wrestle of Spottsylvania; in London, the conference over the Schleswig-Holstein struggle was in session, and the feelings of Great Britain were deeply enlisted on behalf of Denmark, borne down by the united weight of Prussia and Austria. So, in view of immediate possible hostilities, the *Post* now exclaimed, — " We are essentially a maritime power, and are bound by every motive of self-interest to watch with jealousy the observance of neutral maritime obligations. We may be at war ourselves ; we have a future [South Africa !] to which to look forward, and we must keep in mind the precept which inculcates the necessity of doing to others as we would be done by. . . . War is no longer con-

[1] Geneva Arbitration : *Correspondence*, etc., vol. v. p. 583.

sidered by the commercial classes an impossibility;
and the ship-owners of Liverpool are considering what
is to become of their property should we unhappily
become involved in war, and innumerable *Alabamas*
issue from neutral [American] ports to prey upon
British commerce throughout the world.   Suppose that
circumstances obliged us to espouse the cause of Denmark against her ruthless enemies, would not the
German States hasten to follow the bad example set
them by the Confederates, and at which the inefficiency
of our law obliges us to connive?"   And the London
organ of " society " and the " influential classes " then
added this sentence, which, under certain conditions
actually existing thirty-five years later, would have
been of very pregnant significance: — " Some petty
principality which boasts of a standing army of five
hundred men, but not of a single foot of sea-coast
[*e. g.* the Transvaal, the Orange Free State], might
fit out cruisers in neutral [*e. g.* American] ports to
burn, sink, and destroy the commerce of Great Britain;
and the enormous amount of damage which may be
done in a very short time, even by a single vessel, we
know from the history of the *Alabama*." [1]

Thus when the War of the Rebellion closed, the
trans-Atlantic outlook was, for Great Britain, ominous in the extreme.   Just that had come about which
English public men and British newspapers had wearied themselves with asseverating could not possibly
happen.   The *Times* and *Morning Post* especially
had loaded the record with predictions, every one
of which the event falsified; and, in doing so, they
had gone out of their way to generate bitter ill-

[1] The *Post*, May 14 and 18, 1864.

feeling by the arrogant expression of a contemptuous dislike peculiarly British and offensive. For example, the *Times*, " well aware that its articles weigh in America more heavily than despatches," first referred to us as " this insensate and degenerate [1] people," and then proceeded to denounce " this hateful and atrocious war, . . . this horrible war," which it declared was of such a character that its defenders could not find in all Europe a single society where they could make themselves heard.[2] In the same common temper, the *Standard*, reviewing the results of the conflict on the very day that Vicksburg, unknown to it, had sur-

[1] The " degeneracy " of the American was, at this time, the subject of much lachrymose contemplation on the part of British journalistic scribes. A writer in that highly respectable quarterly, the *North British Review*, thus delivered himself, for instance, in its February number for 1862 (p. 248) : — " In nearly every element of political and moral, as distinguished from material, civilization, the deterioration of America since the days of Washington had been appallingly rapid and decisive. It had ceased to be the land of progress, and had become in a peculiar manner the land of retrogression and degeneracy."

[2] July 9, 12, 1862. The course and language of the *Times* at this period were peculiarly ill-advised. American opinion on that point might be considered prejudiced ; but Mr. Leslie Stephen, then a man of thirty-three, has since established a world-wide reputation as a critic on questions of taste. Mr. Stephen, in 1865, thus expressed himself in a pamphlet (pp. 105, 106) entitled *The " Times " on the American War : A Historical Study* ; a production not included in his recognized writings, and long since forgotten : — " But my complaint against the *Times* is that its total ignorance of the quarrel, and the presumption with which it pronounced upon its merits, led to its pouring out a ceaseless flood of scurrilous abuse, couched, indeed, in decent language, but as essentially insulting as the brutal vulgarities of the New York *Herald*. No American — I will not say with the feelings of a gentleman, for of course there are no gentlemen in America — but no American with enough of the common feelings of humanity to resent the insult when you spit in his face could fail to be wounded, and, so far as he took the voice of the *Times* for the voice of England, to be irritated against England."

rendered, declared, — "We have learned to dislike,
and almost to despise the North; to sympathize with,
and cordially to admire, the South. We have learned
that the South is, on the whole, in the right; that
the North is altogether, wilfully and wickedly in the
wrong." But these expressions of heartfelt contempt
were not confined to the London press. Liverpool,
for instance, was conspicuous as a hot-bed of Confederate sympathy; and, as early as August, 1861, the
leading journal of that city expressed itself as follows:
— "We have no doubt whatever that the vast majority of the people of this country, certainly of the people of Liverpool, are in favor of the cause espoused by
the Secessionists. The defeat of the Federalists gives
unmixed pleasure; the success of the Confederates is
ardently hoped, nay, confidently predicted." A year
later, the London *Post* referred in the same tone
to those whom it saw fit, in the rarefied and luminous
atmosphere of its own exalted wisdom, to describe as
"the infatuated people across the Atlantic." "The
whole history of the war is a history of mistakes on
the Federal side. Blinded by self-conceit, influenced
by passion, reckless of the lessons of history, and deaf
to warnings which every one else could hear and
tremble at, the people of the North plunged into hostilities with their fellow-citizens without so much as a
definite idea what they were fighting for, or on what
condition they would cease fighting. They went to
war without a cause, they have fought without a plan,
and they are prosecuting it still without a principle."
It would then pleasantly allude to the "suicidal frenzy"
of a contest in which two sections were striving "with
a ferocity unknown since the times when Indian

scalped Indian on the same continent;" and sorrow-
fully add, — " American pride contemptuously dis-
dains to consider what may be thought of its proceedings by the intelligent in this country; inflated
self-sufficiency scorns alike the friendly advice of the
disinterested and the indignant censures of a disap-
proving world." And then, finally, when its every
prevision had proved wrong, and all its predictions
were falsified, as it contemplated the total collapse of
the Confederacy, this organ of " society " and the
" influential classes " innocently observed : — " The
antipathy entertained by the United States toward
England has, owing to circumstances entirely beyond
our control, and into which it is unnecessary now to
enter, been fanned into a fiercer flame during the
progress of the war;" [1] and it now spoke of Great
Britain as " the mother country ! "

Recorded utterances of this character could be
multiplied indefinitely ; [2] I take these few, selected at

[1] May 15, 1865.

[2] Those of the *Post*, read a generation after the event, and in the
light of passing South African events, are simply inconceivable.
They reflect a degree of ignorance, and a malignity of disposition,
difficult to account for. Take, for instance, the following : — " Yet
what wild tribe, from the Red River or the South Sea Islands, dan-
cing round its fires, and goading each other to fury by its cries, could
exceed in deliberate cruelty and implacability the citizens of Washington on the occasion to which we refer ? " (August 19, 1862.) The
" occasion " was a " war-meeting " at that time held, " under the au-
spices of President Lincoln." " But as the contest went on, it was
soon seen how little slavery had to do with it ; and even Europe, to a
man, has lost every spark of interest in the Federal cause. Sympathy
goes continuously southward." (August 29, 1862.) " We doubt if
there could be found in the entire universe a more degrading spectacle
than that of a regiment of negro soldiers fighting in support of the
Federal government." (September 22, 1862.) " A proclamation would
almost suffice to dislodge Abraham Lincoln. . . . We believe that if

random, merely to illustrate the extreme difficulty
of the position into which the precedents and declara-
tions she herself had established, and put freely on
record, brought Great Britain at the close of our Civil
War.   It is useless to say that, as between nations,
irresponsible utterances through the press and from the
platform are entitled to no consideration, and should
not be recalled.   They, none the less, are a fact; and
they are not forgotten.   On the contrary, they rankle.
They did so in 1865.

Happily, however, for the peace of the world, a few
great facts then stood forth, established and of record;
and it is these prominent facts which influence popular
feeling.   English built ships — English manned and
English armed — had swept the American merchant
marine from the seas; but, most fortunately, an American man-of-war of not unequal size had, within sight
of English shores, sent to the bottom of the British
Channel the single one of those commerce-destroyers
which had ventured to trust itself within the range of

President Davis were to assume the functions of President of the
United States, the population of the North would gladly accept this
ready mode of preserving the integrity of the country, and at once
acknowledge his authority." (September 24, 1862.)   "It is easy to
conceive, though it may be difficult to express, the language in which
future historians will speak of this deplorable contest.   Foolish it has
been, without a parallel in the annals of human folly.   Aimless it
has been, when the utter hopelessness of the object with which it was
prosecuted is borne in mind.   In no previous wars has the sacrifice of
human life been proportionally greater; in none has the expenditure
been so wantonly, so profligately, extravagant.   There remains, however, one term which must still be applied.   It has been profitless.
Life, money, and national credit have all been frittered away to procure — nothing!" (October 2, 1862.)   It is difficult now to recall
these, and endless similar lucubrations, without mirth; then they
hurt.   And they were meant to hurt.   Perhaps the cruelest possible
revenge for such utterances is, subsequently, and in the cold light of
actualities, to confront the utterer with them.

our guns. In this there was much balm. Again, America was weary of strife, and longed for rest; and it could well afford to bide its time in view of the changed tone and apprehensive glances which now came across the Atlantic from those whose forecast had deceived them into a position so obviously false. In common parlance, Great Britain had made her bed; she might now safely be left to a prolonged nightmare as she lay in it. The United States — no longer an " insensate and degenerate people " — could wait in confidence. Its time was sure to come.

Great Britain, also, was most uncomfortably of this same opinion. The more her public men reflected on the positions taken by the Palmerston-Russell Ministry, and the precedents therein created, the worse they seemed, and the less propitious the outlook. The reckoning was long; and it was chalked plainly on the wall. It was never lost to sight nor out of mind. The tendency of events was obvious. They all pointed to retaliation in kind; for, in the summer of 1866, the House of Representatives at Washington passed, without one dissenting vote, a bill to repeal the inhibitions contained in the American neutrality laws against the fitting out of ships for belligerents. The threat was overt; Great Britain deprecatingly met it by the passage, in 1870, of a new and stringent Foreign Enlistment Act.

Just six years elapsed between the close of the War of the Rebellion (May, 1865) and the signing of the Treaty of Washington (May, 1871). For Great Britain those were years of rapid education toward a new code of international law. Considering the interval traversed, the time of traversing it cannot be said to have been long. When, in the midst of the Civil War, tidings of the depredations of the British built Confederate commerce-destroyers reached America, instructions were sent to the Minister of the United States in London to demand reparation. To this demand Earl Russell, then Foreign Secretary, in due time responded. Not only did he deny any liability, legal or moral, but he concluded his reply with this highly significant, not to say petulant remark: — " I have only, in conclusion, to express my hope that you may not be instructed again to put forward claims which Her Majesty's Government cannot admit to be founded on any grounds of law or justice." [1]

The discussion seemed closed; Great Britain had apparently taken her stand. In the words of the Foreign Secretary, — " Her Majesty's Government entirely disclaim all responsibility for any acts of the *Alabama*." [2] This was in March, 1863. On the 19th of June, 1864, the depredations of the *Alabama* were brought to a summary close. When the Confederate Secretary of War at Richmond heard of the loss thus sustained, he wrote immediately (July 18) to the Liverpool bureau of his department: "You must supply her place if possible, a measure [now] of paramount importance." [3] This despatch reached its destination on the 30th of August, and on the 20th of October the head of the bureau had "the great satisfaction of reporting the safe departure on the 8th inst." of the *Shenandoah* from London, and its

[1] *Dip. Cor.*, 1863, p. 380. Russell to Adams, September 14, 1863. Geneva Arbitration: *Correspondence*, etc., vol. iii. p. 164.

[2] Russell to Adams, March 9, 1863. Geneva Arbitration: *Correspondence*, etc., vol. iii. p. 122.

[3] Bulloch, vol. ii. p. 112.

consort, the *Laurel*, from Liverpool, " within a few
hours of each other ; " and this in spite of " embarrassing and annoying inquiries from the Customs
and Board of Trade officials." [1] The *Shenandoah* now
took up the work of destruction which the *Alabama*
was no longer in position to continue. It thus de-
volved on the American Minister to present further
demands on the Foreign Secretary. But, in the mean
time, the situation had materially changed. The correspondence over the depredations of the *Alabama*
was abruptly closed by Earl Russell seven weeks before the unfortunate battle of Chancellorsville ; Lee
surrendered at Appomattox just two days after Mr.
Adams brought to the notice of the Foreign Secretary
the depredations of the *Shenandoah*.

A long correspondence ensued, which was closed on
the 2d of the following December by Lord Clarendon,
Earl Russell's successor as Foreign Secretary. His
despatch was brief ; but in it he observed, " that no
armed vessel departed during the war from a British
port to cruise against the commerce of the United
States ; " and he further maintained that throughout
the war " the British government have steadily and
honestly discharged all the duties incumbent on them
as a neutral power, and have never deviated from the
obligations imposed on them by international law." [2]
And yet in this correspondence the first step in the
direction of a settlement was taken, — a step curiously
characteristic of Earl Russell. As indicative also of
the amount of progress as yet made on the long road to
be traversed, it was the reverse of encouraging. Earl

[1] Bulloch, vol. ii. pp. 131–133.
[2] Geneva Arbitration : *Correspondence*, etc., vol. iii. p. 625.

Russell had brought Great Britain into a position from which she had in some way to be extricated. The events of April and May, 1865, in America were very significant when viewed in their bearing on the fast rising European complications incident to the blood-and-iron policy to which Count Bismarck was deliberately giving shape. Dark clouds, ominous of coming storm, were hanging on the European horizon; while America, powerful and at peace, lowered angrily British-ward from across the Atlantic. It was a continuous, ever-present menace, to be averted only when approached in a large way. One course — one course alone — was open to the British statesmen. But to see and follow it called for an eye and mind and pen very different, and far more quick and facile, than the eye, mind, and pen with which nature had seen fit to endow the younger scion of the ducal house of Bedford.

Had he been equal to the situation, it was then in the power of Earl Russell to extricate Great Britain from the position into which he had brought her, and out of the nettle, danger, to pluck the flower, safety. Nor would it have been difficult so to do; and that without the abandonment of any position he had taken. Weary of battle and satiated with success, America was then in complaisant mood. A complete victor is always inclined to be magnanimous, and that was a time when, as Mr. Sumner afterwards expressed it, "we would have accepted very little." [1] Taking advantage of this national mental mood, it would have been possible for Earl Russell then, while extricating Great Britain from a false position, to have at once

[1] Pierce : *Sumner*, vol. iv. p. 384.

obliterated the recollection of the past and forestalled
the Treaty of Washington, securing at the same time
the adoption at little cost of a new principle of international law obviously in the interest of Great Britain.
Still insisting in his correspondence with the American
Minister that Her Majesty's Government had, in the
language of his successor, "steadily and honestly discharged all the duties incumbent on them as a neutral
power," and hence had incurred no liability under any
recognized principle or precedent of international law
for depredations committed by Her Majesty's subjects
beyond her jurisdiction, — adhering firmly to this contention, he might have gone on to recognize, in the
light of a record which he had already over and over
admitted was a "scandal" and "a reproach to our
laws," that a radical change in the international code
was obviously desirable, and that the time for it had
come. The neutral should be responsible for results
whenever, after due notice of a contemplated infraction was given (as in the cases of the *Florida* and
Alabama), she permitted her territory to be made by
one belligerent the base of operations against another.
The laws ought, he would have admitted, to be adequate to such an emergency; and they should be enforced. He might well then have expressed the honest
regret Great Britain felt that her laws had during our
rebellion proved inadequate, and a proper sense of the
grievous injury the United States had in consequence
sustained. The rest of the way out would then have
been plain. In view of Great Britain's commercial
and maritime interests, she could well afford to incur
large pecuniary sacrifices to secure the future protection involved in the change of international law con-

tended for by the American government. She could
not ask that protection for the future with no regard
to the past. That Great Britain had incurred to a
certain extent a moral obligation through the insuf-
ficiency of her statutes, combined with the unsatisfactory state of international law, could not be denied in
view of the oft recorded admission that the cases of the
Confederate commerce-destroyers were a " scandal "
and a " reproach." Under these circumstances, Great
Britain was prepared to assent to the modifications of
international law now contended for by the United
States ; and, to secure the manifest future advantage
involved in their adoption, would agree, subject to
reasonable limitations as to extent of liability, etc., to
have those principles operate retrospectively in the case
of such Confederate commerce-destroyers as had, after
notice given, sailed from British ports of origin during
the Civil War.

In the light of what afterwards occurred, including
the Treaty of Washington and the results of the
Geneva Arbitration, it is not difficult to imagine the
astonishment with which the American Minister would
have read a despatch couched in these terms, and the
gratification with which the American people would
have hailed it. It would have been, in the reverse, a
repetition of the *Trent* experience, — the honest acknowledgment of a false attitude. The clouds would at
once have rolled away. While the national pride of
Great Britain would have suffered no hurt, that of the
United States would have been immensely flattered.
The one country would have got itself gracefully, and
cheaply, out of an impossible position. It would have
secured an advantage of inestimable future value at a

cost in reality nominal, and a cost which it afterwards had to pay; the other party would have achieved a great diplomatic victory, crowning and happily rounding out its military successes. Most unfortunately, as the result showed, Earl Russell did not have it in him thus to rise to the occasion. On the contrary, with that curious conventional conservatism which seems innate in a certain class of English public men, — an inability to recognize their own interests if presented in unaccustomed form, — the British Foreign Secretary declined to consider those very changes in the law which Parliament five years later voluntarily adopted, and which, seven years later, Great Britain agreed to incorporate in a solemn treaty. The proposed liability for the abuse of neutrality by belligerents, so invaluable to England, Lord Russell now characterized as "most burdensome, and, indeed, most dangerous;" while, with a simplicity almost humorous, he ejaculated, — "Surely, we are not bound to go on making new laws, *ad infinitum*, because new occasions arise."[1]

So, high-toned Englishman as he was, Lord Russell, guided by his instincts and traditions, as Prime Minister characteristically went on to make perceptibly worse what, as Foreign Secretary, he had already made quite sufficiently bad. He did not aggrandize, he distinctly belittled, his case. In reply to the renewed demands of the American Minister, he suggested, in a most casual way, the appointment of a joint commission, to which should be referred "all claims arising during the late Civil War [his note was dated August 30, nearly four months after the cap-

[1] Russell to Adams, August 30, 1865. Geneva Arbitration: *Correspondence*, etc., vol. i. p. 677; vol. iii. p. 561.

ture of Jefferson Davis], which the two powers shall agree to refer." [1]   The correspondence was at once published in the *Gazette ;* and, so general was the proposition of reference, that the *Times,* in commenting editorially on it the morning after publication, admitted the desirability of a settlement, and construed the proposal of a commission as designed to embrace all the American claims.   The " Thunderer's " utterance on this point might be inspired, — a feeler of public opinion ; a possible way out seemed to open. Earl Russell characteristically lost no time in closing it.   At a later day, after the Alabama claims had been arbitrated and paid, his Lordship asserted that he had always been willing to have them assumed, or, as he expressed it, would " at once have agreed to arbitration," could he have received assurances on certain controverted issues, involving, as he considered, the honor and dignity of Great Britain.[2] This was clearly an afterthought in the light of subsequent events. No suggestion of that nature was ever made by him to Mr. Adams ; and when, in October, 1865, such a possible construction was put upon his despatches, he made haste to repudiate it.   In fact, Earl Russell, still Foreign Secretary, but soon to become Premier, was not yet ready to take the first step in the educational process marked out for Great Britain.   The dose was, indeed, a bitter one ; no wonder Lord Russell contemplated it with a wry face.

So the Foreign Secretary, in October, 1865, lost no time in firmly closing the door which seemed opening. The day following the editorial implication of the

---

[1] Geneva Arbitration. *Correspondence, etc.,* vol. iii. p. 562.
[2] *Recollections and Suggestions,* p. 278.

Times, there appeared in its columns an official correction. The correctness of the implication was denied. As Mr. Adams wrote in his diary, the proposal of a joint commission, thus explained, "really stands as an offer to refer the British claims, and a facile refusal to include ours. Wonderful liberality!" And, a few days later, he added: — "The issue of the present complication now is that Great Britain stands as asking for a commission through which to procure a settlement of claims advanced by herself, at the same time that she refuses at the threshold to permit the introduction of all the material demands we have against her. Thus the British position passes all the time from bad to worse. The original blunder, inspired by the over-eagerness to see us divided, has impelled a neutral policy, carried to such extremes of encouragement to one belligerent as seemingly to hazard the security of British commerce, whenever the country shall become involved in a war. The sense of this inspires the powers of eastern Europe with vastly increased confidence in pursuing their particular objects. It is not difficult to see that whatever views Russia may ultimately have on Constantinople will be much fortified by a consciousness of the diversion which it might make through the neutral ports of the United States against the British commerce of one half of the globe. We lose nothing by the passage of time; Great Britain does."

This somewhat obvious view of the situation evidently suggested itself to the mind of Earl Russell's successor in the Foreign Office, for Earl Russell, on the death of Lord Palmerston, in the autumn of 1865, became Prime Minister. So, one day in the following

December, Mr. Adams was summoned to an official interview with the new Secretary. The conversation at this interview, after the matters immediately in hand were disposed of, passed to the general and well-worn subject of the neutrality observed by Great Britain during the struggle which, seven months before, had come to its close. Lord Clarendon, Mr. Adams wrote, insisted that the neutrality "had been perfectly kept; and I signifying my conviction that a similar observation of it, as between two countries so closely adjacent as Great Britain and France, would lead to a declaration of war by the injured party in twenty-four hours. Here we might have closed the conference, but his Lordship proceeded to continue it by remarking that he had it on his mind to make a suggestion. He would do so. He went on to express his long conviction of the expediency of a union of sentiment and policy between two great nations of the same race. He hoped to see them harmonize, after the immediate irritation consequent upon the late struggle should have passed away, more than ever before. There were many things in what was called International Law that are now in a vague and unsatisfactory condition; it would, therefore, seem very desirable that by some form of joint consultation, more or less extensive, these points could be fixed on something like a permanent basis. He inquired of me whether I thought my government would be at all inclined to entertain the idea. I replied that the object was certainly desirable; but that, in the precise state in which things had been left, I could give no opinion on the question proposed. All that I could do was to report it; and that not in any official way. His Lordship talked a

little grandly about our overlooking the past, letting
bygones be bygones, and considering these questions
solely on their abstract importance as settling great
principles. He said that two such very great countries could scarcely be expected to stoop to concessions
or admissions in regard to one another. Would I
reflect upon the whole matter. All this time I was
rather a listener than a speaker, and committed myself
to nothing but vague professions. The fact stares up
that this government is not easy at the way the case
has been left by Lord Russell, and desires to get out
of it without mortification. My own opinion is rather
against any effort to help them out. I ought to note
that yesterday Mr. W. E. Forster called to see me
for the purpose of urging precisely the same tentative
experiment at Washington. He reasoned with me
more frankly, in the same strain, and evidently contemplated a more complete process of rectification of
the blunder than Lord Clarendon could hint. I also
talked to him with more freedom, in a strain of great
indifference about arriving at any result; the advantage was on our side, and I saw no prospect of its
diminishing with time. He ended by asking me to
think a little longer about a mode of running the
negotiation; for, if it could be done, he felt sure that
enough power could be applied to bring this government to consent to it. I replied that all that could
be done now must pass through private channels.
The record was made up, and I had no inclination to
disturb it."

This call of Mr. Forster at that particular juncture was significant; for Mr. Forster less than a
month before had gone into Earl Russell's Ministry,

becoming Under-Secretary for the Colonies ; and Mr.
Forster was well known to be a friend of the United
States. Badly compromised by Lord Russell's blundering committals, the government at last appreciated
the situation, and was feeling for a way out. The
position now taken by the Foreign Secretary and Mr.
Forster was clearly suggestive of the subsequent Johnson-Clarendon Convention. Nothing, however, immediately resulted. Lord Clarendon had, indeed, at the
time of his talk with Mr. Adams, already put his suggestion in shape to be formally submitted to Secretary
Seward through the British Minister at Washington ;
and when, six weeks later, his despatch appeared in
the Blue Book, Mr. Adams wrote : " The object is
now evident. It is to blunt the effect of Lord Russell's original blunder, and try to throw the odium of
it back by a new offer, which we must decline. The
contrivance will scarcely work. It is certainly civil
to propose that we should bear all the consequences
of their policy, and consent to secure them against
any future application of it to themselves."

As showing how very sensitive to the situation in
which they had been placed the English now were,
Mr. Adams two days later mentioned a long conversation with Mr. Oliphant, a member of Parliament, then
just back from a visit to America. The Fenian movement was at that time much in evidence through its
British dynamite demonstrations, and the Irish in the
United States were consequently in a state of chronic
excitement. Mr. Oliphant called in regard to it.
After some discussion of that matter, the conversation
drifted to the policy pursued by the British government toward the United States, of which Mr. Oli-

phant "evidently had not approved. It should have been either positive intervention, or positive amity. The effort to avoid both had excited nothing but ill-will from both parties in the war. One Southern man whom he had met had gone so far as to declare that he was ready to fight England even on the case of the *Alabama*. I briefly reviewed the course taken, and pointed out the time when the cordiality between the countries could have been fully established. It was not improved; and now I had little hope of restoring it for many years." It was during the ensuing summer that the lower house of Congress passed by acclamation the bill already referred to, repealing the inhibitions of the neutrality laws.

A change of ministry at this time took place in Great Britain. Earl Russell, with the Liberals, went out of office, and Lord Derby, at the head of the Conservatives, came in. Lord Stanley, the oldest son of the new Premier, succeeded Lord Clarendon in the Foreign Office, and again the old straw was threshed over. A distinct step was, however, now marked in advance. The new Prime Minister took occasion to intimate publicly that a proposition for the arrangement of the *Alabama* claims would be favorably entertained; and the *Times*, of course under inspiration, even went so far as to admit that Earl Russell's position on that subject was based on a " somewhat narrow and one-sided view of the question at issue. It was not safe," it now went on to say, " for Great Britain to make neutrals the sole and final judges of their own obligations." This was a distinct enlargement of the " insular" view. It amounted to an abandonment of the contention that a petty jury in an English criminal court was the tribunal of last resort on all questions involving the international obligations of Great Britain.

The interminable diplomatic correspondence then began afresh; and, in the course of it, Secretary Seward rested the case of the United States largely on what both he and Mr. Adams termed " the premature and injurious proclamation of belligerency " issued by the British government in May, 1861. This he pronounced the fruitful source whence all subsequent evil came. Lord Stanley took issue with him on that point. He did not deny a responsibility for the going forth of Confederate commerce-destroyers from British ports, and a certain liability for the damages by them caused; but, he contended, the British government could not consent to arbitrate the question whether the Confederacy was prematurely recognized as a belligerent. The recognition of belligerency in any given case was, he contended, a matter necessarily resting in the discretion of a sovereign, neutral power. He intimated, however, a willingness to arbitrate all other questions at issue.

In view of the position always from the commencement taken by the American Secretary of State and his representative in London, this limited arbitration could not be satisfactory. Time and again Secretary and Minister had emphasized the impropriety and unfriendliness of the Queen's proclamation of May 13, 1861, and the consequences thereof, so momentous as scarcely to admit of computation. Accordingly, the discussion again halted. In July, 1868, Mr. Reverdy Johnson of Maryland succeeded Mr. Adams in London; and, once more, negotiations were renewed. But now the British government had so far progressed towards its ultimate and inevitable destination that, a discreet silence being on both sides observed in the matter of the proclamation of May, 1861, a convention was readily agreed to covering all claims of the citizens and subjects of the two countries against the government of each. While this treaty was in course of negotiation, another change of ministry took place in Great Britain; and Mr. Gladstone, who had been Chancellor of the Exchequer throughout the Civil War, became Premier, Earl Russell being now finally retired from official life. Lord Clarendon was again placed in charge of the Foreign Office. Under these circumstances, the form of convention agreed to by Lord Derby was revised by his successor in such a way as to make it satisfactory to Secretary Seward, and, on the 14th of January, 1869, it received the signatures of Mr. Johnson and Lord Clarendon. It was known as the Johnson-Clarendon Convention.

In hurrying this important negotiation to so quick a close, both Secretary Seward and Reverdy Johnson were much influenced by a natural ambition. They both greatly desired that a settlement of the momentous issues between the two English-speaking nations should be effected through their individual agency. Mr. Seward especially was eager in his wish to carry to a final solution the most difficult of the many intricate complications which dated back to the first weeks of his occupation of the State Department. Accordingly, he did not now repeat his somewhat rhetorical arraignment of Great Britain in the correspondence of two years before, because of the proclamation of 1861. No longer did he roar so as to do the genuine American's heart good to hear him, but he did so aggravate his voice as to roar as gently as a sucking dove; he roared as 't were a nightingale. It thus became simply a question of the settlement of the money claims of individual citizens and subjects of one country against the government of another. Lord Stanley's contention on the recognition of belligerency issue was tacitly accepted as sound. This, as will presently appear, implied a great deal. It remained to be seen whether that primal offence — that original sin which

" Brought death into the world and all our woe " —

could thus lightly and in silence be relegated to the limbo of things unimportant, and so, quite forgotten.

The negotiation had been entered upon in September, 1868; the convention was executed in January following. But in the interim a presidential election had taken place in the United States; and, when the treaty reached America, the administration of Andrew Johnson was, in a few weeks only, to be replaced by that of General Grant. Secretary Seward would then cease to be at the head of the Department of State; and, as he now wrote to Reverdy Johnson, " the confused light of an incoming administration was spreading itself over the country, rendering the consideration of political subjects irksome, if not inconvenient." Charles Sumner was at that time chairman of the Senate Committee on Foreign Relations, a position he had held through eight years. As chairman of that committee, the fate of the treaty rested largely with him. The President-elect, with no very precise policy in his mind to be pursued on the issues involved, wished to have the claims convention go over until his administration was installed;

and when, in February, the convention was taken up in the Senate committee, all its members expressed themselves as opposed to its ratification. " We begin to-day," Mr. Sumner then said, referring to the rejection of the proposed settlement as a foregone conclusion, " an international debate, the greatest of our history, and, before it is finished, in all probability the greatest of all history." [1]

III

It was now that Mr. Fish came upon the scene, — the successor of Secretary Seward in the Department of State. And here, perhaps, it would be proper for me to say that I had no personal acquaintance with Mr. Fish. I never met him but once. In the summer of 1890, I think it was, some years preceding his death, I passed a morning with him by appointment at his country home at Garrison, going there to obtain from him, if I could, some information on a subject I was then at work on. Beyond this, I knew him only as a public character, more or less actively engaged in political life through twenty-five exceptionally eventful years.

Held in its Committee of Foreign Relations, the Johnson-Clarendon Convention was not acted upon by the Senate, at the time sitting in executive session, until the 13th of April, 1869. It was then rejected by a practically unanimous vote (54 to 1) following an elaborate speech in condemnation of it by the chairman of the committee having it in charge. That speech was important. It marked a possible parting of the

[1] Pierce: *Sumner*, vol. iv. p. 384.

ways. In that speech, and by means of it, Mr. Sumner not only undid, and more than undid, all that yet had been done looking to an amicable adjustment of the questions at issue between the two nations, but he hedged thick with difficulties any future approach to such an adjustment. To appreciate this, the essential feature of the Clarendon-Johnson Convention must be borne constantly in mind.

As I have already said, that convention provided only for the settlement of the claims of individuals. All questions of liability were to be referred to arbitration. The right of Great Britain to judge for itself as to the time and manner of the recognition of the Confederacy as a belligerent power was not called in question, or submitted to arbitrament. A settlement was thus made possible; indeed, the way to a settlement was opened wide. The concession was also proper; for, viewed historically, and with a calm regard for recognized principles of international law, it must be admitted that the long and strenuously urged contention of Secretary Seward and Mr. Adams over what they described as the " premature and injurious proclamation of belligerency," and the consequences of the precipitancy of Great Britain in the early stages of the Rebellion, was by them carried to an undue length. Indisputably, the British Ministry did issue the very important proclamation of May, 1861, with undue haste; and, in so doing, they were presumably actuated by a motive they could not declare. The newly accredited American Minister had not then reached London; but he was known to be on his way, and, in fact, saw the just issued proclamation in the *Gazette* the morning of his arrival. The intention of the government may fairly be inferred. It apparently was that this question should be disposed of, — be an accomplished fact, — in advance of any protests. It had been decided on; discussion was useless. This was neither usual nor courteous. It was, moreover, in direct disregard of assurances given : and, in the excited state of the American public mind at that time, while it was passionately denounced, evil auguries were drawn from it. Yet it by no means followed that the step was taken in an unfriendly spirit, or that it in fact worked any real prejudice to the Union cause. That it was a grievous blow, given with a hostile intent, and the source of infinite subsequent trouble and loss to the United States government, Secretary Seward and Mr. Adams always afterwards maintained ; and, during the war, very properly maintained. But for it, they asserted and seem even to have persuaded themselves, the Rebellion would have collapsed in its infancy. Because of it, the struggling insurrection grew into a mighty conflict, and was prolonged to at least twice the length of life it otherwise would have attained. For this, they then proceeded to argue, and for the loss of life and treasure in it involved, Great Britain stood morally accountable; or, as Secretary Seward years afterwards saw fit to phrase it, in rhetoric which now impresses one as neither sober nor well considered, it was Her Majesty's proclamation which conferred " upon the insurrection the pregnant baptismal name of Civil War."

There then was, and there now is, nothing on which to base so extreme an assumption. On the contrary, the historical evidence tends indisputably to show that, though designedly precipitate, the proclamation was

issued with no unfriendly intent.   On this point, the
statement of William E. Forster is conclusive.   Mr.
Forster, then a newly elected member of Parliament,
himself urged the issuance of the proclamation, and
looked upon it as a point gained for the cause of the
Union ; [1] and eight years later he declared that " from
personal recollection and knowledge " he could testify
that " the proclamation was not made with unfriendly
animus " to the United States.   On the contrary, he
showed it was issued " in accordance with the earnest
wishes of himself and other friends of the North." [2]

The principle of international law involved is simple,
and founded on good sense.   In no case and under no
circumstances can a declaration of neutrality, which
carries with it of necessity a recognition of the fact
of belligerency, be a wrong to a power which is itself
exercising, or has assumed to exercise against neutrals,
any of the rights of war.   Exclusion by blockade,
search for contraband, and capture as prize on the
high seas are distinct acts of war.   All these rights
the government of the United States claimed, and
exercised, after the 19th of April, 1861.   It is difficult to see how foreign governments, in view of the
consequent interruptions of commerce and seizure of
property, could long ignore such an abnormal state
of affairs.   They might, from an excess of comity, do
so for a few weeks, and until the state of war and its
consequences became fixed and manifold ; but of this
they were of necessity the judges.[3]

Neither is there any ground not admitting of dispute on which to argue that the issuance by the British

---

[1] Reid : *Forster*, vol. i. p. 335.   [2] *Ib.*, vol. ii. pp. 12, 21.
[3] See Appendix A, *infra* p. 199.

government of the proclamation of May, 1861, however premature, and with whatever intent, was productive of any injury to the United States. On the contrary, it has been plausibly contended that it worked in the end most potently in favor of the Union cause.[1] It is obvious that the proclamation could not in any event have been withheld more than ninety days; for within that period the Confederacy had at Manassas incontrovertibly established its position as a belligerent, and the Confederate flag on the high seas, combined with a Union blockade of three thousand miles of hostile coast, was evidence not easily explained away of a *de facto* government on land. Under such conditions, it is idle to maintain that the recognition of belligerency did not fairly rest in the discretion of neutrals. Moreover, had the recognition been delayed until after the disgrace of Bull Run, it would in all probability have been complete, and have extended to a recognition of nationality as well as of mere *de facto* belligerency. Nor, finally, is there anything in the record, as since more fully developed, which justifies a belief that the struggle would have been shorter even by a month, or in any degree less costly as respects either life or treasure, had the Confederacy never been buoyed up by the confident hope of foreign recognition, and consequent aid from without. The evidence is indeed all the other way. As since developed, it is fairly conclusive that, almost to the end, and unquestionably down to the close of 1863, while the Confederates, rank and file as well as leaders civil and military, confidently counted on being able, through the potency of their cotton con-

[1] *Life of C. F. Adams*, American Statesmen Series, pp. 171–174.

trol, to compel an even reluctant European recognition,[1] yet they never for a moment doubted their
ability to maintain themselves in arms and achieve
independence without extraneous aid of any kind.
Thirty years in preparation, calling into action all the
resources of a singularly masterful and impulsive race,
numbering millions and occupying a highly defensible
territory of enormous area, the Confederate rebellion
was never that sickly, accidental foster-child of Great
Britain which, in all their diplomatic contentions,
Secretary Seward and Senator Sumner tried so hard
to make it out, — a mere bantling dandled into premature existence by an incomplete foreign recognition.
On the contrary, from start to finish, it was Titanic
in proportions and spirit. It presented every feature
of war on the largest scale, domestic and foreign. From
the outset, neutral interests were involved; European
opinion was by both sides invoked. In face of such
conditions and facts as these, to go on, to the end of
the chapter, asserting that such a complete and formidable embodiment of all-pervasive warlike energy
should, through years, have been ignored as an exist-

[1] The evidence on this point, though now largely forgotten, is overwhelming. Jefferson Davis, in common with the great mass of the
people of the Confederacy, had an implicit — an almost childlike faith
in the commercial, and consequent political, supremacy of cotton.
They wanted no other ally. They went the full length gone by J.
H. Hammond of South Carolina when, on the 4th of March, 1858,
he thus expressed himself in the Senate at Washington : — "Without
firing a gun, without drawing a sword, should [the States of the North]
make war on us, we could bring the whole world to our feet. What
would happen if no cotton was furnished for three years ? I will not
stop to depict what every one can imagine ; but this is certain, England would topple headlong, and carry the whole civilized world with
her. No, you dare not make war on cotton. No power on earth dares
to make war on it — Cotton is King ! "

ing fact by all foreign nations, and refused a recognition even as belligerent, was, historically speaking, the reverse of creditable — it was puerile. Yet, after this unparalleled struggle had been brought to a close, Secretary Seward had the assurance to assert in a despatch to Mr. Adams, written in January, 1867 : — " Before the Queen's proclamation of neutrality the disturbance in the United States was merely a local insurrection. It wanted the name of war to enable it to be a civil war and to live; " and this was merely the persistent iteration of a similar statement likewise made to Mr. Adams shortly prior to the 1862 disasters at Shiloh and before Richmond : — " If Great Britain should revoke her decree conceding belligerent rights to the insurgents to-day, this civil strife . . . would end to-morrow." [1]

The Johnson-Clarendon Convention was open to criticism at many points, and its rejection by the Senate was altogether defensible. It did, however, have one merit, it quietly relegated to oblivion the altogether untenable positions just referred to. By so much the discussion approached a rational basis. Unfortunately, it was upon that very feature of the settlement Mr. Sumner characteristically directed his criticism, and brought his rhetoric to bear. In so doing he gave the debate a violent wrench, forcing it back into its former impossible phase; and, in so far as in him lay, he put obstacles, well-nigh insuperable, in the way of any future approach to an adjustment. Recurring in his speech, subsequently published by order of the Senate, to the sentimental grounds of complaint because of conjectural injuries resulting

[1] *Dip. Cor.* 1862, p. 43. See Appendix B, *infra*, p. 204.

from precipitate action based on an assumed unfriendly purpose in the issuance of the proclamation
of May 13, 1861, he proceeded to do what his great
model Burke had declared himself unwilling to do,
— he framed an indictment of a whole people, — an
indictment of many counts, some small, others grandiose, all set forth in rhetoric incontestably Sumner-
esque. In 1869 he fairly outdid Seward in 1862.
Because of the proclamation, and because of that
solely, he pronounced Great Britain responsible not
only for the losses incurred through the depredations
of all British built Confederate commerce-destroyers,
but for all consequent losses and injuries, conjectural
and consequential, computable or impossible of computation, including the entire cost of the Civil War
during half its length, and an estimate of the value
of a large and increasing proportion of the world's
carrying trade. The " war prolongation " claim, as
it was called, Mr. Gladstone afterwards estimated as
alone amounting to eight thousand million dollars
(£1,600,000,000).[1] From lack of information only,
Mr. Sumner failed to include a trifle of an hundred
millions, which the Confederate Secretary of the Navy
had, in 1864, put down as the increased expenditure
imposed on the United States by the naval operations set on foot by his department alone;[2] but he
counterbalanced this omission by including an hundred and ten millions on account of " our natural
increase in [a certain] branch of industry which an
intelligent statistician " had told him we might have
looked for, if, etc., etc. He then triumphantly added,
" Of course this ($110,000,000) is only an item in

[1] Reid: *Forster*, vol. ii. p. 24.   [2] Bulloch, vol. ii. p. 112.

our bill." [1] The chairman of the Senate Committee on Foreign Relations then put himself on record deliberately, and not in the heat of debate, as estimating the money liability of Great Britain, because of the issuance of the proclamation of May 13, 1861, at twenty-five hundred millions of dollars ; and he clinched the matter by declaring that " whatever may be the final settlement of these great accounts, such must be the judgment in any chancery which consults the simple equity of the case." And this proposition the Senate of the United States now by formal vote approved, promulgating it to the world as its own.

No one in the United States was at that time so familiar with the issues between the two countries, or so qualified to speak understandingly of them, as Mr. Adams, from his Boston retirement then watching the course of events with a deep and natural interest. On reading Mr. Sumner's speech, and noting the unanimity of the vote by which the Senate had rejected the convention, he wrote, — " The practical effect of this is to raise the scale of our demands of reparation so very high that there is no chance of negotiation left, unless the English have lost all their spirit and character. The position in which it places Mr. Bright and our old friends in the struggle is awkward to the last degree. Mr. Goldwin Smith, who was at the meeting of the [Massachusetts] Historical Society [which chanced that day to be held], spoke of it to me with some feeling. The whole affair is ominous of the change going on in our form of government; for this is a pronunciamento from the Senate as the treaty-making power. There were intimations made to me

[1] *Works,* vol. xiii. p. 83.

in conversation that the end of it all was to be the
annexation of Canada by way of full indemnity.
Movements were going on in that region to accelerate
the result. I suppose that event is inevitable at some
time; but I doubt whether it will come in just that
form. Great Britain will not confess a wrong, and
sell Canada as the price of a release from punishment.
. . . I begin to be apprehensive that the drift of this
government under the effect of that speech will be to
a misunderstanding; and, not improbably, an ultimate
seizure of Canada by way of indemnification." To
the same effect the British Minister at Washington,
Mr. Thornton, was apprising his government that,
in the Senate debate held in executive session, Mr.
Sumner was followed by a few other Senators, all
speaking in the same sense. Mr. Chandler, Senator
from Michigan, seeming to be most violent against
England, indicating his desire that Great Britain
should possess no territory on the American Continent.

General Grant was now fairly entered on his first
presidential term, and Mr. Fish had, for some five
weeks, been Secretary of State. So far as concerned
an amicable settlement between Great Britain and the
United States, the outlook was unpropitious; less propitious, in fact, than at any previous time. The new
President was a military man, and, in the language of
Mr. Sumner, he was " known to feel intensely on the
Alabama question." At the close of the war he had
expressed himself in a way hostile to Great Britain, not
caring whether she " paid ' our little bill ' or not ; upon
the whole he would rather she should not, as that
would leave the precedent of her conduct in full force

for us to follow, and he wished it understood that we should follow it." During the war, he had been accustomed to regard Great Britain as " an enemy," and the mischief caused by her course he thought not capable of overstatement; and, in May, 1869, Sumner wrote that the President's views were in close conformity with those set forth in his speech, and that after its delivery General Grant had thanked and congratulated him.[1] Everything, consequently, now seemed to indicate that events must take the course thus marked out for them. Great Britain would have to face the contingencies of the future weighted down by the policy followed by Palmerston and Russell, and confronted by the precedents of the *Florida*, the *Alabama*, and the *Shenandoah*. She had taken her position in 1861–65, defiantly proclaiming that, for her, conditions could never be reversed, the womb of the future contained no day of reckoning, — no South Africa.

Into the details of what now ensued, it is not necessary here to enter. They are matter of history; and as such, sufficiently familiar. I shall pass rapidly over even the Motley imbroglio, coming directly to the difficulty between Mr. Fish and Mr. Sumner, — high officials both, the one Secretary of State, the other chairman of the Senate Committee on Foreign Relations. In regard to this difficulty much has been written; more said. In discussing it, whether by pen or word of mouth, no little temper has been displayed;[2] but, so far as I am aware, its significance in an historical way has never been developed. As I look upon it, it was an essential element, — almost

[1] Pierce: *Sumner*, vol. iv. pp. 255, 389, 393, 410.
[2] See, for example, Pierce: *Sumner*, vol. iv. p. 469.

a necessary preliminary to that readjustment between the United States and Great Britain now so influential a factor in the international relations of four continents.

The divergence between the two was almost immediate. The position of Mr. Fish, as head of the State Department, was, so far as Mr. Sumner was concerned, one of great and constantly increasing difficulty. The latter had then been seventeen years a member of the Senate, and, during eight of the seventeen, chairman of the Committee on Foreign Relations. Secretary Seward had been Mr. Sumner's senior in the Senate, and afterwards Secretary of State from the commencement of Sumner's chairmanship of his committee. Naturally, therefore, though he had often been bitter in his attacks on the Secretary, — at times, indeed, *more suo*, indulging even in language which knew no limit of moderation,[1] — he regarded him with very different eyes from those through which he cast glances of a somewhat downward kind on Seward's successor in office. In earlier senatorial days, when they sat together in that body during the Pierce administration, Mr. Fish had always evinced much deference to Sumner's scholarly and social attributes, and had treated him with a consideration which the latter not impossibly misconstrued. The evidence is clear and of record that, when unexpectedly called to take charge of the State Department, Mr. Fish was solicitous as to Sumner's feeling towards him, and anxious to assure himself of the latter's coöperation and even guidance. Meanwhile, though wholly unconscious of the fact, Mr. Sumner could not help regarding Mr.

[1] Adams : *R. H. Dana*, vol. ii. pp. 258, 259.

Fish as a tyro, and was not disposed to credit him with any very clearly defined ideas of his own.[1] He assumed, as matter of course, that at last the shaping of the foreign policy of the country would by seniority devolve upon him. The appointment of Mr. Motley to succeed Mr. Reverdy Johnson in the English mission undoubtedly confirmed him in this opinion. Mr. Motley was his appointee. That the new plenipotentiary regarded himself as such at once became apparent; for, immediately after his confirmation, he prepared a memoir suggestive of the instructions to be given him. The Johnson-Clarendon Convention had just been rejected; the course now to be pursued was under advisement; Mr. Sumner's recent speech was still matter of general discussion. The new President was understood to have no very clearly defined ideas on the subject; it was assumed that Mr. Fish was equally susceptible to direction. Mr. Motley, therefore, looked to Mr. Sumner for inspiration. In his memorandum he suggested that it was not advisable at present to attempt any renewal of negotiations. And then he fell back on the proclamation of May, 1861; proceeding to dilate on that wrong committed by Great Britain, — a wrong so deeply felt by the American people! This sense of wrong had now been declared gravely, solemnly, without passion; and the sense of it was not to be expunged by a mere money payment to reimburse a few captures and conflagrations at sea. And here, for the present, he proposed to let the matter rest. A time might come when Great Britain would see her fault, and be disposed to confess it. Reparation of some sort would then nat-

---

[1] Pierce: *Sumner*, vol. iv. pp. 375, 378.

urally follow; but, meanwhile, it was not for the
United States to press the matter further.

Distinct indications of a divergence of opinion as to
the course to be pursued were at once apparent. The
President, acting as yet under the influence of Mr.
Sumner, wished Mr. Motley to proceed forthwith to
his post; Mr. Fish inclined to delay his going.   Meanwhile the Secretary was at work on the new Minister's
letter of instructions; and in them he clearly did not
draw his inspiration from the Motley memoir.   On
the contrary, referring to the fate of the Johnson-
Clarendon Convention in the Senate, he proceeded to
say that, because of this action, the government of the
United States did not abandon " the hope of an early,
satisfactory, and friendly settlement of the questions
depending between the two governments."   The suspension of negotiations, he added, would, the President
hoped, be regarded by Her Majesty's Government, as
it was by him, " as wholly in the interest, and solely
with a view, to an early and friendly settlement."
The Secretary then went on to open the way to such
a settlement by defining, in terms presently to be referred to, the views of the President on the effect to be
ascribed to the Queen's proclamation of May, 1861.

At this point, the reason became apparent why Mr.
Fish was in no haste to have the newly appointed Minister proceed at once to London.   The Secretary was
in a dilemma.   The rule of action he was about to lay
down as that which should have guided the British
government in 1861 must control the United States
in 1869.   That was obvious; but, in 1869, the United
States was itself the interested observer of an insurrection in the neighboring island of Cuba; and, more-

over, the new President was not backward in expressing the warm sympathy he felt for the insurgents
against Spanish colonial misrule. He wished also to
forward their cause. That wish would find natural expression in a recognition of belligerent rights. General
Grant was a man of decided mind; he was very persistent; his ways were military; and, as to principles
of international law, his knowledge of them can hardly
be said to have been so much limited as totally wanting. He inclined strongly to a policy of territorial
expansion; but his views were in the direction of the
tropics, — the Antilles and Mexico, — rather than towards Canada and the north. As the event, however,
showed, once his mind was finally made up and his
feelings enlisted, it was not easy to divert him from his
end. In the matter of foreign policy, the course he
now had in mind, though neither of the two at first
realized the fact, involved of necessity and from the
outset a struggle with Mr. Sumner; and, to one who
knew the men, appreciating their characteristics and
understanding their methods, it was plain that the
struggle would be bitter, prolonged and unrelenting.

As different in their mental attributes as in their
physical appearance, while Mr. Sumner was, intellectually, morally and physically, much the finer and more
imposing human product, Grant had counterbalancing
qualities which made him, in certain fields, the more
formidable opponent. With immense will, he was
taciturn; Sumner, on the contrary, in no way deficient
in will, was a man of many words, — a rhetorician.
In action and among men, Grant's self-control was
perfect, — amounting to complete apparent imperturb-
ability. Unassuming, singularly devoid of self-con-

sciousness, in presence of an emergency his blood never seemed to quicken, his face became only the more set — tenacity personified ; whereas Sumner, — when morally excited, the rush of his words, his deep, tremulous utterance, and the light in his eye did not impart conviction or inspire respect. Doubts would suggest themselves to the unsympathetic, or only partially sympathetic, listener whether the man was of altogether balanced mind. At such times, Mr. Sumner did not appreciate the force of language, nor, indeed, know what he said ; and, quite unconsciously on his part, he assumed an attitude of moral superiority and intellectual certainty, in no way compatible with a proper appreciation of the equality of others. In the mind of a man like Grant, these peculiarities excited obstinacy, anger and contempt. Thus, an agitator and exponent of ideas, Mr. Sumner might and did stimulate masses, but never, man or boy, was he a leader among equals. Moreover, as one of his truest friends and warmest admirers said of him, he was prone to regard difference of opinion as a moral delinquency.[1] Grant, on the contrary, not retentive of enmities, regardless of consistency, and of coarse moral as well as physical fibre, moved towards his ends with a stubborn persistency which carried others along with him, and against which a perfervid, rhetorical opposition was apt to prove unavailing.

Mr. Fish stood between the two. So far as questions of foreign policy, and problems of international law, were concerned, though, as the result unmistakably

[1] " A man who did not believe there was another side to the question, who would treat difference of opinion almost as moral delinquency." George William Curtis, in his oration on Charles Sumner, *Orations and Addresses*, vol. iii. p. 230.

showed, well grounded in fundamental principles and with a grasp of general conditions at once firm and correct, there is no evidence that, before his quite unexpected summons to the Department of State, the new Secretary had felt called upon to form definite conclusions. Mr. Fish was, however, not only a lawyer by profession, but, without any claim to being what is known as a jurist or publicist, his thought had a distinctly legal turn. No more doctrinaire than mercantile or philanthropic, his was essentially a practical mind, strongly infused with saving common sense. By nature cautious and conservative, not an imaginative man, having passed his whole life in a New York social and commercial environment, he would have inclined to proceed slowly in any path of national expansion, most of all in one heading towards the tropics, and an admixture of half-breeds. So far as Great Britain was concerned, he would, on the other hand, be disposed to effect, if he could, an amicable, business-like settlement on rational terms. From the beginning he was inclined to think Mr. Sumner had in his speech gone too far, — that the positions he had taken were not altogether tenable. The British proclamation of May, 1861, he regarded as a " grievous wrong " under all the circumstances of the case ; but he assented to the position of Lord Stanley that issuing it was within the strict right of the neutral, and the question of time was one of judgment. As he wrote to a friend in May, 1869, four weeks after Mr. Sumner had enunciated very different views in his Senate speech, the proclamation could be made subject of complaint only as leading in its execution and enforcement to the fitting out of the *Alabama*, etc., and the moral support given in England to the rebel cause. " Sumner's speech was able and eloquent, and perhaps not without a good effect. . . . Although the only speech made in the debate, it was not the argument of all who agreed in the rejection of the treaty, and we cannot stand upon it in all its points." [1] Within a week of the rejection of the Johnson-Clarendon Convention he wrote to another friend, — "Whenever negotiations are resumed, the atmosphere and the surroundings of this side of the water are more favorable to a proper solution of the question than the dinner-tables and the public banquetings of England."

Thus, from the very commencement, there was an essential divergence of view between the Secretary of State and the Senator from Massachusetts, as well as between the latter and the President. As between Charles Sumner and Ulysses S. Grant, past friendly relations, similar social connections, and common tastes would decidedly have drawn Mr. Fish towards the former ; but, by nature loyal, he was distinctly repelled by Mr. Sumner's demeanor.

I have dwelt on these personal factors, and divergences of view and aim, for they must be kept constantly in mind in considering what was now to occur. They account for much otherwise quite inexplicable. In history as a whole, — the inexhaustible story of man's development from what he once was to what he now is, — the individual as a factor is so far minimized that the most considerable unit might probably have been left out of the account, and yet the result be in no material respect other than it is. Exceptional forces and individual traits counterbalance each other, tend-

[1] See Appendix C, *infra*, p. 206.

ing always to average results. With episodes it is far
otherwise. In them the individual has free play ; and,
accordingly, the personal factor counts. The Treaty
of Washington was an episode. In dealing with the
conditions which led up to that treaty, the minds of
Charles Sumner and Hamilton Fish naturally moved
on different lines ; while it so chanced that the likes
and dislikes, the objectives, surroundings and methods
of Ulysses S. Grant,— disturbing factors, — largely
affected the result.

IV

In the years 1869 and 1870, as indeed throughout
his public life, Charles Sumner was intent on the African, and questions of human right ; and consequently,
while, in the matter of territorial expansion, he might
look vaguely to Canada and a Greater American policy,
he would instinctively be opposed to any movement in
the direction of the tropics. President Grant, on the
contrary, from the beginning of his first presidential
term, was bent on early acquisitions in the West Indies, and disposed to adopt a summary tone towards
Spain. As respects Great Britain, his attitude, one
of comparative indifference, admitted of almost indefi-
nite shaping. Mr. Fish, new, and not comfortable, in
his unsolicited position, was inclined to be influenced,
— almost to be led, by Sumner ; but he at the same
time looked to Grant as the head of an administration,
in which he himself held the place of precedence, and
was disposed to give to his chief a thoroughly loyal
support. New in their positions, and, so far as Grant
was concerned, strange to each other, they had all to

find their bearings.   Under such circumstances, inexperienced in foreign affairs and unduly distrustful of himself on questions of international law, the new Secretary seems in some degree to have turned to Caleb Cushing; nor could he, among men then available at Washington, have found a more competent or tactful adviser.   Of decided parts, with good attainments and remarkable powers of acquisition, Caleb Cushing was a man of large experience, much human insight, and, while given to manipulation, he was not hampered either in council or in action by any excess of moral sensibility.   He understood the situation; and he understood Mr. Sumner.

In the matter of the Queen's proclamation of May, 1861, and the concession of belligerent rights, it was thus a case of alternatives, — the rule of British accountability to be laid down for the new administration must not stand in the way of a more than possible line of aggressive action towards Spain.   That the instructions now prepared for Mr. Motley were more rational than the positions assumed by Mr. Sumner four weeks before, must be admitted; they were also more in accordance with recognized principles of international law.   In his Senate speech Mr. Sumner had contended that, because of the proclamation, the liability of Great Britain must be fixed at amounts scarcely calculable in money, — a damage " immense and infinite," — " a massive grievance," all dependent on " this extraordinary manifesto," the " ill-omened," the " fatal " proclamation which " had opened the floodgates to infinite woes."   Mr. Fish, with the Cuban situation obviously in mind, declared, on the contrary, that the President recognized " the right of every power, when a civil conflict has arisen in another state, and has attained a sufficient complexity, magnitude and completeness, to define its own relations and those of its citizens and subjects toward the parties to the conflict, so far as their rights and interests are necessarily affected by the conflict." Then followed some saving clauses, carefully framed ; but, as already foreshadowed in Mr. Fish's correspondence, the precipitate character of the " unfriendly " proclamation was dwelt upon only as showing " the beginning and the *animus* of that course of conduct which resulted so disastrously to the United States." In the original draught, these instructions had been even more explicit on this point ; and, for that reason, had led to a characteristic remonstrance on the part of Mr. Sumner. Having early got some inkling of their character, he at once went to the house of Mr. Davis, and there, speaking to the Assistant Secretary in a loud voice, tremulous and vibrating with excitement, he had exclaimed, — " Is it the purpose of this Administration to sacrifice me, — me, a Senator from Massachusetts ? " — and later he wrote to the Secretary himself, declaring his dissent " from the course proposed," on the ground that " as chairman of the Senate committee I ought not in any way to be a party to a statement which abandons or enfeebles any of the just grounds of my country as already expounded by Seward, Adams, and myself." To this more than merely implied threat, Mr. Fish had contented himself by replying that, whether the modifications were of greater or of less significance, they could " hardly be of sufficient importance to break up an effort at negotiation, or to break down an Administration."[1] Mr. Cushing here

[1] Davis : *Mr. Fish and the Alabama Claims*, pp. 31–34, 114–116.

intervened, and his skilful hand temporarily adjusted the difficulty.[1] The adjustment was, however, only temporary. The inevitable could not be averted, and coming events already cast their shadows before.

To revive in detail the painful Motley imbroglio of 1870 is not necessary for present purposes. Suffice it to say that, when he reached England, Mr. Motley was, apparently, quite unable to clear his mind of what might, perhaps, not inaptly be described as the Proclamation Legend; and, both in his official interviews with the British Foreign Secretary and in social intercourse, he failed to follow, and apparently did not grasp, the spirit of his instructions. Confessing to a " despondent feeling " as to the " possibility of the two nations ever understanding each other, — of the difficulty, at this present moment, of their looking into each other's hearts," — he, in his first interview with Lord Clarendon, fell heavily back on the ubiquitous and everlasting proclamation, as the " fountain-head of the disasters which had been caused to the American people, both individually and collectively, by the hands of Englishmen." Historically untrue and diplomatically injudicious, this tone and stand evinced, on the part of Mr. Motley, an inability to see things in connection with his mission otherwise than as seen by Mr. Sumner. His misapprehension of the objects his official superior had in view was obvious and complete.

Grant afterwards said that when Mr. Motley's despatch containing his report of this interview reached Washington, it made him very angry, adding, as it did, " insult " to " injury." This statement, though made some eight years after the event,[2] is altogether probable

---

[1] Pierce: *Sumner*, vol. iv. p. 405.

[2] Interview at Edinburgh, New York *Herald*, September 25, 1877.

in view of the somewhat complicated, if extremely interesting, state of affairs then existing at Washington. But to a complete understanding of what can only be described as Mr. Motley's most unfortunate diplomatic *faux pas*, it is necessary here to diverge from the narrative.

The despatch of the new Minister containing the report of his first conference with Lord Clarendon reached the Department of State in due course of time, and was acknowledged by the Secretary on the 28th of June. In the course of the Edinburgh interview of eight years later, just referred to, Grant said, — "As soon as I heard of [the tenor of Motley's conversation with Clarendon] I went over to the State Department, and told Governor Fish to dismiss Motley at once. . . . I have been sorry many a time since that I did not stick to my first determination." Grant was, indeed, as he stated, " very angry " on this occasion. Nor, in the light of what is now known, was the cause of his anger far to seek. It was due to the state of affairs in Cuba, and the course he then had in mind to pursue in respect thereto.

One of the inherent defects of Grant as a civil administrator was what Mr. Sumner, at a later day, termed his " aide-de-campish " tendency. As President he was surrounded, and greatly influenced, by his old field associates, — at once the terror and despair of his constitutional advisers and official associates. The best, and by far the most influential, of this White House staff was General Rawlins, Grant's first Secretary of War. He, at least, held an official position ; most of

The report of the conversation was, in this case, authorized, and prepared by John Russell Young, Grant's recognized travelling companion.

the others were irregular army assignments, holding no position at the White House recognized by law.[1] During the early months of Grant's first administration, the Secretary of War, though in declining health, was greatly concerned over the course of events in Cuba. As afterwards appeared, he had even a money interest in the success of the insurrection then on foot in the island. With his customary energy, he pressed the cause of the insurgents on the President, demanding their recognition as belligerents. For this no grounds existed. As Secretary Fish afterwards privately wrote, — "They have no army, . . . no courts, do not occupy a single town, or hamlet, to say nothing of a seaport, . . . carrying on a purely guerrilla warfare, burning estates and attacking convoys, etc. . . . There has been nothing that has amounted to ' War.' Belligerency is a fact. Great Britain or France might just as well have recognized belligerency for the Black Hawk War." None the less, so far did General Rawlins's urgency prevail on the President that, as Mr. Motley's malign diplomatic star would have it, the detailed report of his arraignment of the Queen's proclamation of 1861 reached Washington at the very time when the President was himself meditating, and the Secretary of State was apprehending, a similar proclamation as respects the Cuban insurgents. Nor merely that. A few weeks later, the President not only caused such a proclamation to be drawn up, but signed it himself, directed the Secretary of State to affix to it the official seal, and then to promulgate it.

---

[1] J. D. Cox: "How Judge Hoar ceased to be Attorney-General," *Atlantic Monthly Magazine* (August, 1895), vol. lxxvi. p. 162 ; Sumner: "Republicanism *vs.* Grantism," *Works*, vol. xv. pp. 131–138.

This was on the 19th of August. Mr. Bancroft Davis, the Assistant Secretary of State, was intrusted with the order for the purpose of affixing the seal, — it having been signed in the cabin of the Fall River boat, — and with it returned to Washington; and there, in obedience to the direction of Mr. Fish, he deposited the document in a safe place, to await further directions. In that "safe place" this proclamation, vital to Cuba's insurrectionists and, probably, to the country's peace, rested for months and years. It never was promulgated.[1]

With Grant, an order was an order; and an order,

---

[1] Some facts concerning this singular episode, copied from Mr. Fish's diary by his son, Hamilton Fish, were published in an Associated Press despatch, from Albany, in the New York papers of March 16, 1896. Writing a year after the occurrences referred to in the text, July 10, 1870, Mr. Fish said that Grant made use of these expressions to him, — "On two important occasions, at least, your steadiness and wisdom have kept me from mistakes into which I should have fallen." Mr. Fish then added, these two occasions were "one preventing the issuing, last August and September, of the proclamation of Cuban belligerency, which he had signed, and which he wrote me a note instructing me to sign (which I did) and to issue (which I did not), and, second, the Cuban message of June 13" (1870). The message last referred to (*Messages*, etc., *of the Presidents*, vol. vii. p. 64), setting forth a definite policy as respects Cuba and Spain, was at the time a great relief to the members of the Cabinet. It amounted to a complete change of administration front, brought about by the insistence of the Secretary of State, and almost as the alternative to his resignation. Though very reluctant to yield on this point, the President finally did so, affixing his signature to the message as drawn up by the Secretary. In response to a request therefor, the family of Mr. Fish have kindly furnished me extracts from the diary relating to this interesting bit of history, supplementary to those already published by Mr. Hamilton Fish, in the Associated Press despatch above referred to. These are of such value, and so extremely creditable to Mr. Fish, that they are printed in full, together with those previously published by Mr. Fish's son, in Appendix E (*infra*, p. 215) of this paper.

something to be obeyed. Why, in this case, the order was not obeyed, or some one held to strict account for disobedience, does not appear. He seems to have forgotten all about it at the time; and, subsequently, he expressed much gratification at this failure of memory. In point of fact he, at that particular juncture, had other things to think of. It was the vacation season, and he was away from Washington, — at Newport, in New York, and in the mountains of western Pennsylvania; Mr. Fish was at his country place, at Garrison on the Hudson; General Rawlins was ill at Washington, — dying, in the last stages of pulmonary consumption. It so chanced that Messrs. Jay Gould and James Fisk, Jr., of New York had made up their minds that this particular period was one favorable for the execution of a great financial stroke. They proceeded accordingly, and their operations culminated in the famous " Gold Corner," and the long-remembered Wall Street " Black Friday " of September 24, 1869. Never fastidious in the selection of his company, the President had been brought into some sort of an association with these men through his brother-in-law, Abel R. Corbin, a resident of New York. Him they had fairly entangled in their meshes; through him they were scheming to ensnare the President.[1] They did not succeed; but they did influence his action as President, and they threw the whole financial machinery of the country, including that of the United States government, into confusion. For some time public attention was concentrated on them and their misdoings, to the utter exclusion of all else,

[1] Henry Adams: *Chapters of Erie, The New York Gold Conspiracy,* pp. 100–134. See, also, *infra,* p. 224.

including Cuba. It was Grant's first experience with
men of that stamp in Wall Street; well for him had
it been his last.

Thus the last formal act preliminary to the issuance
of a proclamation of Cuban belligerency was performed
during the evening of August 19; the Secretary of
War died on the 9th of the month following; fifteen
days later was Wall Street's "Black Friday." The
Rawlins pressure on Grant had then ceased; thenceforth
the proclamation slept, innocuous, in the safe of the
Department of State. But, though thus pigeon-holed,
it might well have been issued at any time subsequent
to the 19th of August; and that it was not so issued
was due, apparently, to the fact that Secretary Fish
withheld it during the President's vacation absence
from Washington. Grant's thoughts chanced then to
be otherwise directed, and subsequent events made the
action he had decided on manifestly inexpedient.

Returning to Mr. Motley and the report of his first
conversation with Lord Clarendon, it is now quite
apparent why Grant was "very angry indeed" when
he first heard of it. The diplomacy of Mr. Motley
certainly was not happy. With a degree of fortuitous
infelicity truly remarkable, it was most nicely calculated to compromise the President and the Secretary
of State. By the merest chance did it fail so to do.
The lesson could not have been lost; and it was small
matter of surprise that Mr. Motley was promptly
relieved from the necessity of further discussing the
Alabama claims, and the Queen's proclamation of
May, 1861, in its connection therewith. However
Mr. Fish felt about Cuba, — and on that subject his
views were quite well defined, — he could have enter-

tained no wish to have his representative in London get him into a position which might not improbably demand of him much awkward explanation, founded on distinctions not at once apparent.[1]   However, as it was almost immediately decided that, so far as the settlement of outstanding difficulties between the two nations was concerned, any future negotiations should be conducted in Washington, Mr. Motley ceased at this point to be a factor in the course of events.

Now, however, an extremely adroit, though unofficial, intermediary appeared on the stage; and his presence almost immediately made itself felt.   Born in Scotland in 1820, and emigrating with his parents

---

[1] Though a man of extensive research, Mr. Sumner, unlike Mr. Fish in that respect, had not a legal mind.   He prided himself on his acquaintance with International Law; but, when occasion arose, he instinctively evolved his law from his inner consciousness, and it rarely failed to meet the emergency.   The difficulty with it was that it was apt to be of a code peculiarly his own, and not found in the books usually accepted as authoritative.   It was so in the case of foreign built Confederate cruisers; it was so as respects the Queen's proclamation of May, 1861; it was so as respects national, as contradistinguished from private, claims.   An accomplished littérateur and brilliant historian, Mr. Motley was unacquainted with law, and quite innocent of any legal instinct.   When, therefore, Mr. Motley undertook to expound Mr. Sumner's jurisprudence, the result might not improbably be something for which a matter-of-fact government would not care always to be held responsible.   In the present case, Mr. Motley in June descanted most eloquently to Lord Clarendon on the sin of commission involved in the premature recognition of Confederate belligerency by the British government; but, six months later, President Grant declared that a "nation is its own judge, when to accord the rights of belligerency, either to a people struggling to free themselves from a government they believe to be oppressive, or to independent nations at war with each other." (*Messages and Papers of the Presidents*, vol. vii. p. 32.)   Even this discrepancy was unquestionably embarrassing; a Cuban proclamation actually outstanding would obviously have aggravated the embarrassment.

to America at the age of sixteen, Sir John Rose, or Mr. Rose as he still was in 1869, had been for a number of years prominent in Canadian public life. A natural diplomat of a high order, he was at this time acting as British commissioner on the joint tribunal provided by the treaty of 1863 to arbitrate the claims of the Hudson's Bay and Puget Sound companies. Mr. Caleb Cushing was of counsel in that business, and relations of a friendly nature grew up between him and the British arbitrator. Whether already privately authorized so to do or not, Mr. Rose, who was very solicitous of an arrangement between the two nations, skilfully instilled into Mr. Cushing a belief that he, Mr. Rose, might be of use in the delicate work of reopening negotiations on new lines. Accordingly, on the 26th of June, — not eleven weeks from the rejection of the Johnson-Clarendon Convention, and sixteen days after Mr. Motley's despondent interview with Lord Clarendon just referred to, — Mr. Cushing, then in Washington, wrote to Mr. Rose, in Ottawa. Referring to previous letters between them, he now told him that he had that day seen Secretary Fish, and had arranged for Mr. Rose to meet him. "I am," he wrote, "not sanguine of *immediate* conclusion of such a treaty as either you or I might desire. But I think the time has arrived to *commence*, trusting that discretion, patience, and good-will on both sides may eventuate, in this important matter, satisfactorily to the two governments."[1]   Accordingly, on the 8th of July, Mr. Rose

[1] In this letter Mr. Cushing significantly went on to say, — "In view of the disposition which the Senate of the United States has recently shown to assume more than its due, or at least than its usual part, in the determination of international questions, you will appreciate the unreadiness of the Executive, at the present time, to take upon itself

called on the Secretary in Washington. The first of the interviews which led up to the Treaty of Washington two years later took place next day at Mr. Fish's dinner-table. The basis of a settlement was then discussed, and that subsequently reached outlined by Mr. Fish, who laid especial emphasis on the necessity of "some kind expression of regret" on the part of Great Britain over the course pursued in the Civil War. The two even went so far as to consider the details of negotiation. The expediency of a special commission to dispose of the matter was discussed, and, among others, the names of the Duke of Argyll and John Bright were canvassed in connection therewith.

Immediately after this interview Mr. Rose went to England. His official and personal relations with men high in influence were close; and, moreover, another personage of growing consequence in English ministerial circles was now at work laboring earnestly and assiduously to promote an adjustment. In 1869 William E. Forster was fast rising into the front rank of English public men. President of the Privy Council in Mr. Gladstone's first Ministry, he was acting as Minister of Education. Nine years later, in the second Gladstone Ministry, he was to occupy the crucial position of Secretary for Ireland. Always, from his first entrance into public life in 1861, an earnest, out-

any spontaneous or doubtful ventures, especially on the side of England." The reference was, of course, to Mr. Sumner, and pointed to an already developing source of trouble. Grant's first presidential term was yet in its fourth month only. On the "disposition" referred to by Mr. Cushing, see the paper by A. M. Low, entitled "The Oligarchy of the Senate," in the *North American Review* for February, 1902, vol. 174, pp. 238-243.

spoken, consistent and insistent friend of democratic United States, — during the Civil War the one in that small group of friends held by Mr. Adams in "most esteem," [1] — Mr. Forster was now strenuous in his advocacy of a comprehensive settlement of the issues arising out of the Rebellion, and the honest admission by Great Britain of the ill-considered policy then pursued. His name also had been discussed by Mr. Fish and Mr. Rose as one of the proposed special mission.

Within less than two months, therefore, of the rejection of the Johnson-Clarendon Convention, the Treaty of Washington was in the air ; and, curiously enough, within a month of the time when Mr. Motley in London was confessing to Lord Clarendon his "despondent feeling" in view of the "path surrounded by perils," and talking of "grave and disastrous misunderstandings and cruel wars," Secretary Fish and Mr. Rose, comfortably seated at a dinner-table in Washington, were quietly paving the way to a complete understanding. Nothing more occurred during that summer ; but, in the course of it, Mr. Fish thus expressed his views in a letter to a correspondent, — an expression at this early date to which subsequent events lent much significance : — " The two English-speaking progressive liberal Governments of the world should not, must not, be divided — better let this question rest for some years even (if that be necessary) than risk failure in another attempt at settlement. I do not say this because I wish to postpone a settlement — on the contrary, I should esteem it the greatest glory, and greatest happiness of my life, if it could be settled while I remain in official position ;

---

[1] Reid : *Forster*, vol. ii. p. 10.

and I should esteem it the greatest benefit to my
country to bring it to an early settlement. . . . I want
to have the question settled. I would not, if I could,
impose any humiliating condition on Great Britain.
I would not be a party to anything that proposes
to ' threaten' her. I believe that she is great enough
to be just; and I trust that she is wise enough to
maintain her own greatness. No greatness is inconsistent with some errors. Mr. Bright thinks she was
drawn into errors — so do we. If she can be brought
to think so, it will not be necessary for her to say so ;
— at least not to say it very loudly. It may be said
by a definition of what *shall* be Maritime International
Law in the future, and a few kind words. She will
want in the future what we have claimed. Thus she
will be benefited — we satisfied." Written in the
early days of September, 1869, this letter set forth
clearly the position of Mr. Fish : it also correctly
foreshadowed the course of the diplomacy which had
already been entered upon.

During the autumn of 1869 the *Alabama* claims,
and the unsatisfactory relations of the country with
Great Britain, were discussed at more than one Cabinet meeting in Washington. At this time, while the
Secretary of State professed himself as ready to negotiate whenever England came forward with a fairly
satisfactory proposition, the President favored a policy
of delay. Presently, Mr. Rose was again heard from.
The letter he now wrote has since often been referred
to and much commented upon, though it was over
twenty years before its authorship was revealed.[1]   In

[1] By Mr. J. C. Bancroft Davis, in his *Mr. Fish and the Alabama
Claims*, p. 48.

it he said, — " I have had conversations in more than one quarter, — which you will readily understand without my naming them, and have conveyed *my own belief*, that a kindly word, or an expression of regret, such as would not involve an acknowledgment of wrong, was likely to be more potential than the most irrefragable reasoning on principles of international law." Mr. Rose then went on to touch upon a very delicate topic, — Mr. Motley's general London presentation of his country's attitude. " Is your representative here," he added, " a gentleman of the most conciliatory spirit ? . . . Does he not — perhaps naturally — let the fear of imitating his predecessor influence his course so as to make his initiative hardly as much characterized by consideration for the sensibilities of the people of *this* country, as of his own ? . . . I think I understood you to say, that you thought negotiations would be more likely to be attended with satisfactory results, if they were transferred to, and were concluded at, Washington ; because you could from time to time communicate confidentially with leading Senators, and know how far you could carry that body with you. . . . But again is your representative of that mind ? — and how is it to be brought about ? By a new, or a special envoy — as you spoke of — or quietly through Mr. Thornton ? . . . If I am right in my impression that you would prefer Washington and a new man, and you think it worth while to enable me to repeat that suggestion as one from myself in the proper quarter, a line from you — or if you prefer it, a word by the cable, will enable me to do so."

Eight days later, on the 11th of the same month, Mr. Rose again wrote to Mr. Fish, calling his attention to the speech of Mr. Gladstone at the Guildhall, which, he said, "hardly conveys the impression his tone conveyed with reference to United States affairs. There was an *earnest* tone of friendship that is hardly reproduced." [1]

At the time these letters reached Mr. Fish, the relations between him and Mr. Sumner were close, and still friendly. The Secretary spoke to the Senator freely of Mr. Rose's visits, and consulted with him over every step taken. Knowing that Mr. Sumner and Mr. Motley were constantly interchanging letters, he took occasion to advise Mr. Sumner of the intimations which had thus reached him, giving, of course, no names, but saying simply that they were from a reliable quarter. The well-meant hint was more than disregarded, Mr. Sumner contenting himself with contemptuous references to the once celebrated McCracken episode.[2] Years afterwards, in the same spirit, Mr. Motley's biographer sneeringly referred to the still unnamed writer of the Rose letters as "a faithless friend, a disguised enemy, a secret emissary, or an injudicious alarmist." [3]

The reply of Mr. Fish to the letters of Mr. Rose revealed the difficulties of the Secretary's position. The individuality of Mr. Sumner made itself felt at every point. In London, Mr. Motley reflected the views of the chairman of the Senate Committee on Foreign Relations rather than those of the Secretary of State; in Washington, the personal relations of Mr. Sumner with the British Minister were such as

[1] See Appendix D, *infra*, p. 212.
[2] Davis: *Mr. Fish and the Alabama Claims*, p. 128.
[3] O. W. Holmes: *Memoir of John Lothrop Motley* (1879), pp. 178, 179.

to render the latter undesirable at least as a medium of negotiation. Referring first to his intimations concerning Mr. Motley, Mr. Fish replied to Mr. Rose as follows : —

" Your questions respecting our Minister, I fear may have been justified by some indiscretion of expression, or of manner, but I hope only indiscretions of that nature. Intimations of such had reached me. I have reason to hope that if there have been such manifestations, they may not recur. Whatever there may have appeared, I cannot doubt his desire to aid in bringing the two Governments into perfect accord. . . . I have the highest regard for Mr. Thornton, and find him in all my intercourse, courteous, frank, and true. A gentleman with whom I deal and treat with the most unreserved confidence. He had, however, given offence to Mr. Sumner (chairman of the Senate Committee on Foreign Relations), whose position with reference to any future negotiation you understand. I chance to know that Mr. Sumner feels deeply aggrieved by some things which Mr. Thornton has written home, and although he would not consciously allow a personal grief of that nature to prejudice his action in an official intercourse with the representative of a State, he might unconsciously be led to criticism unfavorable to positions which would be viewed differently, if occupied by some other person. . . . I am very decidedly of opinion that whenever negotiations are to be renewed, they would be more likely to result favorably here than in London. I have so instructed Mr. Motley to say, if he be questioned on the subject."

Such was the posture of affairs at the close of the

year 1869. Events now moved rapidly, and the general situation became more and more complicated. In Europe, the war-clouds which preceded the Franco-Prussian storm-burst of 1870 were gathering; in America, President Grant was, persistently as earnestly, pressing his schemes of West Indian annexation. In London, Mr. Rose was informally sounding the members of the government to ascertain how far they were willing to go; in Washington, Mr. Thornton was pressing the Secretary " with much earnestness to give him an intimation of what would be accepted " by the United States. The outbreak of hostilities between France and Germany six months later brought matters, so far as Great Britain was concerned, fairly to a crisis. In presence of serious continental complications, — in imminent danger of being drawn into the vortex of conflict, — Great Britain found itself face to face with the *Alabama* precedents. Like " blood-bolter'd " Banquo, they would not down. The position was one not likely to escape the keen eye of Count Bismarck. England's hands were tied. Internationally, she was obviously a negligible quantity. The principles laid down and precedents established only six years before were patent, — fresh in the minds of all. Her Majesty's Government remembered them; Count Bismarck was advised of them; each was well aware of the other's knowledge. The Ministry were accordingly in an extraordinarily receptive mental condition.

On this side of the Atlantic the situation complicated itself no less rapidly. Colonel Babcock, one of the group of young army officers already referred to, who, having been members of General Grant's mili-

tary staff, were retained, under detail, near his person
during his presidency, had been sent down by him to
examine, as an engineer, the bay of Samana, and to
report upon it as a coaling station. Presently he got
back, and, at the next meeting of the Cabinet, the
President paralyzed his official advisers by announcing, in a casual sort of way, " Babcock has returned,
as you see, and has brought a treaty of annexation."
To say that never before in the whole history of the
government had any President made such a naïve
exhibition is quite within safe bounds. Ignorance
of law and usage, and an utter absence of the sense
of propriety, were about equally pronounced. A subordinate officer of engineers, sent to a West Indian
island to make a report on a coaling station, had not
only undertaken to negotiate a formal treaty for the
annexation of an entire foreign country to the United
States, but had actually executed it, entitling himself
in the solemn instrument " Aide-de-camp " to His Ex-
cellency, and his " special agent to the Dominican Republic." Instead of charitably concealing the mingled
assurance and incompetency of the young man under
a private rebuke, the President now adopted as his
own this pronounced opéra bouffe performance, irresistibly suggestive of the Grand Duchy of Gerolstein.
Sent to examine a harbor, the President's aide had
undertaken to annex a negro republic! This being so,
there is small occasion for surprise that, when the
President brought the matter up in cabinet meeting,
the gaze of all about the table involuntarily turned
toward the Secretary of State. Mr. Fish sat " impas-
sive, and his eyes were fixed on the portfolio before
him." Had it not been somewhat appalling, the sit-

uation would have been farcical in the extreme. As
it was, it may well be doubted whether even Judge
Hoar's strong sense of humor rose to the occasion.
The startling bit of information thus conveyed by the
President was received in expressive silence, broken
at last by a single hesitating query, which remained
unanswered. The atmosphere of general disapproval
was, however, pervasive, and painfully apparent; so
nothing more was then said, nor was the matter ever
again submitted to the assembled Cabinet.[1] None
the less, the idea of annexation had taken possession
of the presidential mind, and from that time Grant
became intent upon it; and intent in his characteristic way. It was a cardinal point in his policy.
Obviously, the support of the chairman of the Senate
Committee on Foreign Relations was very necessary
to the success of the scheme, for the treaty, however
irregularly negotiated, must go to the Senate for ratification; a foreign country and its people could not
be annexed by a proclamation of the Commander-
in-chief, even though countersigned by an aide-de-
camp. So, warned by his Cabinet experience, as well
as by the fate of the Johnson-Clarendon Convention,
the President-General made up his mind to exert all
his influence on the chairman of the committee; and,
consequently, in the early days of January, he, the
Chief Executive of the United States, dropped in one
evening at Mr. Sumner's house, while the latter was
at dinner with some friends, and sought to enlist his
influence, — designating him repeatedly as chairman
of the "Senate Judiciary Committee," — in support of

[1] Cox: "How Judge Hoar ceased to be Attorney-General," *Atlantic Monthly Magazine* (August, 1895), vol. lxxvi. pp. 165–167.

what afterwards became known as President Grant's
Dominican policy. What followed is familiar history. During the immediately ensuing months there
took place a complete division between the two men.
They thereafter became not only politically opposed,
but bitter personal enemies.

To all outward appearances, during those months,
no advance whatever was being made towards an
adjustment with Great Britain ; but, in point of fact,
both time and conditions were rapidly ripening. In
the early days of September, 1870, the Imperial government of France collapsed at Sedan ; and, on the
13th of that month, M. Thiers arrived in London
soliciting on behalf of the new French republic the
aid and good offices of Great Britain. His mission
was, of course, fruitless ; but, none the less, it could
not but emphasize in the minds of those composing
the Ministry the difficulty of England's position. If
it failed so to do, a forcible reminder from America
was imminent, and followed almost immediately. In
December, with Paris blockaded by the Prussians,
France was brought face to face with dismemberment.
The general European situation was, from an English
point of view, disquieting in the extreme. At just
this juncture, within one week of the day on which his
Parliament called on the Prussian King to become
Emperor of Germany, and the French delegate government, to avoid a German army operating in the
heart of the country, removed its sittings from Tours
to Bordeaux, — at just this juncture (December 5)
President Grant took occasion to incorporate the following distinctly minatory passage, draughted by his
Secretary of State, into his annual message : —

" I regret to say that no conclusion has been reached for the adjustment of the claims against Great Britain growing out of the course adopted by that Government during the Rebellion.   The cabinet of London, so far as its views have been expressed, does not appear to be willing to concede that Her Majesty's Government was guilty of any negligence, or did or permitted any act during the war by which the United States has just cause of complaint.   Our firm and unalterable convictions are directly the reverse.   I therefore recommend to Congress to authorize the appointment of a commission to take proof of the amount and the ownership of these several claims, on notice to the representative of Her Majesty at Washington, and that authority be given for the settlement of these claims by the United States, so that the Government shall have the ownership of the private claims, as well as the responsible control of all the demands against Great Britain.   It cannot be necessary to add that whenever Her Majesty's Government shall entertain a desire for a full and friendly adjustment of these claims, the United States will enter upon their consideration with an earnest desire for a conclusion consistent with the honor and dignity of both nations."

The hint thus forcibly given was not lost in London.   The educational process was now complete.   The message, or that portion of it which most interested the British public, appeared in the London journals of December 6, and was widely commented upon. It was characterized as " menacing " in tone, and " thoroughly unpromising of any friendly settlement." Significantly enough, in another column of the same issue of the *Times* appeared the headline, " Rouen and Orleans have fallen! " while the paper was crowded with letters descriptive of the conflicts at Gravelotte and Metz, together with accounts of the investment of Paris and of Gambetta's harangues at Tours. The general continental situation was even more " menacing " than the message of the American President. In any event, the steps of diplomacy, ordinarily so very sedate, were now quickened to an unusual, not to say unprecedented, pace. Indeed, the gait now struck in London bore, so to speak, a close resemblance to a run. Exactly five weeks later, on the 9th of January, 1871, Mr. Rose was again in Washington. Coming ostensibly on business relating to the Dominion of Canada, he was in reality at last fully empowered to open negotiations looking to an immediate settlement. The very evening of the day he arrived, Mr. Rose dined with Mr. Fish. The after-dinner talk between the two, lasting some five or six hours, resulted in a confidential memorandum.[1] More carefully formulated by Mr. Rose the following day, this paper reached Mr. Fish on the 11th of January. He expressed himself, on acknowledging its receipt, as inspired with hope.

Hamilton Fish was no more ambitious than imaginative. Though he held the position of Secretary of State during both of the Grant administrations, he did so with a genuine and well-understood reluctance, and was always contemplating an early retirement. At this juncture, however, there can be no doubt his ambition was fired. That which a year before he had pronounced as, among things possible,

[1] Davis: *Mr. Fish and the Alabama Claims*, p. 59.

"the greatest glory and the greatest happiness" of his life, was within his reach. He was to be the official medium through which a settlement of the questions between "the two English-speaking, progressive liberal" countries was to be effected. That was to be his monument. To a certain extent, also, conditions favored him. Mr. Sumner and his Senate speech on the Johnson-Clarendon Convention were the great obstacles in the way. For, as Mr. Fish had himself expressed it a year previous, — "The eloquence, and the display of learning and of research in [that] speech, and — perhaps above all — the gratification of the laudable pride of a people in being told of the magnitude of wealth in reserve for them in the way of damages due from a wealthy debtor, captivated some, and deluded more." Of this widespread popular feeling, reinforced by the anti-British and Fenian sentiment then very prevalent, account had to be taken. Strangely enough, moreover, Mr. Sumner's lukewarmness as respects any settlement at that time, much more his possible opposition to one originating with the State Department, indirectly forwarded that result; for, as already seen, the President and the Massachusetts Senator were now in open conflict over the former's Dominican policy. In that struggle Secretary Fish had most properly, if he remained in office, reconciled himself to siding with his official head. The Motley imbroglio had followed. With the most friendly feeling towards Mr. Motley personally, and sincerely desirous of avoiding so far as possible any difficulty with Mr. Sumner, Mr. Fish's expressed wish was to continue Mr. Motley in his position, taking from him all part in the proposed negotiation, and giving him explicit instructions in no way to refer to it, or seek to influence it. He was practically to be reduced to a functional representative. To this the President would not assent. He insisted that Mr. Motley represented Mr. Sumner more than he did the Administration, and he declared in a cabinet meeting, at which the matter was discussed, that he would "not allow Sumner to ride over" him. The Secretary continued to plead and urge, but in vain. The President was implacable. It was then suggested that Mr. Sumner should himself be nominated to succeed Motley, and General Butler, then in the House of Representatives, and Mr. Cameron, Senator from Pennsylvania, called on the Secretary to advocate this solution of the difficulty. They pronounced Sumner unpractical and arrogant, and urged that he should be got out of the way by any practicable method. This suggestion also was discussed at a cabinet meeting, and the President expressed a willingness to make the nomination, on condition that Sumner would resign from the Senate; but he also intimated a grim determination to remove him from his new office as soon as he had been confirmed in it. At last Mr. Fish was compelled to yield; and, under the President's explicit direction, he wrote to Mr. Motley a private letter, couched in the most friendly language, in which he intimated as clearly as he could that so doing was most painful to him, but he must ask for a resignation. The incident had no historical significance, but was very characteristic of Grant. The method of procedure was his, — less abrupt, less marked by military curtness than three similar dismissals from his Cabinet; but, owing to Mr. Motley's international position and literary prestige,

such an unwonted proceeding at the time excited much
comment, while it has since been exhaustively discussed.   Grant gave his own explanation of it,[1] and
diplomatists,[2] biographers,[3] and essayists[4] have each
in turn passed judgment upon it.   Under these circumstances, it is sufficient here to say that whatever
was then done, was done by General Grant's impera-
tive order, and solely because of Mr. Motley's intimate personal relations with Mr. Sumner, and the
latter's opposition to the President's Dominican policy.
The urgent and repeated remonstrances of the Secretary of State were of no avail.   Utterly unqualified for
political life, and only partially adapted for diplomacy,
Mr. Motley was thus doomed to illustrate the truth of
Hamlet's remark as to the danger incurred by him of
lesser weight who chances

> " Between the pass and fell incensed points
> Of mighty opposites."

It may, however, be pertinent to say, that, in view of the
close personal relations existing between Mr. Sumner
and Mr. Motley, it is not easy to see how the latter
could have been allowed to remain at London, the
supposed representative of the United States, with the
Massachusetts Senator in open opposition to the Administration.   Indeed, bearing in mind the whole situation as it then existed, there seems reason to conclude
that the President, with his instinctive strategic sense,

[1] In the conversation, already referred to, with Young, at Edinburgh, September 11, 1877, three months after Mr. Motley's death;
reported in the New York *Herald* of the 25th of the same month.

[2] " Motley's Appeal to History," by John Jay.   An Address before
the New York Historical Society; subsequently printed in the *International Review* (1877), vol. iv. pp. 838–854.

[3] Pierce: *Sumner*, vol. iv. pp. 446–451.

[4] O. W. Holmes: *Memoir of Motley* (1879), pp. 155–190.

grasped the essential fact in the case more firmly than did the Secretary. The immediate control of the external relations of the government, and the shaping of its foreign policy, were fast passing out of the hands of the executive, and into those of a Senate committee. This tendency had to be checked. The correspondence between Senator Sumner and Minister Motley has never been published, and it is questionable whether it now exists. A few brief extracts from Sumner's letters to Motley are to be found in Pierce's biography of the former; but Motley's letters to Sumner were looked upon by Mr. Pierce as " absolutely confidential," and of them he made no use. Those are not now to be found in the files ; but the few short excerpts from the Sumner letters, which have been printed, are very suggestive. They show conclusively the nature of the intercourse. It was intimately semi-official. Difficulty from this source had from the outset been foreseen ; for when, immediately after his appointment to the English mission, Mr. Motley was in Boston, he naturally called on Mr. Adams, seeking light on the course best to be pursued in his new position. Referring to the interview, Mr. Adams then wrote,— " His embarrassment is considerable in one particular which never affected me, and that is in having two masters. Mr. Seward never permitted any interference of the Senate, or Mr. Sumner, with his direction of the policy." Under these circumstances, when the break between Grant and Sumner became pronounced, the displacement of Motley almost of necessity followed. The executive had to resume its functions ; and, to do so effectively, it must be represented by agents in whom it had confidence, and who were not in the confidence of its opponents. It is somewhat strange that Mr. Motley should have had no suspicion of so obvious a fact.

His failure to suspect it, and follow the reluctant suggestion of the Secretary, affronted, none the less, the military instincts of the President, whose anger towards the Massachusetts Senator was now at white heat. It was even publicly said that he had declared to a Senator that, were he not President, he "would call [Mr. Sumner] to account."[1] He had, also, cause for wrath; not only was there notoriously very "free talk" about the President at Mr. Sumner's table,[2] but those holding confidential relations at the White House — the military household — openly asserted that Mr. Sumner had more than intimated that he, Grant, was intoxicated when, early in January, 1870, he had made his memorable after-dinner call at his, the Senator's, house. The Senator from Massachusetts could not forthwith be called "to account;" the Minister to Great Britain could, in a way. So, when Mr. Motley refused to resign, his removal was ordered. This the Secretary delayed, for he expected then himself shortly to retire, and was more than willing to leave the final act of displacement to his successor. At the last moment he was, however, prevailed upon to continue in office, sorely against his own wishes; and what then, as respects the English mission, occurred, is matter of record. That the patience of the Secretary had been sorely tried during the intervening time, does not admit of question. To this subject, and the probable cause of

[1] Sumner: *Works*, vol. xiv. p. 256.
[2] Davis: *Mr. Fish and the Alabama Claims*, p. 56.

his irritation, I shall have occasion to refer presently.
Unfortunately, as is apt to be the case with those of
Netherlandish blood, though slow to wrath, Mr. Fish's
anger, once aroused, was neither easily appeased nor
kept within conventional bounds; and now it extended
beyond its immediate cause. He felt aggrieved over
the course pursued by Mr. Motley. In it he saw no
regard for the difficulties of the position in which
he himself stood; and he was especially provoked by
the minister's voluminous record of the circumstances
attending his displacement, placed by him on the files
of the Department, and entitled " End of Mission."
Accordingly, Mr. Fish's long-contained anger found
expression in the well-known letter, addressed to Mr.
Moran, secretary of the legation at London, and then
acting as *chargé d'affaires*. This letter, in a first
draught, was read by the Secretary to the President,
in presence of Vice-President Colfax and Senator
Conkling, before it was despatched; and, while the
last-named gave to it his approval, the President not
only declined to allow certain alterations suggested by
Mr. Colfax to be made, but expressed his wish that
not a word in the paper be changed.

Immaterial as all this may at first seem, it had a
close and important bearing on the negotiations preliminary to the Treaty of Washington, now fairly
initiated. In this case, indeed, one negotiation may
be said to have hung upon the fate of another; for,
though the outcome of Colonel Babcock's diplomacy
had not again been brought to the attention of the
Cabinet, it was an open secret that all those composing
it were by no means earnest in support thereof. The
White House hangers-on and tale-bearers were also

abnormally busy, even for them. The newspapers consequently teemed with rumors; the atmosphere was rife with gossip. General Grant was not the man long to submit to this state of things; if nought else, he was a disciplinarian. So he presently intimated, with much show of feeling, that certain members of his Cabinet — more particularly the Secretary of the Treasury, the Attorney-General, and the Secretary of the Interior — Messrs. Boutwell, Hoar, and Cox — were not giving the support he deemed proper to the San Domingo treaty. The first he declared was opposed to the treaty; the second said " nothing in its favor, but sneers at it ; " the third did not open his mouth to utter a word in its support. A few days later he brought up this cause of complaint in a cabinet meeting, plainly saying that he wished all the members of his Cabinet, and all his friends, to use every proper effort to aid him. He went on to state that he did not propose to let those who opposed him in this matter " name Ministers to London," etc., etc., and he then entered on a warm defence of Colonel Babcock, proclaiming his belief in the utter falsity of the charges made against that officer. After some further discussion, and a general expression of approval of the plan of holding members of the party to the support of an administration policy, the matter was allowed to drop. This was on the 14th of June. The very next day the resignation of the Attorney-General was called for, in the way and under the circumstances his colleague, General Cox, afterwards described in the pages of *The Atlantic Monthly*. Evidently, the President-General was disciplining his Cabinet.[1] A

[1] It is proper to say that the President assigned for this proceeding

day or two later he called in the evening on Mr. Fish
at his house, and, in the course of the conversation
which ensued, took occasion to express his sense of the
support the Secretary had given his favorite measure,
and to intimate a sense of obligation therefor. He
probably felt this the more, as he was not unaware
that Secretary Fish had taken the course he did solely
from a sense of loyalty, and in opposition to his own
better judgment. Mr. Fish had finally brought himself to regard the treaty as a measure of policy
inaugurated by the head of the Administration; and,
after that policy was fairly entered upon, did what
he properly could to forward it. This, also, notwithstanding the fact that the treaty had been most
irregularly negotiated in derogation of the Department of State, and that it was in charge of persons
whose standing had in no degree increased public
confidence.[1] But, in dealing historically with President Grant, and seeking to explain both the influences which operated upon him and his methods of
procedure, the fact must ever be kept in mind that
he was essentially a soldier, and not a civilian. As a
soldier, he achieved all his successes, and they were
great; as a civilian, his life was a conspicuous failure.

different reasons to various people. The reason stated in the text was
that clearly intimated to Secretary Fish. Secretary Boutwell was
given to understand that the change was made because divers Senators declared themselves as not on speaking terms with the Attorney-
General, and refused to visit his department while he was at its head;
on the other hand, Secretary Cox was told that it was thought desirable
to have one representative from the South in the Cabinet, rather than
two from Massachusetts. All these reasons may have had weight in
the President's mind; and, in selection for immediate use, he took
into more or less careful consideration the individual with whom he
was talking.

[1] See Appendix E, *infra*, p. 222.

In his military capacity, exacting obedience, he appreciated loyalty. As a civilian, he looked upon the members of his cabinet as upon a headquarters staff, and, while he enforced discipline by curt dismissal, he rewarded fidelity by return in kind. It was so now: Hoar, he abruptly dismissed; to Fish, he gave a reciprocal support. As the Secretary of State had proved loyal to him in the Dominican matter, he, in return, stood ready to adopt any policy towards Great Britain the Secretary might see fit to recommend. If, moreover, such a policy implied of necessity a conflict with Mr. Sumner, it would, for that very reason, be only the more acceptable. The President thus became a tower of strength in the proposed negotiation.

Still while, on the whole, the conditions contributing to success seemed to predominate, the fate of the Johnson-Clarendon Convention had to be borne in mind. Mr. Sumner was chairman of the Senate Committee on Foreign Relations. To defeat the result of a negotiation, it was necessary to control but a third of the Senate; and his influence in that body had recently been emphasized by the rejection of the Dominican treaty, in favor of which the President had made use of every form of argument and inducement within the power of an executive to employ. So, after the proposal of Sir John Rose had been discussed by the Secretary with Senator Conkling and General Schenck, the newly designated minister to England, it was agreed that Mr. Fish should seek an interview with the Massachusetts Senator, and, by a great show of consideration, see if he could not be induced to look favorably on the scheme.

What ensued was not only historically interesting, but to the last degree characteristic; it was, moreover, altogether unprecedented. The Secretary of State actually sounded the way to an interview with the chairman of a Senate committee through another member of that committee, — a species of "mutual friend," — the interview in question to take place, not at the Department of State, but at the house of the autocratic chairman.[1] The meeting was arranged accordingly; and, on the morning of the 15th of January, six days only after Sir John Rose's arrival in Washington, Mr. Fish, with Sir John's confidential memorandum in his pocket, stood at Mr. Sumner's door. In the meeting that ensued the business in hand was discussed. At the close of the interview, Mr. Sumner expressed a wish to take further time in which to consider the matter, but promised an answer shortly. Thereupon the Secretary took his leave.[2]

---

[1] Davis: *Mr. Fish and the Alabama Claims*, p. 133.

[2] In answer to a request for any entry in the diary of Mr. Fish relating to what passed at this interview, I have received the following from the family of Mr. Fish, with permission to use it: —

"1871. January 15. Sunday. Call upon Sumner; introduce the question and read to him Rose's 'Confidential Memorandum.' He declaims; Boutwell comes in at this point, conversation continued. Sumner insists that it should be understood in advance what Great Britain is willing to agree to, on the several questions. Boutwell says he has learnt through the Bankers that Great Britain intends to concede the inshore Fisheries in consideration of our yielding San Juan. I say that cannot be conceded; the West will be united against the cession of San Juan.

"I try to obtain from Sumner an expression of opinion as to the answer to be given to Rose; ask what will be the candid judgment of the world when it is known that Great Britain makes the overtures she has made, if she accompany them with a distinct understanding that her liability for the acts of the *Alabama* is to be admitted if the United States decline the negotiation. Refer to the danger of actual collision on the Fishery grounds, and the serious complications that would ensue.

Then, in due time, followed one of the most curious incidents in diplomatic history, an incident than which few could more strikingly illustrate the changes which in a comparatively short space of time take place in public opinion, and the estimate in which things are held. Two days later, on the 17th of January, Secretary Fish received from Senator Sumner a brief, initialed memorandum, embodying this, to those of the present time, fairly astounding proposition : [1] —

"Finally I tell him that I have come officially to him as chairman of the Senate Committee on Foreign Relations to ask his opinion *and* advice ; that I am entitled to it, as I must give an answer, etc.

"He says that it requires much reflection, etc.

"I then on leaving him request him to consider the subject, and to let me know his opinion within a day or two.

"In the evening I call upon Gov. Morton at the National. Explain the proposition to him, and read him Rose's 'Confidential Memorandum.' He thinks the Alabama question ought to be settled, and the sooner the better ; that it would justify the President in convening an extra session of the Senate. Thinks the country would regard the recognition by Great Britain of liability for the *Alabama*, and reference of the question of liability as to the other vessels as satisfactory ; that the public mind considers the *Alabama* as embracing the whole class of questions ; but he says that beside the actual losses by the *Alabama*, Great Britain should assume the expenses of this Government in endeavoring to capture her ; that this would be regarded as 'consequential' damage, and would satisfy the public expectation on that point.

"I ask whether a treaty on that basis could be ratified by the Senate against Sumner's opposition. He thinks it would. Says Casserly follows Sumner, so does Schurz and Patterson ; on mentioning that Patterson had been consulted and approved, he replies, that 'gives a majority of the committee, and there can be no doubt of the Senate.' "

In the Appendix to the American Case, submitted to the tribunal at Geneva, the expenses incurred by the United States government in its efforts to capture the British built commerce-destroyers was estimated, and reimbursement on that account was demanded as a consequential injury. The expense incurred was estimated at $7,080,478.70. (Geneva Arbitration ; *Correspondence*, etc., vol. vii. p. 120, table.) The claim was disallowed.

[1] Moore : *International Arbitrations*, vol. i. p. 525.

" First. — The idea of Sir John Rose is that all questions and causes of irritation between England and the United States should be removed absolutely and forever, that we may be at peace really, and good neighbors, and to this end all points of difference should be considered together. Nothing could be better than this initial idea. It should be the starting-point.

" Second. — The greatest trouble, if not peril, being a constant source of anxiety and disturbance, is from Fenianism, which is excited by the British flag in Canada. Therefore the withdrawal of the British flag cannot be abandoned as a condition or preliminary of such a settlement as is now proposed. To make the settlement complete, the withdrawal should be from this hemisphere, including provinces and islands."

V

Since his death, nearly thirty years ago, Charles Sumner has been made the subject of one of the most elaborate biographies in the language. Patient and painstaking to the last degree, nothing seems to have escaped the notice of Mr. Pierce, and the one conspicuous fault of his work is its extreme length. Conceived on a scale which assumes in the reader an interest in the subject, and an indifference to toil, commensurate with those of the author, it was carried to completion in strict conformity with the initial plan. The official biography of Lincoln by Messrs. Nicolay and Hay is not inaptly called by them " A History ; " and its ten substantial volumes, averaging over 450 pages each, defy perusal. Life simply does not suffice for literature laid out on such a Brobdingnagian scale; all sense of proportion is absent from it. Yet the ten volumes of the Lincoln include but a quarter part more reading matter than Mr. Pierce's four. On a rough estimate, it is computed that these fourteen volumes contain some two million words. The most remarkable, and highly characteristic, memorandum just quoted is expressed in about 220 words; and yet for it Mr. Pierce found no space in his four solid volumes. He refers to it indeed, showing that he was aware of its existence; but he does so briefly, and somewhat lightly, in his text,[1] though laboring painfully over it in an appendix.[2] Mr. Storey, in his smaller biography of Sumner, makes no reference at all to it; apparently it had failed to attract his notice. And yet, that memorandum is of much historical significance. A species of electric flash, it reveals what then was, and long had been, in Sumner's mind. It makes intelligible what would otherwise remain well-nigh incomprehensible; if, indeed, not altogether so.

To those of this generation, — especially to us with the war in South Africa going on before our eyes, — it would seem as if the first perusal of that memorandum of January 17 must have suggested to Mr. Fish grave doubts as to Mr. Sumner's sanity. It reads like an attempt at clumsy ridicule. The Secretary of State had gone to an influential Senator in a serious spirit, suggesting a business settlement of grave international complications; and he was met by a proposition which at once put negotiation out of the question. What could the man mean? Apparently, he could

[1] Pierce : *Sumner*, vol. iv. pp. 480, 481.
[2] *Ib.*, pp. 635–638.

only mean that he did not intend to permit any adjustment to be effected, if in his power to prevent. Such unquestionably is the impression this paper now conveys. Meanwhile, strange as it seems, when received it could have occasioned Mr. Fish no especial wonder; except, perhaps, in its wide inclusiveness, it suggested nothing new, nothing altogether beyond the pale of reasonable expectation, much less of discussion. It brought no novel consideration into debate. Surprising now, this statement measures the revolution in sentiment as respects dependencies which has taken place during the last thirty years.

"From 1840 to, say, 1870, the almost universal belief of thoughtful Englishmen was that the colonies contributed nothing or little to the strength of England. We were bound, it was thought, in honor, to protect them; the mother country should see that her children were on the road to become fit for independence; the day for separation would inevitably come; the parting, when it took place, should be on friendly terms; but the separation would be beneficial, for both parent and children. Even a Conservative minister spoke, or wrote, it is said, about our 'wretched colonies.' To-day the whole tone of feeling is changed; her colonies are, it is constantly asserted, both the glory and the strength of Great Britain. Not the extremest Radical ventures to hint a separation."[1] To similar effect another authority, an American, referring to the same period, says, — "We find England declining to accept New Zealand when offered to her by English settlers; treating Australia as a financial

[1] Letter signed "An Observer," dated Oxford, August 22, 1901, in New York *Nation* of September 12, 1901.

burden, useful only as a dumping-ground for crimi-
nals ; discussing in Parliament whether India be
worth defending; questioning the value of Hong-
Kong, and even refusing to be responsible for territories in South Africa." [1] So late even as 1881, ten
years after the negotiation of the Treaty of Washington, there can be little doubt that this feeling — the
conviction of the little worth of dependencies — inspired the policy pursued towards the South African
republics by the second Gladstone administration,
after the disaster of Majuba Hill.

In the mind of Mr. Sumner, the ultimate, and, as
he in 1870 believed, not remote withdrawal of all
European flags, including, of course, the British, from
the western hemisphere, was a logical development of
the Monroe doctrine. That doctrine, as originally set
forth, was merely a first enunciation, and in its sim-
plest form, of a principle which not only admitted of
great development, but was in the direct line of what
is known as Manifest Destiny. Secretary Seward's
Alaska acquisition, bringing to an end Russian dominion in America, created a precedent. One European flag then disappeared from the New World.
Covering areas of consequence, those of Spain and
Great Britain only remained ; and more than twenty
years before, Richard Cobden had written to Sumner,
— " I agree with you that Nature has decided that
Canada and the United States must become one for
all purposes of inter-communication. . . . If the people of Canada are tolerably unanimous in wishing to
sever the very slight thread which now binds them
to this country, I see no reason why, if good faith and

[1] Poultney Bigelow: *The Children of the Nations*, p. 332.

ordinary temper be observed, it should not be done amicably." Charles Sumner did not belong to the Bismarckian school of statesmanship, — he was no welder in blood and iron ; and these words of Cobden furnished the key of the situation as it lay in his essentially doctrinaire mind. He, accordingly, looked forward with confidence to the incorporation of the British possessions into the American Union ; but, as Mr. Pierce truly enough says, he always insisted that it "should be made by peaceful annexation, by the voluntary act of England, and with the cordial assent of the colonists." [1] Nor, in April, 1869, when he delivered his National Claims or Consequential Damages speech in the Senate, did this result seem to him remote. Five months later, still borne forward on the crest of a flooding tide, — little prescient of the immediate future, — he quoted before the Massachusetts State Republican convention Cobden's words of prophecy, and triumphantly exclaimed, — " The end is certain ; nor shall we wait long for its mighty fulfilment. In the procession of events it is now at hand, and he is blind who does not discern it." [2]

Read with this clue in mind, Mr. Sumner's utterances between 1869 and 1871 — including his speech on the Johnson-Clarendon negotiation, his address before the Massachusetts Republican convention in the following September, and his memorandum to Secretary Fish of sixteen months later — become intelligible, and are consecutive. The claims against Great Britain, mounting into the thousands of millions, were formulated and advanced by him as no vulgar pot-

---

[1] Pierce : *Sumner*, vol. iv. p. 637.
[2] *Works*, vol. xiii. p. 129. See, also, vol. xii. p. 173.

house score, to be itemized, and added up in the form of a bill, and so presented for payment. On the contrary, they were merely one item in the statement of a "massive grievance," become matter of gravest international debate. The settlement was to be commensurate. Comprehensive, grandiose even, it was to include a hemispheric flag-withdrawal, as well as a revision of the rules of international law. The adjustment of mere money claims was a matter of altogether minor consideration; indeed, such might well in the end become makeweights, — mere pawns in the mighty game.

It is needless to say that the unexpected was sure to occur in the practical unfolding of this picturesque programme. Indeed, a very forcible suggestion of the practical danger involved in it, just so long as the average man is what he is, was brought home to the Senator from Massachusetts when he resumed his seat in executive session after completing his speech on the Johnson-Clarendon Convention, — the carefully prepared opening of the great world debate. Mr. Zachariah Chandler of Michigan subsequently took the floor. He was a Senator much more closely than Mr. Sumner representative of the average American public man. And Mr. Chandler proceeded unconsciously to furnish an illustration of the practical outcome of Mr. Sumner's scheme as he, the average American, understood it. He entirely concurred in Mr. Sumner's presentation of national injuries, consequential damages, and a sense of "massive grievance." "If Great Britain," he then went on to say, "should meet us in a friendly spirit, acknowledge her wrong, and cede all her interests in the Canadas in settlement of these claims, we will have perpetuate peace with her; but, if she does not, we must conquer peace. We cannot afford to have an enemy's base so near us. It is a national necessity that we should have the British possessions. He hoped such a negotiation would be opened, and that it would be a peaceful one; but, if it should not be, and England insists on war, then let the war be 'short, sharp, and decisive.'"[1] The

---

[1] See report of debate in New York *Tribune*, April 21, 1869. There is reason to believe that, in this utterance, Mr. Chandler more nearly reflected the original views of General Grant than did Mr. Sumner, or, subsequently, Mr. Fish. Always military, Grant, as President, looked upon the accession of the British Dominion to the American Union as both inevitable and highly desirable for all concerned. He was what is now known as a thorough expansionist. Hence, when the Civil War closed, he was in favor of an immediate invasion of Mexico. (*Around the World with General Grant*, vol. ii. p. 163.) As President, he later proceeded to annex islands in the West Indies in the wholly unceremonious fashion already described in this paper. He had fully considered a Canadian campaign, and was of opinion that " if Sheridan, for instance, with our resources, could not have taken Canada in thirty days, he should have been cashiered." (*Ib.*, p. 167.) Mr. Sumner never contemplated forcible annexation as the result of a war with Great Britain growing out of his theory of national injuries. He did look to a voluntary and peaceable consolidation of adjacent English-speaking territories and their inhabitants. Grant also looked for such a consolidation, but was quite ready to have it come about as the result of a campaign, and incidental beneficent compulsion. Again, Secretary Fish stood between the two. Mr. Sumner's policy was, under the circumstances, fraught with immediate danger. He was for keeping the questions at issue open, a cause of possible rupture at any moment; and for that rupture Grant always stood ready. This the English Minister (Sir Edward Thornton) perfectly understood. Hence his eagerness to effect a settlement. Grant, meanwhile, was indifferent, and Sumner, unconsciously, was playing into his hands. Finally, as the result of a quarrel with Sumner, Grant gave Fish a free hand. He might effect a settlement if he could ; but if, for any reason, he failed in so doing, recourse would be had to the other plan of procedure. The Secretary might then stand aside, and the Commander-in-chief would settle the question of claims against Great Britain, individual and national, through a process never contemplated by the

report of these utterances was at once transmitted by the British Minister to his government; and, taken in connection with Mr. Sumner's arraignment, and his presentation of consequential damages, furnished those composing that government, as well as Professor Goldwin Smith, with much food for thought.[1]

The policy proper to be pursued in the years following 1869 rapidly assumed shape in Mr. Sumner's mind. He worked it out in every detail. As, shortly after, he wrote to his friend, Dr. S. G. Howe, — " I look to annexation at the North. I wish to have that whole zone from Newfoundland to Vancouver." It was with this result distinctly present to him, and as a first step thereto, that he secured the English mission for Mr. Motley. Through Motley he thought to work. He, chairman of the United States Senate Committee on Foreign Relations, was to mould and shape the future of a hemisphere, — President, Secre-

Massachusetts Senator. It is not suggested that evidence in support of this statement can be adduced; or even exists. That, however, Grant's extreme personal dislike for Mr. Sumner, and his sense of obligation to Mr. Fish, greatly influenced his action on the question of a settlement with Great Britain, admits of no doubt. It gave Mr. Fish the opportunity, of which he availed himself. The alternative Grant always had in mind in the event of his Secretary's failure, or British recalcitrancy, is alone open to question.

[1] It was unquestionably to this utterance of Senator Chandler's, and to counteract its effect, that Mr. Sumner used the following language, in his speech of five months later, just referred to: — " Sometimes there are whispers of territorial compensation, and Canada is named as the consideration. But he knows England little, and little also of that great English liberty from Magna Charta to the Somerset case, who supposes that this nation could undertake any such transfer. And he knows our country little, and little also of that great liberty that is ours, who supposes that we could receive such a transfer. On each side there is impossibility. Territory may be conveyed, but not a people. I allude to this suggestion only because, appearing in the public press, it has been answered from England."

tary of State, and Her Majesty's Ministers being as clay in his potter hands, with Motley for the deftly turning wheel. Concerning this project he seems during the summer of 1869 to have been in almost daily correspondence with his friend near the Court of St. James, and in frequent conference with Secretary Fish at Washington. On June 11 he wrote to the former that the Secretary had, two days before, sounded the British Minister on the subject of Canada, the American claims on Great Britain being too large to admit of a money settlement. Sir Edward Thornton, he went on, had replied that England " did not wish to keep Canada, but could not part with it without the consent of the population." The Secretary next wanted Mr. Sumner to state the amount of claims; to which he had replied that he did not regard it as the proper time for so doing. This letter, it so chanced, was dated the very day after Mr. Motley's first unfortunate interview with the British Foreign Secretary; and that diplomatic jeremiad might not inaptly have concluded with a premonitory hint of what his mentor and guide was on the morrow to write, — a hint of the nature suggested by Mr. Schurz in a letter to Secretary Fish,[1] written at this very time. Then, only four days later, — on the 15th of June, — Mr. Sumner again advises his correspondent of a dinner-table talk with men in high official circles, and significantly adds, — " All feel that your position is as historic as any described by your pen. England must listen, and at last yield. I do not despair seeing the debate end — (1) In the withdrawal of England from this hemisphere ; (2) In remodelling maritime international law.

[1] *Infra*, Appendix C, p. 209.

Such a consummation would place our republic at the head of the civilized world." Here was no whisper of mere money claims; and, five days after, he writes in the same spirit, referring apparently to the Secretary of State, — "With more experience at Washington, our front would have been more perfect." [1] The "debate" referred to was, of course, that "international debate, the greatest of our history, and, before it is finished, in all probability the greatest of all history." Thus, in June, 1869, the chairman of the Senate Committee on Foreign Relations was sending what were in effect unofficial instructions to a facile national representative, couched, be it noticed, in the very words used by the writer eighteen months later in the memorandum just quoted.

In one of these letters, it will be observed, Mr. Sumner told Motley that Secretary Fish had that day sounded the British Minister as to a possible cession of Canada in liquidation of our national claims, and appeasement of our sense of "massive grievance." [2] The statement was correct; and not only at this juncture, but repeatedly, was a comprehensive settlement on such a basis urged on the British government. Both President and Secretary were thus of one mind with Mr. Sumner. In November, 1869, for instance, four months after Sir John Rose's first visit to Washington, and at the very time he was writing to Mr. Fish about Mr. Motley's attitude in London, an entire cabinet meeting was occupied in a discussion of the *Alabama* claims. The President then suggested the possibility of Great Britain quitting Canada; and he intimated

---

[1] Pierce: *Sumner*, vol. iv. pp. 409–412.
[2] *Ib.*, vol. iv. p. 400.

his belief that, in such case, we ought to be satisfied with the payment for the losses actually sustained through the Confederate commerce-destroyers, combined with a settlement satisfactory to us of the principles of maritime neutrality law. A few days later he expressed his unwillingness at that time to adjust the claims; he wished them kept open until Great Britain was ready to give up Canada. When certain members of the Cabinet thereupon assured him that Great Britain looked upon Canada as a source of weakness, quoting Lord Carlisle and Sir Edward Thornton, the President at once replied, — "If that be so, I would be willing to settle at once." During the following weeks, — December, 1869, and January, 1870, — the subject was frequently discussed between Secretary Fish and Sir Edward Thornton. The former urged on the latter the entire withdrawal of Great Britain from Canada, and an immediate settlement of all claims on that basis. To this Sir Edward replied, — " Oh, you know that we cannot do. The Canadians find fault with me for saying so openly as I do that we are ready to let them go whenever they shall wish; but they do not desire it." In its issue of December 18, 1869, while these conversations, taking place in Washington, were duly reported in Downing Street, the *Times*, probably inspired, expressed itself as follows : — " Suppose the colonists met together, and, after deliberating, came to the conclusion that they were a very long way off from the United Kingdom, . . . and that every natural motive of contiguity, similarity of interests, and facility of administration induced them to think it more convenient to slip into the Union than into the Dominion. Should we oppose their de-

termination ? We all know we should not attempt
to withstand it, if it were clearly and intelligibly pronounced. . . . Instead of the Colonies being the dependencies of the Mother Country, the Mother Country
has become the Dependency of the Colonies. We are
tied, while they are loose. We are subject to danger,
while they are free." And a few months later, when
the Dominion undertook to find fault with some of the
provisions of the Treaty of Washington, the same
organ of English opinion thus frankly delivered itself:
— " From this day forth look after your own business
yourself ; you are big enough, you are strong enough,
you are intelligent enough, and, if there were any de-
ficiency in any of these points, it would be supplied by
the education of self-reliance. We are both now in a
false position, and the time has arrived when we should
be relieved from it. Take up your freedom ; your days
of apprenticeship are over." In view of such utterances as these from the leading organs of the mother
country, Mr. Sumner certainly had grounds for assuming that a not unwilling hemispheric flag-withdrawal by Great Britain was more than probable in the
early future.

Returning to what took place in Washington in
March, 1870, on the eve of the Franco-Prussian war,
Secretary Fish had another long conversation with Sir
Edward Thornton, which showed forcibly how conscious
those composing the English Ministry were of the
falseness of Great Britain's position, and of the immi-
nence of danger. The Secretary again urged on the
Minister that her American provinces were to Great
Britain a menace of danger ; and that a cause of irri-
tation, and of possible complication, would, especially

in those times of Fenianism, be removed, should they be made independent.   To this Mr. Thornton replied, — " It is impossible for Great Britain to inaugurate a separation.   They are willing, and even desirous, to have one.   Europe may at any moment be convulsed ; and, if England became involved, it would be impossi-ble to prevent retaliation, and the ocean would swarm with *Alabamas*.   England would then be compelled to declare war."   The Secretary consoled him by agree-ing that commerce-destroyers would then be fitted out in spite of all the government might, or could, attempt to prevent them.

Up to this point the chairman of the Senate Com-mittee on Foreign Relations, the President, the Sec-retary of State, and the members of the Cabinet generally had gone on in happy concurrence.   They had the same end in view.   But now the cleavage between President and Senator rapidly widened.   A week only after the conversation with Sir Edward Thornton last referred to, General Grant cautioned Mr. Fish against communicating to Mr. Sumner any confidential or important information received at the State Department.   Later, he became persuaded that the Massachusetts Senator was constitutionally un-truthful; but, as yet, he considered him only unfair and inaccurate.   The chairman of the Senate Committee on Foreign Relations ceased, however, to be thereafter a direct factor in the negotiation with Great Britain.

Thus far, in pursuance of the policy dimly outlined in the executive session debate on the Johnson-Clar-endon Convention, the two questions of a settlement of claims and Canadian independence had been kept closely associated.   They were now to be separated.

Yet the change was gradual; for Mr. Sumner's policy had a strong hold on the minds of both President and Secretary.[1] Even as late as September, 1870, only five months before the Treaty of Washington was negotiated, Secretary Fish and Sir Edward Thornton had another conversation on the subject of Canadian independence. It originated in one of the endless squabbles over the Fisheries. The Secretary intimated his belief that the solution of that question would be found in a separation of the Dominion from the mother country. Thereupon Mr. Thornton repeated what he had, he declared, often said before, — that Great Britain was willing, and even anxious, to have the colonies become independent; but could do nothing to force independence on them. He then added, — " It is impossible to connect the question of Canadian independence with the Alabama claims; not even to the extent of providing for the reference of the question of independence to a popular vote of the people of the Dominion. Independence," he added, " means annexation. They are one and the same thing." This conversation, it will be observed, took

---

[1] In his first annual message to Congress, December 6, 1869 (*Messages of the Presidents*, vol. vii. p. 32), General Grant thus expressed himself, — the Secretary of State undoubtedly having draughted the paragraph : — " The United States have no disposition to interfere with the existing relations of Spain to her colonial possessions on this continent. They believe that in due time Spain and other European powers will find their interest in terminating those relations, and establishing their present dependencies as independent powers — members of the family of nations." Seven months later (July 14, 1870), the President transmitted to the Senate, in reply to a resolution, a report from the Secretary of State, in which was the following : — " This policy . . . looks hopefully to the time when, by the voluntary departure of European governments from this continent and the adjacent islands, America shall be wholly American." (*Ib.*, p. 74.)

place on the very day the investment of Paris by the victorious German army was pronounced complete. In the existing European situation everything was possible, anything might be anticipated.

Though his resignation had been requested, Mr. Motley still remained in London. His early removal was contemplated by the President, and the question of who should replace him was under consideration. The appointment was offered to O. P. Morton, then a Senator from Indiana. Wholly the President's, the selection was the reverse of happy. Governor Morton was inclined to accept; but he desired first to know whether he would, as Minister, have the *Alabama* claims settlement intrusted to him. The President then talked the matter over with Secretary Fish, and what he said showed clearly the hold which Sumner's views had on him. He proposed that the new Minister should attempt a negotiation based on the following concessions by Great Britain : (1) the payment of actual losses incurred through the depredations of British Confederate commerce-destroyers ; (2) a satisfactory revision of the principles of international law as between the two governments ; and (3) the submission to the voters of the Dominion of the question of independence. In commenting immediately afterwards on this conversation, Mr. Fish wrote, — " The President evidently expects these Provinces to be annexed to the United States during his administration. I hope that it may be so. That such is their eventual destiny, I do not doubt ; but whether so soon as the President expects may be a question." Owing to the result of an election in Indiana held shortly after, it was deemed inexpedient for Governor Morton to vacate his seat in the Senate. He consequently declined further to consider a diplomatic position. Though in no way germane to the subject of this paper, it is interesting to know that it was to fill the vacancy thus existing that General Butler shortly after brought forward the name of Wendell Phillips. The President, Mr. Fish noted, " very evidently will not consider him within the range of possibilities of appointment."

The pressure for some settlement now brought to bear on the British government was day by day becoming greater. About the middle of November the Russian Minister took occasion to suggest to Secretary Fish, in a neighborly sort of way, that the present time — that of the Franco-Prussian war — was most opportune to press on Great Britain an immediate settlement of the *Alabama* claims. Two weeks later the message of the President was sent to Congress, with the significant paragraph already quoted. In his next talk with Sir Edward Thornton, Secretary Fish alluded to the suggestion made to him by the Russian Minister, and Sir Edward, in return, frankly asked him what the United States wanted. And now at last the negotiation took a new and final turn. The Secretary, dropping Canada from the discussion, asked merely an expression of regret on the part of Great Britain, an acceptable declaration of principles of international law, and payment of claims. This conversation took place on the 20th of November ; nineteen days later, on the 9th of December, at a cabinet meeting held that day, Secretary Fish read in confidence a private letter to him from Sir John Rose, " intimating that the British cabinet is disposed to enter on negotiations." It would thus appear that the obstacle in the way of a renewed negotiation had been the purpose of the United States to combine in some way a settlement of money claims, private and national, with a movement looking to the withdrawal of the British flag, in whole or in part, from the North American continent. The moment this suggestion was withheld, the British cabinet lost no time in signifying its readiness to negotiate. None the less, the whole scheme of Mr. Sumner, underlying his famous speech of April 13, 1869, and the appointment of Mr. Motley to the English mission, was thereby and thenceforth definitely abandoned. In his memorandum, therefore, the chairman of the Senate Committee on Foreign Relations demanded nothing altogether new; he merely, stating the case in its widest form, insisted upon adherence to a familiar policy long before formulated. None the less, there is a wide difference between the concession of its independence to a particular dependency, no matter how considerable, and the somewhat scenic, and obviously compulsory, withdrawal of a nation's flag from half the globe. In Mr. Sumner's imagination, the British drum-beat was no more to follow the rising sun.

VI

The narrative now returns to the point when Mr. Sumner's memorandum of January 17 reached the Secretary of State. Mr. Davis says, " I well remember Mr. Fish's astonishment when he received this document. At first he almost thought any attempt

at negotiation would prove futile." [1]   Probably the
word "dismay" would describe more accurately than
"astonishment" Mr. Fish's state of mind at this
juncture.   Undoubtedly, he had, time and time again,
discussed with Mr. Sumner the whole question of
European withdrawal from America, altogether or in
part, whether from Canada alone or from the hemisphere.   He had referred to it publicly in the passages already quoted from the President's messages.
The proposition, therefore, can have excited no "astonishment" in him.   It might well, however, have
caused a feeling of dismay, for it threatened to bring
to an abrupt close the incipient negotiation he so
much had at heart.   It was phrased also as an ultimatum.   Closing the door to discussion, it precipitated
into the immediate present the academic problem of a
possibly remote future.   After full talk, and subsequent mature reflection, the chairman of the Senate
Committee gave it as his judgment that the demand,
known to be at that time impossible of concession,
"cannot be abandoned as a condition or preliminary."
Language could scarcely be stronger.   The Secretary had cause for discouragement.   His failure had
been complete.   But, whatever may have been the
sensations of the Secretary when gasping under the
first effects of this icy douche, those of the President must also be taken into account.   He was essentially the man for that situation.   He was in his
element.   What followed bore unmistakably the impress of his handiwork; for, to the military eye, one
thing must at once have been apparent.   The situation was simplified; his opponent had put himself

[1] Davis: *Mr. Fish and the Alabama Claims*, p. 137.

in his power. Instinctively, he grasped the opportunity. The natural, indeed the only inference to be
drawn from the memorandum, was that the chairman
of the Senate Committee on Foreign Relations intended to put an immediate stop to the proposed
negotiation, if in his power so to do. The considerations influencing him were obvious. The course of
procedure now suggested was wholly at variance with
the policy outlined by him. In June, 1869, he had
written to Mr. Motley, — "I should make no 'claim'
or 'demand' for the present;" and to Caleb Cushing
a month later, — "Our case, in length and breadth,
with all details, should be stated to England without
any demand of any kind." And now, in January,
1871, he did not regard the conditions of a successful and satisfactory settlement with Great Britain, on
the basis he had in view, as being any more propitious than in June, 1869. Eighteen months only
had elapsed. The fruit was not yet ripe; — then why
shake the tree? That "international debate, the
greatest of our history, and before it is finished, in all
probability the greatest of all history," seemed drawing to a lame and impotent, because premature, conclusion. His memorandum was, therefore, an attempt
at a checkmate. By formulating demands which he
knew would not be entertained, he hoped at once
to end the proposed negotiation. The country would
then await some more convenient occasion, when,
Great Britain being entirely willing, a mild compulsion in favor of independence could be brought
to bear upon her American dependencies. On the
other hand, the issue presented in this memorandum
was clear and not to be evaded, — Was the Executive

to shape the foreign policy of the United States; or was it to receive its inspiration from the room of the Senate Committee on Foreign Relations? Either that committee must be brought into line with the State Department, or the Secretary of State should accept his position as a chairman's clerk.

A delicate question between the executive and legislative departments of the government — a question as old as the Constitution — was thus involved. What constituted an attempt at improper interference by one department with the functions and organization of the other? It is obvious that, in a representative government under the party system, where both the legislative and the executive departments are controlled by the same party organization, the legislative committees should be so organized as to act in reasonable accord with the responsible executive. It is a purely practical question. The executive cannot, of course, directly interfere in the organization of the legislative body; but it has a perfect right to demand of its friends and supporters in the legislative bodies that those having charge through committees of the business of those bodies should be in virtual harmony with the Administration. Certainly, they should not be in avowed hostility to it. As Grant himself later said,[1] it was indeed a singular spectacle " to find a Senate with the large majority of its members in sympathy with the Administration, and with its chairman of the Foreign Committee in direct opposition to the foreign policy of the Administration, in theory and detail." There was force in this statement, and the President was fully justified in asking of his party a

[1] At Edinburgh, New York *Herald*, September 25, 1877.

release from a position of such obvious embarrassment. Indeed, under any proper construction of functions, those thus finding themselves in virtual opposition might well decline committee appointments necessarily placing them in a position where they feel under compulsion to thwart and hamper the measures of the party of which they nominally are members. Such should, in parliamentary parlance, take their places below the gangway. In the winter of 1870–71 Mr. Sumner was in that position. Chairman of the Senate Committee on Foreign Relations, on cardinal features of foreign policy he was notoriously in proclaimed opposition. Such being the case, it is at least an open question whether, in view of the executive functions of the Senate, he should not have voluntarily declined longer to serve as chairman of that particular committee. His serving was clearly an obstruction to the Administration, and its friends constituted a large majority of the Senate ; it would, moreover, be perfectly possible for him to exert his influence both in the chamber and in the committee-room without being the official head of the committee, intrusted as such with the care of measures on the defeat of which he was intent. He was in an obviously false position. The practice under our government is the other way. Senatorial courtesy and seniority, it is well known, prevail ; and Secretaries must govern themselves accordingly. Nevertheless, in the case of Mr. Sumner and his chairmanship in 1870–71, this practice was carried to its extreme limit ; and, after the presidential canvass of the following year, he must necessarily, and by common consent, have been superseded. Even now, indeed, when, having been active in opposition to one measure of foreign policy by which the President set great store, he declared himself in advance opposed to another measure of yet greater moment, the future was plainly foreshadowed. A wholly impossible preliminary condition to the proposed measure must, he declared, be insisted upon, — or, once more to quote his own words, " cannot be abandoned."

In January, 1871, the Forty-first Congress was fast drawing to its close. Chosen at the election which made Grant President for the first time, that Congress was overwhelmingly Republican ; so much so that, of seventy-two Senators admitted to seats, sixty-one were supporters of the Administration. And yet, in a body thus made up, — a body in which the opposition numbered but eleven members, — not one in six, — a treaty in behalf of the ratification of which the President had exerted all his influence, personal and official, had failed to secure even a majority vote. The chairman of the Committee on Foreign Relations, regardless of private personal solicitation on the part of the chief Executive wholly unprecedented in character, had been not only unrelenting but successful in his opposition. The President-General looked upon this action on the part of a Senator at the head of the Committee on Foreign Relations as, during war, he would have regarded the action of a department commander who, refusing to coöperate in the plan of general campaign laid down from headquarters, should exert himself to cause an operation to fail. Such a subordinate would be summarily relieved. He seems actually to have chafed under his inability to take this course with the chairman of a Senate committee ; and so he primarily relieved his feelings at the expense of the friend of the chairman, the Minister to England. He was within his power, and him he incontinently dismissed.

This distinctly savored of Jackson rather than of Washington. The White House had, in truth, become a military headquarters. But the President's personal feelings, as well as the General's instinct for discipline, had been outraged, and he was intent on the real offender, — the Senator from Massachusetts. Hence it followed that, when Secretary Fish, with Mr. Sumner's memorandum in his hand, went to the White House for instructions, the President's views as to the independence, and subsequent early annexation, of the British possessions at once underwent a change. As he welcomed an issue with his much-disliked antagonist upon which he felt assured of victory, hemispheric flag-withdrawals ceased to interest him. A great possible obstruction in the path of the proposed negotiation was thus suddenly removed. The General-President promptly instructed the Secretary to go to Sir John Rose, and advise him that the Administration was prepared to accept the proposal for a commission to settle all questions between the countries. That was, however, a preliminary move only. By it, the Administration was committed to action of great import. A crucial case was presented; one on which no unnecessary risk would be incurred. The next and really vital step remained to be taken.

When the first Congress of Grant's earlier administration met in its final session at the usual date in December, 1870, an attempt was made foreshadowing what occurred four months later. A partial reorganization of the Senate Committee on Foreign Relations was discussed, with a view to the introduction into that committee of some element less under its chairman's influence, and holding more intimate relations with the Executive. A place was to be found for Roscoe Conkling of New York. If possible, Mr. Conkling was to be substituted for Mr. Sumner ; but if Mr. Sumner was found too firmly fixed, Mr. Schurz was to be replaced as a member of the committee; or, as a final resort, Mr. Patterson of New Hampshire, if Mr. Schurz also proved immovable. The last change was finally decided upon ; but, when the committee as thus altered was reported in caucus, Sumner objected. Senatorial courtesy then prevailing, the scheme was for the time being abandoned.[1] Charles Sumner was, however, yet to learn that, in civil as in military life, Ulysses S. Grant was a very persistent man.

Two weeks later Mr. Sumner did what he had hitherto refrained from doing. Up to this time he had expressed himself with characteristic freedom, denouncing the President in conversation and in letter,[2] but he had not opposed him in debate. He now openly broke ground against him in a carefully prepared speech on the Dominican question. In the position he took, he was probably right. He would certainly be deemed so in the light of the views then generally taken of the world-mission of the United States ; but that was during the country's earlier period, and before the universality of its mission was so plainly disclosed as it now is. Whether correct, however, in his position or not, his manner and language were characteristic, and unfortunate. The

---

[1] Pierce : *Sumner*, vol. iv. p. 456.
[2] *Ib.*, pp. 448, 454; *Forum*, vol. xxiv. p. 406.

question on both sides had become personal; the feeling uncontrollable : and, throughout his career, — early and late, — Mr. Sumner did not appreciate the significance of words. He failed to appreciate them in the speech now made, entitled by him " Naboth's Vineyard," wherein he accused the President of seeking surreptitiously to commit the country to a " dance of blood." On the 9th of January, less than three weeks after this outbreak, the papers relating to the recall of Mr. Motley were, by order of the President, sent to the Senate. This was on a Monday ; and it was on the following Sunday morning that Mr. Fish called on Mr. Sumner by arrangement, with the Sir John Rose memorandum. The climax was then at hand. Among the papers relating to the removal of Mr. Motley was one in which the Secretary had referred to some unnamed party as being " bitterly, personally, and vindictively hostile " to the President ; while, in another passage, he had spoken of the President as a man than whom none " would look with more scorn and contempt upon one who uses the words and the assurances of friendship to cover a secret and determined purpose of hostility."

The allusion was unmistakably to Sumner. It was so accepted by him. There is nothing in the record which justifies it ; and, while it indicates a deep personal feeling on the part of Mr. Fish, it was unnecessarily offensive. Mr. Sumner had a right to take offence at it ; nor, indeed, could he well help so doing. On the other hand, Mr. Fish was not improbably equally incensed at some denunciatory remarks of Mr. Sumner's brought to his ears by White House intermediaries, then abnormally active. However this may be, and the record is silent on the point, the Motley papers were laid before the Senate on the very Monday upon which Sir John Rose reached Washington. A week from Tuesday, the eighth day after the transmission of those papers, the memorandum of Mr. Sumner of January 17 reached the Secretary. The break between the two officials was complete; they were no longer on speaking terms.

January was now more than half over, and, in six weeks' time, the Forty-first Congress was to pass out of existence. When, on the 4th of March, the new Congress came into being, the committees of the Senate would . have to be reappointed, and, of necessity, largely remodelled, nineteen newly elected members of the body replacing a similar number whose terms had expired. Mr. Sumner's deposition from the chairmanship he would then have filled through five successive Congresses had meanwhile become a fixed idea in the presidential mind; [1] and Secretary Fish shaped his course accordingly. On the 24th of January he again met Sir John Rose. A week had intervened since the receipt of Mr. Sumner's memorandum, and during that week the Secretary had been holding consultations with Mr. Sumner's senatorial colleagues; of course, absolutely ignoring that gentleman. While so doing, he had carefully informed himself as to the attitude of the Democratic minority in the chamber,

---

[1] Mr. Davis says (Mr. Fish and the Alabama Claims, p. 67) : — "Mr. Fish and the President thought it unwise to make the change. When, however, this ultimatum [the Rose memorandum of January 17] was received from Mr. Sumner, Mr. Fish, with the assent of the President, withdrew all opposition." But, elsewhere (Ib., p. 139), Mr. Davis says, "No Senator has ever told me what induced the Senate to make the change."

now increased to seventeen in a body numbering in all seventy-four. Mr. Bayard and Mr. Thurman were the recognized leaders of the opposition ; and, from both, he received assurances of support. Upon the other side of the chamber, the administration Senators could, of course, be counted on ; and through their leaders, Messrs. Conkling and Edmunds, it was well known that they were ripe for revolt against the Sumner committee-régime. The personal relations of Mr. Sumner with General Grant and Mr. Fish, or rather the absence of all personal relations between the chairman of the Senate Committee on Foreign Relations and the President and Secretary of State, was matter of common knowledge. The several Senators consulted were also informed as to Mr. Sumner's attitude towards the proposed negotiations, and a carefully drawn memorandum in relation thereto was submitted to them by the Secretary. No precaution was neglected.[1]

Charles Sumner was a man with whom it is difficult to deal historically. His is a large figure ; senatorially viewed, perhaps none is larger. He projects himself from the canvas. In referring also to any considerable public character, it is not easy to call attention to his foibles and limitations, as affecting results, without appearing to lay undue emphasis upon them. It is especially so in the case of Mr. Sumner ; for he was a man of intense individuality, and, as he grew in years, his foibles were always more in evidence. In the matters now under consideration, also, they seem to have affected his public conduct and his relations with others to a peculiar extent ; and this was, perhaps, to be in a

[1] Moore : *International Arbitrations*, vol. i. pp. 525, 529.

degree accounted for by the fact that he had then recently passed through a most trying domestic experience, well calculated to disturb a temperament never
disposed to placidity.[1] Though highly respected, Mr.
Sumner was not a favorite among his colleagues.   In
many respects a man of engaging personality, kind,
sympathetic, and considerate, essentially refined and
easy of approach, he could not brook sustained opposition on any question which to his mind involved the
moral issue.   Recognizing superiority in no one, he then
became restive in presence of any assertion of equality.
The savor of incense was sweet in his nostrils; while he
did not exact deference, habitual deference was in later
life essential to his good-will.   Among his colleagues,
especially those not politically opposed but more or less
lacking in sympathy, his unconsciously overbearing
habit when what was ever present to his mind as "*the*
cause" was involved almost necessarily made him enemies.   In those days, also, "*the* cause" was never quies-
cent; and, when intent upon it, Mr. Sumner's language
became rhetorically intemperate and his temper implacable.   These terms seem strong; and yet they are not
so strong as those used of him at the time by men of his
own age, and friends of years' standing.   One instance
will suffice.   "Sumner," wrote R. H. Dana not long
before, "has been acting like a madman . . . in the
positions he took, the arguments he advanced, and the
language he used to the twenty out of twenty-five Republican Senators who differed from him.   If I could
hear that he was out of his head from opium or even
New England rum, not indicating a habit, I should be

[1] See on this point the suggestive incident mentioned by Mr. Davis:
Mr. Fish and the Alabama Claims, p. 55.

relieved. Mason, Davis, and Slidell were never so in-
solent and overbearing as he was, and his arguments,
his answers of questions, were boyish or crazy, I don't
know which." Again, in June, 1861, the same excellent authority describes, in the familiarity of private
correspondence, the Senator as coming from Washington "full of denunciation of Mr. Seward. . . . He
gave me some anxiety, as I listened to him, lest he
was in a heated state of brain.¹ He cannot talk five
minutes without bringing in Mr. Seward, and always
in bitter terms of denunciation. . . . His mission is
to expose and denounce Mr. Seward, and into that
mission he puts all his usual intellectual and moral
energy." Two years later Mr. Dana was in Washington. In the interim he, an old personal as well as
political friend, had ventured to question the Senator's
policy. He now, as was his wont, at once called on
Mr. Sumner, leaving his card. The call was not returned, nor did Mr. Dana hear anything from Mr.
Sumner during the succeeding twenty days while in
Washington, or see him, except once when, by chance,
they encountered each other at a friend's house. All
this was characteristic of the man. To any question
in which he was deeply concerned, there was but one
side.² As it was his mission to denounce Seward in

---

¹ Mr. J. C. Bancroft Davis, under similar circumstances, records the
same impression. "Mr. Sumner seemed to be in a state of great excitement. His tremulous manner and loud voice made upon me the
impression that his mind was affected." (*Mr. Fish and the Alabama
Claims*, p. 32.)

² "Once, in later days, when I argued with him that opponents
might be sincere, and that there was some reason on the other side,
he thundered in reply. 'Upon such a question there *is* no other side.'"
(Eulogy of George William Curtis, *Massachusetts Memorial of Charles
Sumner*, p. 148.) "But at the time of [the San Domingo affair], all he

1861, ten years later it was his mission to denounce
Grant; and he fulfilled it. As he "gave the cold
shoulder" to Dana in 1863, so he gave it to Fish in
1871.[1] Consequently, in 1871, more than half the
body of which he was in consecutive service the senior
member were watching for a chance to humiliate him.

As Mr. Fish looked at it, Mr. Sumner had now
taken his position squarely across the path the Administration proposed to pursue on a momentous question
of foreign policy, — a government measure. He
understood, or thought he understood, Mr. Sumner's
mental processes, and his methods of parliamentary
action. Assuredly, he was not without recent experience of them. He shaped his course accordingly; deciding to give, in the first place, to those now possibly
being invited to another diplomatic humiliation, frank
and full notice of the difficulties they must expect to
encounter, and the danger they would incur. There
was to be no ground on which to rest against him a
future charge of deception, or even of suppression of
facts. So, at his next meeting with Sir John Rose on
the 24th of January, — a meeting which took place at
the Secretary's house, and not at the State Department, — Mr. Fish began by quietly, but in confidence,
handing Sir John the Sumner hemispheric flag-withdrawal memorandum. Sir John read it; and, having

---

said was so deeply grounded in his feeling and conscience, that it
was for him difficult to understand how others could form different
conclusions. . . . It was difficult for him to look at a question or
problem from more than one point of view, and to comprehend its
different bearings, its complex relations with other questions or problems; and to that one point of view he was apt to subject all other
considerations." (Eulogy of Carl Schurz, *Ib.*, pp. 241, 255.)

[1] Pierce: *Sumner*, vol. iv. p. 468; Adams: *R. H. Dana*, vol. ii. p. 265.

done so, returned it, apparently without comment. Mr. Fish then informed him that, after full consideration, the government had determined to enter on the proposed negotiation ; and, should Great Britain decide to send out special envoys to treat on the basis agreed upon, the Administration would spare no effort " to secure a favorable result, even if it involved a conflict with the chairman of the Committee on Foreign Relations in the Senate." [1]

The die was cast. So far as the chairman of the Senate Committee on Foreign Relations was concerned, the man of Donelson, of Vicksburg, and of Appomattox now had his eye coldly fixed upon him. As to the settlement with Great Britain, it was to be effected on business principles, and according to precedent ; " national " claims and hemispheric flag-withdrawals were at this point summarily dismissed from consideration.

The purport of the last interview between Mr. Fish and Sir John Rose was immediately cabled by the latter to London ; and, during the week that ensued, the submarine wires were busy. The Gladstone Ministry, thoroughly educated by fast-passing continental events, — France prostrate and Germany defiant, — was now, heart and soul, intent on extricating Great Britain from the position in which it had, ten years before, put itself under a previous administration of which Mr. Gladstone had been a prominent, as well as an active and an influential, member. Before the seven days had expired an agreement was reached ; and, on the 1st of February, Sir Edward Thornton notified Secretary Fish of the readiness of his government to send a special mission to Washington

[1] Moore : *International Arbitrations*, vol. i. pp. 528–530.

empowered to treat on all questions at issue between the two countries. The papers were duly submitted to Congress, and, on the 9th of February, President Grant sent to the Senate the names of five persons, designated as commissioners to represent the United States in the proposed negotiation. The nominations were promptly confirmed. The question was now a practical one: — Would Great Britain humble its pride so far as to avail itself of the chance of extrication thus opened? — and, if it did humble its pride to that extent, could the administration of President Grant so shape the negotiation as to get the United States out of the position in which Mr. Sumner had partially succeeded in putting it? His more than possible opposition to any settlement at that time had to be reckoned with; if necessary, overborne.

For present purposes, it is needless to enter into the details of the negotiation which ensued. If not familiar history, I certainly have no new light to throw on it. Under the skilful business guidance of Mr. Fish, the settlement moved quietly and rapidly to its foreordained conclusion. It is, however, still curious to study, between the lines of the record, the extent to which the Sumner memorandum influenced results, and how it in the end only just failed to accomplish its author's purpose. It rested among Mr. Fish's private papers, a bit of diplomatic dynamite, the existence of which was known to few, and mentioned by no one. Not a single allusion is to be found to it in the debates, the controversies, or the correspondence of the time. Mr. Pierce, in his life of Sumner, earnestly combats [1] Mr. Bancroft Davis's statement [2] that

[1] Pierce: *Sumner*, vol. iv. p. 481.
[2] Davis: *Mr. Fish and the Alabama Claims*, p. 137.

certain Senators were fully, if confidentially, advised
of the existence of the memorandum and of the attitude of Mr. Sumner. In this he is clearly in error.[1]
At least four Senators knew of both, but, not without
reason, seem to have been afraid of the former. The
danger, of course, lay in the direct and forcible appeal
to Fenianism contained in the memorandum; for the
Irish-Americans then constituted a much more formidable political factor than now, and they were in a
highly inflammatory condition. The echoes of the
last raid on the Dominion had hardly died away in the
press,[2] and it would not have been a difficult task, especially for Mr. Sumner, to have excited an outburst
of Irish-American feeling which would have so affected
a minority at least of the Senate as effectually to seal
the fate of any treaty. In view of this fact, George
F. Edmunds of Vermont, then serving in his second
senatorial term, and one of those in Mr. Fish's confidence and on whom he most depended, had good cause
subsequently to allude in a somewhat mysterious way
to the Sumner propositions as " most astonishing and
extravagant, . . . the mere statement of [which]
would have put an end to all negotiations at once." [3]
As a rule, United States Senators have not been regarded as, among mortals, exceptionally discreet or
secretive. In this case, however, they proved so.
The references to Fenianism and hemispheric flag with-
drawals were few, and, confined to the press and street

---

[1] Moore: *International Arbitrations*, vol. i. p. 529.

[2] *Papers Relating to the Treaty of Washington* (1872), vol. ii. p. 258.
The last Fenian move on the Dominion, calling for action on the part
of the United States government, occurred as late as October, 1871.

[3] *Memorial Address before the Legislature of New York*, April 5,
1894, p. 47.

gossip, elicited no response from the Senate. Yet when it came to the preparation of what is known as " the American case " for the Geneva Arbitration, there can be little doubt that the knowledge of Mr. Sumner's attitude, and the desire to forestall the effect of any possible later appeal to the Irish-American element, contributed sensibly to that extreme presentation of national injuries, indirect claims, and consequential damages which, in the following autumn, startled Great Britain from its propriety, and brought the treaty to the verge of rejection. Had it led to that result, the possible consequences might now, did space permit, be interesting to consider; but such a result, whether an advantage or otherwise to the world at large, would have been a singular tribute to the influence of Charles Sumner. In all human probability, also, a calamity to Great Britain.

But to return to the narrative. General Grant was now handling a campaign. He did it in character-istic fashion. His opponent and his objective were to him clear, and he shaped his plan of operations accordingly. So rapidly did events move, so ready ripe for action were all concerned, that the Joint High Commission, as it was called, organized in Washington on the 27th of February, exactly seven weeks from the arrival there of Sir John Rose. On the 8th of the following May, the treaty was signed; and, on the 10th, the President sent it to the Senate. It was at once referred to the Committee on Foreign Relations. Mr. Sumner was, however, no longer chairman of that committee. On the 8th of March, — two months be-fore, — the negotiators were struggling with the vexed question of indirect claims, Mr. Sumner's special senatorial thunder; and, on the day following, at a Senate Republican caucus then held, he was deposed. As the story has been told in all possible detail, it is needless here to describe what then occurred. The step taken, like the situation because of which it was taken, was one almost without precedent, and there is reason to conclude that it had been decided upon in the councils of the Administration Senators, acting in harmony with inspiration from the White House, quite irrespective of the fate of any possible treaty which might result from negotiations then in progress. However that may be, its complete justification can be found in facts now known in connection with that negotiation. Upon certain points there is no longer room for controversy. As already pointed out, in the conduct of the foreign policy of the country, the chairman of the Senate Committee on Foreign Relations was, and is, virtually, and in everything but name, a part of the Administration. He is, or should be, its confidential mouthpiece, both in dealing with the committee, and upon the floor of the Senate sitting in executive session. He should accordingly be wholly and intimately in the confidence of the State Department on all questions of foreign policy. No other chairman of any congressional committee is similarly placed; for, as respects the treaty-making power, the Senate is not a legislative body, it is the council of the Executive. In March, 1871, a settlement with Great Britain had become a cardinal feature, — it might be said *the* cardinal feature in the President's foreign policy, as represented by his official organ, the State Department. With the head of that department the chairman of the Senate Committee on Foreign

Relations was no longer on speaking terms; while, in private, his denunciation of both Secretary and President was unsparing. Mr. Sumner had, moreover, been consulted in advance as to the negotiations; and, in reply to an official demand therefor, had expressed it as his fixed opinion that " the withdrawal of the British flag " from Canada at least, if not from the hemisphere altogether, could not " be abandoned as a condition, or preliminary," of a settlement such as was now proposed. The conclusion thus reached had then been communicated to the head of the State Department in an informal, but a written, memorandum. The fate of the Johnson-Clarendon Convention was still fresh in memory. Solemnly executed in London by the fully accredited representative of the United States, it had with short shrift, and by a vote practically unanimous, been set contemptuously aside by the Senate. In view of this experience, Mr. Fish privately communicated the memorandum of the chairman of the Senate committee to the confidential agent of the British government. Under the circumstances, this was manifestly the only course open to him to pursue. Its recent experience had been mortifying; and, in view of it, the British government of right ought to be, — in ordinary good faith had to be, advised of this danger, known only to the Secretary, before being invited to enter upon a fresh negotiation, which, not improbably, might result in another rebuff. When so advising him, the Secretary had also intimated to its agent that, should Great Britain still decide to proceed with the negotiation, the Administration would spare no effort to secure a favorable result, " even if it involved a conflict " with Mr. Sumner. To any one who knew the President and his methods, mental and military, such a committal admitted of no misconstruction. Unquestionably, the contents of Mr. Sumner's memorandum were well known to every one of the British plenipotentiaries, as also was the pledge of the Administration in connection therewith. This premised, the course now pursued was more than justifiable ; it was necessary, as well as right.[1] For the Administration, in face of the notice thus given, to have permitted the continuance of Mr. Sumner in his chairmanship, if to prevent was in its power, would have been worse than childish; it would have distinctly savored of bad faith with the British negotiators: and neither General Grant nor Mr. Fish was ever chargeable with bad faith, any more than the record of the former was indicative of a proneness to indecisive or childish courses of procedure.

On the 9th of March, therefore, in accordance with the understood wishes of the President, Mr. Sumner was deposed by his senatorial colleagues from the chairmanship of the Senate Committee on Foreign Relations. But when, some two months later, the treaty was reported back to the Senate by the committee as now organized, with a favorable recommendation, the question of interest was as to the course Mr. Sumner would pursue. Would he acquiesce ? It was well understood that on all matters of foreign policy the Senate, if only from long habit, gave a more than attentive ear to his utterances. Almost daily, after the treaty was transmitted to the Senate and until it was reported back from committee, intimations from this person and from that — callers on Mr. Sumner, or guests at his

[1] See Appendix F, *infra*, pp. 225-244.

table — reached the Department of State, indicating
what the deposed chairman proposed to do, or not to
do.   One day Judge Hoar, now serving as one of the
Joint High Commissioners, would announce that Mr.
Sumner had declared himself the evening before in
favor of the treaty, and was preparing a speech accordingly ; on the evening of the very day of this
reassuring announcement another gentleman would
come to Mr. Fish directly from Mr. Sumner's table
to say that his host had just been criticising the
treaty, and proposed to urge amendments.   The British commissioners were especially solicitous.   They
even went so far as to ignore their instructions to
leave Washington as soon as possible after the treaty
was signed.   The Administration wished them to remain there, as one of the Englishmen wrote, on the
ground that they might be able to influence "particular Senators, such as the Democrats and (still
more) Sumner, over whom [the Administration has]
no party control."   Sir Stafford Northcote then goes
on to say of Mr. Sumner, — " We have paid him a
great deal of attention since he has been deposed, and
I think he is much pleased at being still recognized
as a power." [1]   Sir Stafford might well say that they
had paid him a great deal of attention.   Mr. Sumner's
egotism and love of flattery were tolerably well understood ; and the Englishmen, realizing that he was
" very anxious to stand well with England," humored
him to the top of his bent.   Lord de Grey, for instance,

---

[1] Sir Stafford Northcote added, — "He certainly is [a power], for
though I think the Government could beat him in the Senate, he could
stir up a great deal of bad feeling in the country, if he were so
minded."   (Lang : *Northcote*, vol. ii. p. 23.)

presently to be made Marquis of Ripon, the head of the British side of the commission, went out of his way to inform the deposed chairman that, without his speech on the Johnson-Clarendon Convention, "the treaty could not have been made, and that he [Lord de Grey] worked by it as a chart." Nor were the American commissioners less solicitous, though they went about it in a more quiet way. For, hardly was the ink of the signatures to the treaty dry before Judge Hoar called at Mr. Sumner's door with a copy, which he commended to the Senator's favorable consideration " as meeting on all substantial points the objections he had so well urged against the Johnson-Clarendon Convention."

That Mr. Sumner, had he, on consideration, concluded that it was his duty to oppose the ratification of the treaty, could, placed as he now was, have secured its rejection, is not probable. As chairman of the Committee on Foreign Relations it would almost unquestionably have been in his power so to do; not directly, perhaps, but through the adoption of plausible amendments, — that practice of " customary disfigurement," according to President Cleveland, which treaties undergo " at the hands of the United States Senate." [1] This course Mr. Fish apprehended. On the 18th of May, Mr. Trumbull, then Senator from Illinois, and deservedly influential, called at the Department to inquire whether an amendment would jeopardize the treaty. In reply he was assured that any amendment, however trivial, would, in all probability, destroy the treaty, as it would enable Great

[1] See paper of A. M. Low, " The Oligarchy of the Senate," *North American Review* (February, 1902), vol. 174, p. 242.

Britain either to withdraw entirely, or, in any event, to propose counter-amendments. In point of fact, Mr. Sumner, while advocating approval, did offer amendments ;[1] but, no longer chairman of the committee, he was shorn of his strength. Up to the very time of voting, he was enigmatical. He would intimate a sense of great responsibility, inasmuch as he realized the extent to which the country was looking to him for guidance ; and he would then suggest doubts. His mind was not clear, etc., etc. On the direct issue of approval the solid phalanx of administration Senators would unquestionably have been arrayed against him ; and, on the Democratic side of the chamber, he was far from popular. None the less, had he even remotely resembled his contemporary then in the House of Representatives, Benjamin F. Butler,[2] it would have been in his power, playing on the Hibernian element, and the anti-English feeling then very rife, to have made much trouble. The treaty bears distinct marks of having been framed with this in view. In its provisions, not only did Mr. Sumner find the ground in great degree cut away from under him, but he could not help realizing that, in view of his speech on the Johnson-Clarendon Convention, he stood to a certain extent committed. It was not open for him to take the hemispheric flag-withdrawal attitude. So doing was impossible. He had not taken it before ; and, though his reasons for not taking it then were obvious, to take it now would, under the circumstances, inevitably expose him to ridicule. He was thus fairly and plainly circumvented.

[1] Pierce : *Sumner*, vol. iv. pp. 489, 490.
[2] General Butler subsequently made two public speeches in opposition to the Treaty of Washington.

But, more and most of all, Charles Sumner was, be it ever said, no demagogue. Somewhat of a doctrinaire and more of an agitator, he was still in his way an enlightened statesman, with aspirations for America and mankind not less generous than perfervid. His egoism was apparent ; nor has his rhetoric stood the test of time. A hearty hater, and unsparing of denunciation, he hated and denounced on public grounds only ; but his standards were invariably high, and he was ever actuated by a strong sense of obligation. His course now was creditable. In his belief, an unsurpassed opportunity had been lost. A rejection of the proposed adjustment, manifestly fair so far as it went, could, however, result only in keeping alive a source of acute irritation between two great nations. That involved a heavy responsibility ; a responsibility not in Mr. Sumner's nature to assume. Accordingly, he accepted the inevitable ; and he accepted it not ungracefully. General Grant numbered him with Buckner, Pemberton, Johnston, Bragg, and Lee, — among his vanquished opponents. As to Mr. Fish, the two were never afterwards reconciled ; but the Secretary now had his way.[1]

Into the subsequent difficulties encountered by Secretary Fish in his work of saving Great Britain in spite of Great Britain's self, it is needless to enter. Suffice it to say they can all be traced back to the positions assumed by Mr. Sumner in April, 1869. As already pointed out, it was obviously from an over-desire to forestall Mr. Sumner that Secretary Fish's Assistant Secretary of State, Mr. Bancroft Davis, a little later jeopardized the whole treaty by the

[1] See Appendix G, pp. 245-255.

extreme grounds taken on the subject of national injuries, indirect claims, and consequential damages, and the somewhat intemperate way in which the same were urged. It is wholly unnecessary here to enter into the question of responsibility for this portion of what was known as " The Case of the United States." In preparing it, Mr. Davis unquestionably acted under instructions from Secretary Fish, and in coöperation with the very able counsel who had the matter in charge. Whatever was done by him was done subject to approval; and was, undoubtedly, fully considered before being approved. Those thus responsible for the presentation of the case naturally felt that, with Mr. Sumner's historic indictment of the Johnson-Clarendon Convention fresh in memory, the full record of grievance had to be set forth, or the American people might resent a tacit abandonment of what they had been taught to regard as their just demands. With an eye to this possibility, — Sumner always in mind, — Mr. Fish had at an early stage of the negotiations significantly intimated to his colleagues that " he supposed it was pretty well agreed that there were some claims which would not be allowed by the arbitrators, but he thought it best to have them passed upon." [1] So, in avoiding the senatorial Scylla, the counsel of the United States subsequently brought the ark of settlement squarely up against the British Charybdis. Six years later, when both Mr. Sumner and Mr. Motley were dead,[2] General Grant made contemptuous refer-

[1] Davis : *Mr. Fish and the Alabama Claims*, p. 77.

[2] In the interview at Edinburgh, published in the New York *Herald* of September 25, 1877. Another conversation with Grant on this topic is given by Young in his *Around the World with Grant* (vol. ii. p. 279). It illustrates the utter worthlessness of unverified recollections

ence to the " indirect damage humbug," as he then phrased it; and, as set forth in the American " case " presented at Geneva, it was a " humbug," — a by no means creditable " humbug." As such it had by some

as a basis for the statement of historic details. He was at the time of this interview on a steamship in Asiatic waters, far from books, records, and memoranda. He is reported as then saying : — " When Mr. Fish prepared our case against England, and brought it to me for approval, I objected to the indirect claim feature. Mr. Fish said he entirely agreed with me, but it was necessary to consider Mr. Sumner. Mr. Sumner was at the head of the committee in the Senate that had charge of foreign affairs. He was not cordial to the treaty. . . . Mr. Sumner had also laid great stress upon indirect claims. Not to consider them in our case, therefore, would offend him. . . . The argument of Mr. Fish convinced me, but somewhat against my will. I suppose I consented because I was sincerely anxious to be on terms with Sumner." It is not easy to conceive anything much more mistaken than these utterances. Grant had quarrelled with Sumner, and ceased to be on speaking terms with him, a year before the negotiations, which preceded the treaty, were initiated. When the case for the Board of Arbitration under the treaty was prepared, Mr. Sumner had ceased to be chairman of the Senate Committee on Foreign Relations. He had spoken and voted for the treaty ; and, while the treaty was no longer at issue, neither President nor Secretary cared to conciliate him. The indirect claims were inserted in the case by direction of Fish, and for reasons which he put on record, wholly at variance with those attributed to him by Grant. Finally, Grant, as President, never objected to the claims, and, subsequently, was wholly unwilling that they should be withdrawn from the consideration of the Geneva tribunal. Indeed, in February, 1872, when it seemed probable that Great Britain would, because of our insistence on those claims, refuse to go on at Geneva, he actually wanted Secretary Fish to instruct Mr. Adams to remain at Geneva, and to sign the award alone should all the other arbitrators withdraw. It was necessary for Mr. Fish to call his attention to the fact that, under the terms of the treaty, the award had to be signed by a majority of the arbitrators. The suggestion of Mr. Adams remaining behind, after all the others were gone, and then proceeding to mulct Great Britain in satisfactory damages was again suggestive of opéra bouffe performances and Gerolstein methods. There can, however, be no doubt that Grant was, in 1879, giving a perfectly truthful statement of his recollection of the events of 1871. Merely, his recollection deceived him as to every particular.

means to be got rid of; and at Geneva it was, with general acceptance, so got rid of.[1]   Be it always, how-

[1] There is, however, another side to the question of indirect claims as presented in the " case " at Geneva.   It is well put in the following extracts of a despatch from Secretary Fish to Minister Schenck, of April 23, 1872 (*Papers relating to the Treaty of Washington* (1872), vol. ii. pp. 475, 476): — " Neither the Government of the United States, nor, so far as I can judge, any considerable number of the American people, have ever attached much importance to the so-called ' indirect claims,' or have ever expected or desired any award of damages on their account. . . . You will not fail to have noticed that through the whole of my correspondence we ask no damages on their account; we only desire a judgment which will remove them for all future time as a cause of difference between the two Governments.   In our opinion they have not been disposed of, and, unless disposed of, in some way, they will remain to be brought up at some future time to the disturbance of the harmony of the two Governments. . . . In the correspondence, I have gone as far as prudence will allow in intimating that we neither desired nor expected any pecuniary award, and that we should be content with an award that a State is not liable in pecuniary damages for the indirect results of a failure to observe its neutral obligations.   It is not the interest of a country situate as are the United States, with their large extent of sea-coast, a small Navy, and smaller internal police, to have it established that a nation is liable in damages for the indirect, remote, or consequential results of a failure to observe its neutral duties.   This government expects to be in the future, as it has been in the past, a neutral much more of the time than a belligerent.   It is strange that the British Government does not see that the interests of this government do not lead them to expect or to desire a judgment on the ' indirect claims ; ' and that they fail to do justice to the sincerity of purpose, in the interests of the future harmony of the two nations, which has led the United States to lay those claims before the tribunal at Geneva."

The above contains a sufficient defence of the presentation of the " claims."   The defect in the American " case " was rather one of taste.   Its contentions were advanced with an aggressiveness of tone, and attorney-like smartness, more appropriate to the wranglings of a quarter-sessions court than to pleadings before a grave international tribunal.   In this respect they do not compare favorably with the British papers.   As Sir Roundell Palmer truly says, in these last " no pains were spared to avoid the use of any language which could wound the susceptibilities, or offend the high spirit of a generous nation. . . . In all these respects, the American ' Case ' was in the most marked contrast with our own. . . . Its tone was acrimonious,

ever, remembered, the vulgarized bill then presented
was not the sublimated balance-sheet Charles Sumner
had in mind. His was no debit-and-credit account,
reduced to dollars and cents, and so entered in an
itemized judgment; nor was this better understood
by any one than by President Grant. It is but fair
to assume that, in the rapid passage of events between
1870 and 1877, the facts now disclosed had been by
him forgotten.

In Wemyss Reid's " Life of William E. Forster "
is a chapter devoted to this subject. I think it may
not unfairly be said that Mr. Forster now saved the
treaty. In the first outburst of indignation over the
resurrection in the American " case " of Sumner's self-
evolved equities and incalculable claims, a special
meeting of the British cabinet was summoned, at
which a portion of the members were for withdrawing
forthwith from the arbitration. Though he himself,
unadvised as to the real motive for so emphasizing the
demand on account of national injuries, held the whole
thing to be a case of " sharp practice," yet Mr. Forster counselled a moderate and prudent course, — as
he put it, "a cool head and a cool temper wanted ; "
adding, " I never felt any matter so serious." He
then drew up a special memorandum for the use of
his colleagues, looking to such action as would be most
likely to leave open the way to an understanding.
Upon this all the ministers, save four, were against
him. Mr. Forster next met Mr. Adams, then passing through London on his way home from the pre-

totally wanting in international courtesy." (*Memorials Personal and
Political*, 1865–95 ; vol. i. p. 229.) The truth, as well as the contained force, of this censure cannot be gainsaid.

liminary meeting of the tribunal of arbitration at
Geneva, he being a member of it; and Mr. Adams
fairly told him that, for Great Britain, it was a case
of now or never. If, Mr. Adams said, Great Britain
insisted on the absolute exclusion of the indirect
claims, America must withdraw; and, if it did, "the
arbitration was at an end, and America would never
make another treaty."

During those anxious weeks the British cabinet
was the scene of more than one heated discussion;
and, so severe was the tension, the very existence of
the Ministry was threatened. On the afternoon of
April 24, Forster intimated to General Schenck, the
American Minister, that, unless something was done,
he and the Marquis of Ripon "could not keep the
treaty alive." Mr. Adams was now once more in
London on his way to Geneva, and Mr. Forster again
saw him, receiving the assurance that "Fish and the
President had the Senate well in hand;" yet, this
notwithstanding, when an article supplemental to the
treaty, obviating the cause of trouble, was agreed on
and submitted to the Senate, that body so amended
it before ratification that the English government
professed itself unable to concur. It seemed as if
the last chance of a pacific settlement was about to
vanish.

On the 15th of June, the Court of Arbitration met
at Geneva, pursuant to adjournment. Everything was
in the air. At Geneva, however, the policy of the
State Department was understood; and, intrusted to
experienced hands, it was, at the proper time, skilfully forwarded. A way out of the last and most
serious of all the dangers which imperilled the settle-

ment was thus devised, and the arbitration moved on thenceforth upon common-sense business lines to a practical result.

Times change, and with them the estimate in which nations hold issues. Recollecting the levity, at times marked by more than a trace of sarcasm and petulance, with which the British Foreign Secretary had received our earliest reclamations because of injuries inflicted on our mercantile marine by British built commerce-destroyers, I cannot refrain, before closing, from .a few words descriptive of the very different mood in which the Ministry then in power awaited tidings of the final results reached at Geneva. It was the 15th of June, 1872. The treaty was in question. The Court of Arbitration met at Geneva at noon ; in London, at the same hour, a meeting of the cabinet was in session, — a meeting almost unique in character. The members waited anxiously for tidings. For two hours they attended listlessly to routine parliamentary work; and then took a recess. When, at 3 o'clock, the time for reassembling came, no advices had been received. Thereupon, a further adjournment was taken until 5.30. Still no telegram. All subjects of conversation being now exhausted, the members sat about, or faced each other in silence. It was a curious situation for a ministry. Had England humiliated herself by an expression of fruitless regret? Those present contemplated the situation in the true parliamentary spirit. " The opposition would snigger if they saw us," remarked one ; and the speaker soon after sent for a chess-board, and he and Mr. Forster took chairs out on the terrace in front of the cabinet-room, and there sat down to a game, using one of the chairs as a table. Three games were played; but still no tidings. So the company dispersed for dinner. As the tribunal adjourned over until Monday, no tidings came that night; the method of procedure had, however, been arranged, and Mr. Fish communicated with. His assent to what was proposed came immediately; and meanwhile Mr. Forster was bestirring himself in London to " urge help to Adams," and a " short, helpful telegram" was forwarded. "After all," wrote Mr. Forster that night, " this treaty, which has as many lives as a cat, will live." On the afternoon of the fourth subsequent day, this staunch friend of America and of peace scribbled, from his seat in the ministerial benches of the House of Commons, this note to his wife : " Hip, hip, hip, hooray ! the final settlement of the indirect claims came during questions to-day, and Gladstone announced it amid great cheers on our side and the disgust of the Tories. This is a good year now, whatever happens." It was the 20th of June, 1872, — one month over eleven years since the issuance of the famous proclamation. A heavy shadow was lifted from off the future of the British Empire. That it was thus lifted must in all historic truth be ascribed to Hamilton Fish.

In discussing the developments of history, it is almost never worth while to waste time and ingenuity in philosophizing over what might have been. The course of past events was — as it was ! What the course of subsequent events would or might have been, had things at some crucial juncture gone otherwise than as they actually did go, no one can more than guess. Historical consequences are not less strange than remote. For instance, the lessons of our own War of Independence, closed six-score years ago, are to-day manifestly influencing the attitude and action of Great Britain throughout her system of dependencies. Should the system ever, as now proposed, assume a true federated form, that result, it may safely be asserted, will be largely due to the experience gained a century and a quarter ago on the North American continent, supplemented by that now being gained in South Africa. In view of the enormous strides made by science during the last third of a century, it cannot be assumed that, as respects warfare on land or on sea, what was possible in 1863 would be possible now. The entire globe was not then interlaced with electric wires, and it may well be that another *Alabama* is as much out of the range of future probabilities as a ship flying the black flag, with its skull and crossed bones, was outside of those of 1861. This, however, aside, it is instructive, as well as interesting, to summarize the record which has now been recalled, and to consider the position in which Great Britain would to-day find itself but for the settlement effected and principles established by means of the Treaty of Washington.

So far as the international situation is concerned, the analogy is perfect. Every rule of guidance applicable in our Civil War of 1861–65 is *a fortiori* applicable in the South African war of 1899–1902. The contention of Great Britain from 1861 to 1865 was that every neutral nation is the final judge of its own international obligations; and that, in her own case, no liability, moral or material, because of a

violation of those obligations was incurred, no matter
how scandalous the evasions might subsequently prove
to have been, unless the legal advisers of the government pronounced the ascertainable evidence of
an intention to violate the law sufficient to sustain a
criminal indictment.   In view of the "lucrative"
character of British shipbuilding, it was further maintained that any closer supervision of that industry,
and the exercise of "due diligence" in restraint of
the construction of commerce-destroyers, would impose
on neutrals a "most burdensome, and, indeed, most
dangerous" liability.   Finally, under the official construction of British municipal law, — a law pronounced by Her Majesty's government adequate to
any emergency, — there was "no necessity that a naval
belligerent should have a port, or even a seashore."
The South African republics, for instance, "might
unite together, and become a great naval power,"
using the ports of the United States as a base for their
maritime operations.   "Money only was required for
the purpose."   Then came the admission of Sir Edward Thornton that, in case Great Britain were engaged in war, retaliations in kind for the *Alabama* and
the *Florida* would naturally be in order ; commerce-
destroyers would be fitted out on the Pacific coast as
well as the Atlantic, in spite of all the United States
government might, or could, do to prevent them ; and,
with them, the high seas would swarm.   War must
follow ; and then Canada was "a source of weakness."
On land and on sea, Great Britain was equally vul-
nerable.

From such a slough of despond was Great Britain
extricated by the Treaty of Washington.   That much

is plain ; all else is conjecture. But it is still curious to consider what might well have now resulted had the United States, between 1869 and 1871, definitely for its guidance adopted the policy contemplated by Charles Sumner instead of that devised by Hamilton Fish, and had then persistently adhered to it. In the hands and under the direction of Mr. Sumner, the method he proposed to pursue to the end he had in mind might have proved both effective and, in the close, beneficent. So long as all things are possible — Who can say ? But Mr. Sumner died in 1874 ; and with him must have died the policy he proposed to inaugurate. Characteristically visionary, he was wrong in his estimate of conditions. He in no wise foresaw that backward swing of opinion's pendulum, from the " wretched colonies " estimate of 1870 to the *Imperium et Libertas* conceptions of 1900. Mr. Fish, on the other hand, less imaginative, was more nearly right. He effected a practical settlement ; and, in so doing, he accomplished a large result. For to-day it is apparent to all who carefully observe that, as the direct outcome of the American Civil War, the world made a long stride in advance. It is a great mistake to speak of the *Florida*, the *Alabama*, and the *Shenandoah* as " privateers." They were not. No " privateer," in the proper acceptation of the word, ever sailed the ocean under the Confederate flag ; the commerce-destroyers of that conflict, whether fitted out on the Mersey and Clyde, or in home ports, were, one and all, government ships-of-war, owned and regularly commissioned by the belligerent whose flag they flew, and commanded by its officers. Their single mission was, none the less, to burn, sink, and destroy private prop-

erty on the high seas. They were engaged in no legitimate — no recognized operation of modern warfare ;
unless it be legitimate for an invading army wholly to
devastate a hostile country, leaving behind it a smok-
ing desert only. On the ocean, the archaic principle
still obtains that the immunity of private property
from capture or destruction is confined to times of
peace ; and, when war intervenes, mankind reverts to
piracy, as the natural condition of maritime life. So
the commerce-destroyers were not pirates, — common
enemies of mankind ; but, as a result of the Treaty of
Washington, a new and broad principle will inevitably,
in some now not remote hereafter, replace this relic
of barbarism, — the principle that private property,
not contraband of war, is as much entitled to immunity
from destruction or capture on water as on land. It
is, accordingly, not unsafe even now to predict that the
Florida, the *Alabama*, and the *Shenandoah* will go
down in history, not as themselves pirates, but as the
last lineal survivals of the black-flagged banditti of the
olden time. If this so prove, it will in the close be
apparent that the Treaty of Washington supplemented
the Proclamation of Emancipation, rounding out and
completing the work of our Civil War. The verdict of
history on that great conflict must then be that the blood
and treasure so freely poured out by us between Sumter and Appomattox were not expended in vain ; for,
through it and because of it, the last vestiges of piracy
vanished from the ocean, as slavery had before disappeared from the land.

APPENDIX A[1]

THE grounds on which the British government proceeded in May, 1861, when it issued the proclamation of belligerency, were clearly set forth by Lord Palmerston in the course of a debate in the House of Commons, exactly four years later; when, the Civil War having been brought to a close, the proclamation was withdrawn. Throughout that period Lord Palmerston was Premier; and, on the 15th of May, 1865, — the proclamation having been issued on May 13, 1861, — he said, in answer to a question in the House, — " The President of the United States issued a proclamation declaring a blockade of all the coasts and certain ports of the Southern Confederacy, in accordance, as he said, with the law of nations. Now a blockade, according to the law of nations, is a belligerent right, which can only accrue to a State which is at war; and I need not say that if there is one belligerent there must be two at least, and therefore the fact of the President of the United States declaring that he established a blockade in accordance with the law of nations gave him all those rights which belong to a belligerent in declaring a blockade — the right of capture, and condemnation, and the right of search in regard to neutral vessels. The British government had only one of two courses to pursue; the first, to refuse to submit on the part of British vessels to

1 See *supra*, p. 98.

those belligerent rights, on the ground that there was no formal belligerent on the other side. That was not a course which was at all expedient to pursue, and therefore the only course left us was to acknowledge and submit to those belligerent rights; and that necessarily involved the recognition that the other party was also a belligerent." . . .

Looking at the facts in the case through a vista of forty years, and in connection with all accepted principles of international law, it must now be acknowledged that there was much truth, as well as sound legal sense, in the dictum on this point of Chief Justice Cockburn, in his extremely unconventional " opinion " filed in connection with the Geneva award: — " The pretension that the Federal Government could treat the contest as a war, so as to declare a blockade, and thereby exclude neutral nations from access to the blockaded ports for the purpose of trade, while neutral governments, on the other hand, were not entitled to treat the war as one going on between two belligerent powers, is a proposition which is, I say it with all respect for Mr. Adams, really preposterous." [1] But to appreciate the full audacity of the positions on this point assumed by Secretary Seward, — the correctness of which, largely through the utterances of Senator Sumner, yet has vogue as a species of American article of historic faith, — it is necessary to bear certain facts and dates distinctly in mind. The Rebel-

---

[1] *Papers relating to the Treaty of Washington* (1872), vol. iv. p. 321. On this point, see also a forcible exposition of the correct principles of international law in the letter of Earl Russell to Mr. Adams of May 4, 1865. Geneva Arbitration : *Correspondence*, etc., vol. i. p. 295. The whole subject is thoroughly discussed by Lord Cockburn, in his " opinion." *Papers*, etc., pp. 313-326.

lion assumed the shape of a fully developed civil war on April 12, 1861, when the Confederates opened fire on Fort Sumter. April 19, seven days later, the President issued his proclamation, announcing the blockade of some 2700 miles of sea-coast, " in pursuance of the laws of the United States and of the law of nations in such case provided." [1] The appeal was thus made to " the law of nations," and the step was not taken as a matter of mere municipal regulation. At the same time, Secretary Seward informed foreign ministers to this country, and instructed our own representatives abroad, that the blockade would " be strictly enforced upon the principles recognized by the law of nations ; " and, further, provided for the treatment of the " armed vessels of neutral states." [2] The Queen's proclamation of May 13 was published fourteen days after the receipt in London of the news of the surrender of Sumter, and of information that the Confederate government had taken steps looking to the issue of letters of marque ; twelve days after receipt of intelligence of President Lincoln's proclamation of blockade ; and three days after the official communication of the fact by Mr. Dallas, the American Minister in London, to Lord John Russell, Secretary for Foreign Affairs. [3] One of the most considerable branches of British commerce — that to and from the American cotton ports — was thus, at a moment's notice, not only interfered with, but broken up ; British vessels were, under the law of nations, subjected to search, and liable to capture ; the law of contraband

[1] *Messages and Papers of the Presidents*, vol. vi. p. 14.

[2] *Papers relating to Treaty of Washington* (1872), vol. i. p. 213.

[3] *Ib.*, p. 218.

and prize applied, and was enforced. Almost at once the struggle involved armaments, by sea and land, of the first magnitude, and conflicts marked by an almost unparalleled loss of life. Yet Secretary Seward persistently maintained that this struggle — well-nigh the fiercest on record — in no way concerned foreign nations, and that they had no right to even recognize it as existing. So far as the world at large was concerned, — though its commerce was broken up, its vessels searched, seized and condemned, and its property confiscated as contraband, — the disturbance was merely local and insignificant in character, concerning no one but ourselves. Most assuredly, official effrontery could go no further.

That the recognition by the British government of a state of belligerency, of necessity involving two parties, should, if possible, have been in courtesy deferred until the arrival of the newly appointed American Minister, known to be on his way, is indisputable. Most fortunately for the United States, it was not so deferred. On the other hand, every hour of delay in the recognition of the blockade by neutral governments involved the possibility of unauthorized search, and consequent seizures, due to hostilities, the existence of which was stoutly denied by the United States, and, therefore, not notified to those concerned by neutral governments. The situation was, in the language of Lord Cockburn, " preposterous," and could only continue for a brief period, and that at great risk, through the exercise of extreme comity on the part of neutrals.

And yet, so strong is tradition, the question is still asked, — how could that proclamation have been considered by Mr. Forster, or any one else, as a point gained for the United States? The answer seems obvious. It was given by Lord Palmerston in the speech above quoted. The United States declared an extensive blockade, under and by virtue of international law and usage. By the Queen's proclamation, that blockade was recognized. This was of vital importance to the United States, and an important concession on the part of foreign powers. A recognition of the blockade, with all that recognition implied, was, therefore, in May, 1861, the point gained for the cause of the Union " in accordance with the earnest wishes of [William E. Forster] and other friends of the North." As to Secretary Seward's contention that our Civil War was no affair of any nation but the United States, it will not, in the light of history and of international law, bear an instant's examination. The British proclamation of belligerency of May 13, 1861, was the logical and legal sequence of the President's proclamation of blockade of the 19th of the previous month. By the nations whose commerce was affected by it, the blockade had either to be recognized or disallowed; and its recognition was essential to the Union cause.

The difficulty with Secretary Seward was one not at all uncommon among men, whether in public station or private life. He claimed for the side he represented all and every right known to the code; he then vehemently protested against the application to himself, by those affected by his action, of its logical and necessary consequences under that code. His contentions may have been wise, as well as bold, under the circumstances and at the time; but American historians and publicists cannot afford to profess responsibility for them now. They are quite untenable.

APPENDIX B [1]

THIS assertion seems to have been a favorite one with Secretary Seward; and he repeated it so often, in terms only slightly varied, that he evidently persuaded himself of its truth. He thus wrote to Mr. Pike, the Minister at the Hague, — "This domestic war . . . would come to an end to-morrow if the European States should clearly announce that expectations of favor from them must be renounced." [2] To the same effect he wrote to Mr. Sanford, at Brussels, May 23, 1862, — "Europe has thus put this beneficent government upon an ordeal more solemn and fearful," [3] etc. On the 19th of February, 1862, he wrote to Mr. Dayton, at Paris, — "Let the European States . . . concede now to the Union half as much toleration as they have practically, though unintentionally, shown to disunion, and the Civil War will come to an end at once." [4] Even a year later, after the battle of Gettysburg, he wrote to Mr. Adams, — "The insurrection . . . has now descended so low that manifestly it would perish at once, if it were left like the late insurrection in India, like the insurrection which a few years ago occurred in Canada . . . to stand by means of its own strength, not as a recognized belligerent." [5] The Sepoy mutiny of 1857 was undoubtedly a fierce struggle for supremacy; but it now seems in-

[1] *Supra*, p. 101.
[2] *Dip. Cor.* 1862, p. 597. See, also, pp. 597, 612.
[3] *Ib.*, p. 656.
[4] *Ib.*, p. 317; see, also, pp. 320, 327, 332, 337, 338.
[5] *Dip. Cor.* 1863, p. 328.

credible that an American Secretary of State could, in the summer of 1863, with Grant's Wilderness campaign and Sherman's march to the sea in the womb of the immediate future, have gravely put our Civil War on an equal footing with the Canada " six-county insurrection " of 1837, effectually suppressed by militia and one regiment of infantry, after a single repulse of a fourth of a regiment from a brewery extemporized into a stronghold. But the same lack of any correct sense of proportion is apparent in all the discussions of the Rebellion period, and of the period immediately succeeding the Rebellion, whether diplomatic and parliamentary, or legal and historical. It permeates the United States "Case," prepared for submission to the Geneva tribunal. Seward and Sumner, Motley and Davis, seemed all affected by it, the difference being only one of degree and temperament. It was. a psychological phenomenon. America still hung on the lips of Europe, as the old colonial, dependency spirit, continually asserting itself, died slowly out. In the case of Secretary Seward, it must be said that, though he overdid the thing grossly, he yet wrote and talked largely for effect; but there is no reason to think Mr. Sumner did not fully and actually believe what he said, when, in April, 1869, he asserted in the Senate that a certain paper manifesto, recognizing a fact of common knowledge, put forth in London in May, 1861, and followed by no act, added " not weeks or months, but years to our war." It is not easy to see how the genuine, innate, provincial spirit could have gone further. The moment " Her Majesty's Proclamation " entered into account, the nascent rebellion, no longer a Palladian giant, was suddenly transformed into a puny, workhouse British bastard.

APPENDIX C[1]

WRITING privately to his friend, S. B. Ruggles of New York, on May 18, 1869, — just five weeks after the delivery of Mr. Sumner's National Claims speech, — Mr. Fish thus explains himself, covering the whole situation, and indicating, on his part at least, a clear comprehension of the law governing it : —

"Public law recognizes the right of a sovereign power, when a civil conflict has broken out in another country, to determine when that conflict has attained sufficient complexity, magnitude, and completeness, to *require* (not merely to *excuse*) for the protection of its own interests and peace, and of the interests and relations and duties of its own citizens or subjects, a definition of its relations, and of the relations of its citizens or subjects to those of the parties to the conflict.

" In the exercise of this right, the foreign power is responsible to the general obligations of right, and must be guided by *facts*, not by prejudice for or against the parent country, or the insurgents — least of all against the parent country, when well established, and a friendly power.

" Having defined its relations to the parties in the civil conflict as one of neutrality, it must enforce its neutral position, and allow no infraction thereof : give no favor.

[1] See *supra*, p. 112.

" England professes to have exercised *only* what is a recognized right of a sovereign foreign power.

" We have held she was precipitate; much may well be said on this side — she had promised to await Mr. Adams's arrival, but anticipated it, and of course any information or explanation he might make. Still England says — the United States had declared a blockade — which is ' war ' — the Confederates had announced ' letters of marque ' and ' prize courts ' which mean ' war ' — both sides had levied large armies; forts had been seized, etc., etc.

" This would *seem* to give some justification to her concession of belligerency, and disprove the complaint of this act [of concession] of some of its force. Then, again, France and other powers were contemporaneous with England in the same concession. *The United States make no claim against them, and it is important to separate them* from any *intent* to unite with England in resisting the claim.

" The complaint against England is, that she subsequently allowed acts inconsistent with neutrality, and these acts (to a certain extent) reflect back upon the act of concession of belligerency, and to this extent alone should the complaint be limited of the proclamation of neutrality. No other nation which conceded belligerency (even at or about the same time with England) was guilty of such *subsequent* causes of injury.

" The British proclamation of neutrality is, therefore, subject of complaint, *only as leading to, as characterized by, and authorizing in its execution and enforcement* the fitting out of the *Alabama*, etc., etc., the acts of hospitality, etc., given in their colonial ports, to those piratical cruisers, and as *leading* to the moral support given in England to the Rebel cause.

" Mr. Sumner makes the act of concession *per se*, a grievance; he draws a distinction not recognized by publicists, between belligerency on land and what he terms ' ocean belligerency.' Belligerency is war, and whether on land or on the ocean, or on both, is *a fact*, and not susceptible of division — certainly not, when the parties to the conflict each have seaboard, and ports and commerce.

" This is (perhaps) the *main* point in his argument, and is one which it will be difficult to maintain — difficult, at least, to establish now, as applicable to Prize Courts.

.   .   .   .

" Pray let me hear from you. The newspapers seem *shy* of dissent from what seems to be the controlling argument in bringing the Senate to its vote.

" *But the fact is*, many Senators dissented from the argument while agreeing in the conclusion."

As to the influence of Mr. Sumner's position and legal contentions as contributing to the defeat of the Johnson-Clarendon Convention, Mr. Fish at the same time (May 17) wrote to Senator W. P. Fessenden, then at his home in Portland, Maine, where he died early in the following September. Mr. Fessenden, on May 25, replied as follows: —

" As to Sumner's speech, I can only say that it would not, in my judgment, be safe to look at it in the light of an ultimatum. Such an idea would be simply preposterous.

" When delivered, I considered it as intended for a

statement of our grievances, not of our claims. I perceive that the language is stronger than I had supposed and in some particulars unguarded and exceptionable, and calculated to give a wrong impression. I was pleased with the *tone* of the speech, and so said; though it would have been vastly better to have made none at all, and trusted to the effect of *such* a vote. But it was not possible for Sumner to omit availing himself of such an occasion. On the whole, I think no great harm will be done by it.

"It is absurd to suppose that the offence of recognizing belligerency can be atoned for by the payment of money. Still, under the circumstances, it was a grievous wrong, and coupled with subsequent avowals and conduct would have justified a declaration of war. The occasion for that, however, has gone by. Yet we are entitled to something in the nature of a plaster for the sore — a little of 'Mrs. Winslow's Soothing Syrup' at least. The fault of the treaty was that it offered absolutely nothing, and might have left matters in a worse condition than they now are."

Mr. Carl Schurz, then in the Senate, writing confidentially from St. Louis, said to Secretary Fish: —

"We shall then endeavor to find *a form of settlement as regardful of the national pride of England, and of her material interests*, as possible. (Distant hint at Canada.) In the mean time we prefer not to indulge in possibly exciting discussions, but, for the present, we are content *to leave the question open*, giving the British Government a fair chance for quiet consideration.

. . . .

" Mr. Motley might furthermore be instructed, when by Lord Clarendon a point of international law is urged upon him, never to reply promptly, to refer the matter to his Government whenever there is a chance for it, and, when he cannot avoid giving an answer, to be very short. He ought to produce the impression that we are rather inclined to take the matter very easy and are in no haste whatever. He might, when very hard pressed, occasionally ask the question, whether England would be content to have us follow the precedent set by her ? In private conversation he might freely speak of the annexation of the North American provinces as being the decided wish of the American people in settlement of the claims, leaving the Government uncommitted. It is our interest to familiarize them gradually with the idea."

George F. Edmunds of Vermont was, at the time of the rejection of the Johnson-Clarendon Convention, a member of the Senate. In a private letter, written thirty-three years later, he thus gave his recollections of the effect of Mr. Sumner's speech on the minds of his colleagues : —

"I am confident that the Johnson-Clarendon treaty was not rejected by reason of its failure to embrace the stupendous claims of Mr. Sumner based upon Great Britain's recognition of belligerency. I do not believe there were more than ten Senators, if as many, who stood upon any such ground. I am sure the majority of the Senate acted upon the ground that the making of such a treaty, and in such a form, would not only be a very small piecemeal toward the restoration of good relations, but would be a kind of recognition of the fact that we had nothing more to complain of than the ordinary and accidental wrongs that the government of one country continually commits or permits against the citizens of another. Nobody who possessed even a moderate knowledge of the principles of international law, and their practice, would, unless laboring under some great emotion, maintain for a moment that Great Britain had violated international law, or had done an act in that sense hostile to the United States. It was only valuable and important as throwing light upon the later conduct of that Government in permitting the building and departure of Confederate vessels and munitions of war from her ports."

APPENDIX D [1]

THE following is the speech referred to in the text, so far as it related to the United States. It was delivered at the Lord Mayor's banquet, November 9, 1869, and printed in the London *Times*, of the following day.

"Without arrogating influence, I think we are bound on every occasion that may offer to make every effort towards composing those differences and allaying those disturbances which may arise in different portions of the world ; and I rejoice to think that, on more than one occasion since his return to office, my noble friend who holds the seals of the Foreign-office has had the satisfaction of receiving the liberal and handsome acknowledgments of foreign Governments for the useful contributions he has made towards the accommodation of their relations. One exception, per-haps — one partial exception — I ought to name. It is an exception of the deepest interest. I refer to our relations with the United States. But there is no occasion, my Lord Mayor, that I should refer to those relations in any terms except those of peace and concord. (Cheers.) Were I tempted to depart from that friendly strain I should, indeed, be admonished to judge more correctly and to speak more wisely by an event which has happened in the city in the course of the last few days. Your quick associations will out-

[1] See *supra*, p. 128.

run my allusions. You will know that I refer to the death of Mr. Peabody, a man whose splendid benefactions — which, indeed, secure the immortality of his name in that which he regarded as his old mother country, but which, likewise, in a broader view, is applicable to all humanity — taught us in this commercial age, which has witnessed the construction of so many colossal fortunes, at once the noblest and most needful of all lessons — namely, he has shown us how a man can be the master of his wealth instead of being its slave. (Cheers.) And, my Lord Mayor, most touching it is to know, as I have learnt, that while, perhaps, some might think he had been unhappy in dying in a foreign land, yet, so were his affections divided between the land of his birth and the home of his early ancestors, that that which had been his fond wish has, indeed, been realized — that he might be buried in America, but that it might please God to ordain that he should die in England. (Cheers.) My Lord Mayor, with the country of Mr. Peabody we are not likely to quarrel. (Loud cheers.) It is true, indeed, that the care and skill of diplomacy, animated by the purest and most upright feelings, though they have not imperilled, yet have failed to lead to a final issue at this moment the tangled questions of law that have been in discussion between the two countries ; but the very delay that has taken place, instead of being a delay tending to anger, has been a delay promoted by kindred good-will and by the belief that the intervention of a limited time may be likely to obviate any remaining difficulty. (Cheers.) My Lord Mayor, I speak with confidence in anticipating that that which the whole world would view with horror and amazement, namely, a parricidal strife between England and America, — is above all things the most unlikely to grow out of this state of affairs. My confidence is, in the first place, in the sentiment which I know animates the Government of the United States as well as our own, it is in the sentiment which we believe to pervade the mind of the people of these two great countries; and, permit me to add, I have yet another source of confidence, connected with some of those changes which we are witnessing in the age in which we live. I mean this change in particular, that as in every country there has long been, and especially in the best governed countries, not only a force of law, but also of opinion that has tended to restrain it, so with the augmenting intercourse of nations there is now growing up what I may term an international opinion, a standard of international conduct higher than the standard which a particular nation sets up for itself, and to which it becomes more and more from year to year as we live necessary that each country should conform consistently with the rights and duties of the whole mass of the civilized community of the world."

APPENDIX E[1]

THE condition of affairs in Cuba became matter of discussion again in 1896. Senator Sherman then stated, in the course of a Senate debate, that, in 1870, there had been a conflict of opinion between President Grant and Secretary Fish. Mr. Hamilton Fish, son of the Secretary, who had died three years before, was, in 1896, Speaker of the New York House of Assembly, and he permitted the publication of an Associated Press despatch, dated Albany, March 15, which threw much light on this question, — a question always of interest, inasmuch as Cuban complications gave its shape to the whole foreign policy of the government during General Grant's first administration, including the country's attitude towards Great Britain, after the rejection of the Johnson-Clarendon Convention.

The younger Hamilton Fish then said, — " During his eight years' service in the State Department Mr. Fish kept, chiefly as a reference record for his own use, a diary in his own handwriting, containing a minute of important transactions and of his conversations with the President, members of the Cabinet, Senators, and other leading public men in regard to the more prominent of the foreign questions with which he had to deal. From May 31 to June 13, 1870, the date of President Grant's special message to Congress on Cuban belligerency, the entries in the diary are many,

[1] *Supra*, p. 119.

and very full, in regard to the origin, preparation, discussions in the Cabinet, and final completion of the special message."

The following passages from the diary were then given to the correspondent of the Associated Press, his despatch appearing, in whole or in part, in many journals of the following day (March 16, 1896) : —

February 19, 1870. "Called this morning, by appointment, to see Senator John Sherman on subject of the unit of coinage. After conversing on that question, I referred to his resolution introduced in the Senate, and his speech in favor of recognizing the belligerency of Cuba, and asked if he had recently examined the treaty with Spain of 1795. He said he had not; was not aware of the existence of such a treaty. I referred to its provisions, and to the probable consequences of the exercise by Spain of the right of visit (or of search); thought our people would not submit to it, and that the consequences would soon develop in war; said that fighting was not belligerency; there is fighting, but no belligerency in Cuba; there is no government of the insurrectionary party, no political organization, etc. He admitted that he had not examined the subject closely, but said there is a good deal of excitement in the country on the subject. I advised him, in connection with the passing of his resolution of belligerency, to prepare bills for the increase of the public debt, and to meet the increased appropriation which will be necessary for the army, navy, etc."

June 10, 1870. "Judge Orth and General Butler called in the evening to urge the sending of a message by the President on the question of Cuban belligerency. Orth says the vote will be close. Banks will make the closing speech, but there are some twenty or thirty quiet members who may be decided by his speech, but would not go against the President's views."

June 12, 1870. "Stay at home and prepare a message on the Cuban belligerency question, to be submitted for the President's consideration, in case he agreed to send one. He has not yet returned from his fishing excursion."

June 13, 1870. "It was generally admitted that if war is to be resorted to it should be by a direct declaration, and not by embarrassing Spain by a declaration of belligerency; agrees unanimously that no condition of facts exists to justify belligerency. Finally the President amends his sentences by referring in general terms to seizures on the high seas, embargoes of property, and personal outrages. Robeson adds the concluding sentences, claiming that the question of belligerency is distinct from those questions of wrongs which are being pressed for indemnification, and, if not satisfied, they will be made the subject of a future message. And thus it is agreed that the message shall be sent in."

In view of the close bearing of the policy at this time pursued towards Spain on the policy pursued towards Great Britain, I asked the representatives of Mr. Fish for any further entries from the diary made at that time on this topic. In compliance with my request, the following were furnished.

A cabinet meeting was held on the day following that of the last passage from the diary quoted in the Associated Press despatch above referred to: —

June 14, 1870. " Also read Clinton J. Trues'
(Consul at St. Thomas) despatch, not numbered,
dated April 16. . . . President thinks he may be
removed, and wishes to give the place to a nominee
of Governor Morton. He has wished to give almost
every place, for some weeks past, to some friend of
Morton. He then speaks of the San Domingo treaty;
his desire for its ratification; that he wishes all the
members of his Cabinet, and all his friends, to use all
proper efforts to aid him; that he will not consider
those who oppose his policy as entitled to influence
in obtaining positions under him: that he will not
let those who oppose him 'name Ministers to London,' etc., etc.; refers warmly and affectionately to
Babcock, whose innocence of the charges against him
he confidently believes; speaks very strongly against
Perry, against whom he says grave charges were made
while in the army. . . .

" A general approval is expressed by the members
of the Cabinet, on the announcement of his determination to hold members of the party to the support
of the policy of the Administration. (I did not say
so, but hope it may mean something more than San
Domingo.) I did say that I was glad to hear this (it
is what I had recommended some months ago when the
President said he would remove men from New York
Custom House and Post Office, who had been appointed
on recommendation of Evarts and others connected
with the New York *Sun;* but Boutwell interposed
and prevented the carrying out of this determination),
and hoped it would be applied to the general policy of
the Administration, and referred to the paper read a
short time before from D. C. Forney, and said that

while J. W. Forney supported the Cuban policy, etc."

June 17, 1870. "Not an allusion was made at the Cabinet to Judge Hoar's resignation, or to the proceedings in the House on the 'Cuba' message; after the meeting (Hoar, Cox, Robeson and I, on the portico) Hoar and Cox congratulated me most cordially, saying it was 'the greatest triumph the Administration had yet achieved.' Robeson said, 'Yes — the *first* triumph.' All concur in the opinion that the movement was wise, and beneficial in its results, that it has served to concentrate and consolidate the party, and to exhibit a policy, and the capacity of rallying the party. This in truth has been the great want of the party; the presentation of some issue on which they should be required, as party men, to say 'yes' or 'nay' distinctly upon some issue presented by the Administration; we have not done it before. Each man has been allowed to follow his own peculiar views. Consequently all the measures presented by the Administration thus far have failed. I felt that the 'Cuban' question was the one on which perhaps more than on any other, the sensational emotions of the party and of the country might be arrayed in opposition to what is honest and right. Believing, as I do, that the public sentiment, however much influenced by questions of sentiment, and of supposed popular impulse, is sure eventually to be just and correct, I have pressed this question in the way I have done, and first tried the proposed message submitted a short time since; finding the President would not adopt it, I tried the latter message, and he was induced with great hesitation, and with much reluc-

tance, to sign it, and after it was sent in he told me
that he feared he had made a mistake. I never
doubted the propriety of it, nor the 'policy' of it,
in the mere sense of ordinary politics. It evoked a
fierce debate, and much denunciation, but it evoked
also much good sense, in the speeches of those who
sustained it; an expression of good, sound international law, and of honesty of purpose, and it brought
the gravity of the case to the consideration of Congress; and the Administration, after the severest
debate on a question of. *Foreign Policy* which has
occurred for years, was triumphantly sustained. In
the mere and the low sense, of a political or partisan
question, it has consolidated the party, and those who
are the demagogues and the disorganizers, — the men
who follow a party so long as they can control it. In
a higher view, it has shown that the representatives
of the country can rise above the temporary and fer-
vent appeals of a momentary excitement of popular
sympathy in support of the obligations of national
duties, and in the line and direction of honesty and of
right, even when opposed by clamor, and by appeals
to passion. Most sincerely am I thankful for the
result, and that I have been a very humble instrument
in bringing it to its conclusion. I have been most
grossly maligned and assailed. At times I have been
inclined to retire and abandon the cause, but I have
felt it a duty to stand or fall with what I felt to be a
principle. The office I hold has no attractions for
me; it is attended with immense labor, with great
sacrifices of comfort, and of personal and family associations, with privations of pursuits with which I had
surrounded myself, and which were congenial to my

tastes and my years. . . . Most gladly would I· be relieved of its honors, and its labors, its responsibilities, and the constant criticisms and misrepresentations to which its incumbent is exposed. If I could, now, to-day, when the vote of Congress has emphatically sustained me, with a consciousness of duty, resign, I would follow Hoar's example, and send a written note, declaring myself once more free from official duties and responsibilities. I do not *quite yet* see the road clear. I hope to do so soon. I certainly shall find it open before long.

" While at dinner Judge Hoar called. He goes home this evening, to return, and remain in office until the end of July.

" The public announcement of his resignation, he tells me, was ' owing to one of the leaks at the White House — that the President had given his reply to one of the *confidential* clerks to be copied, and thus it had gotten out ; ' hearing it had been telegraphed to the public prints in New York, and thus given to the world, he had advised the immediate nomination of his successor, to relieve the President from the importunity which would otherwise follow. He said that he called for the purpose of urging me ' under all circumstances to hold fast,' and added most kindly and flatteringly, that I was ' the bulwark now standing between the Country and its destruction.'

" This may be very complimentary, but while I am trying to do my duty, I can by no means accept either the compliment or the responsibility — (I mean before very long to retire from the Cabinet, and from all public position). I told the Judge that I did not feel that I could much longer stand the labor, and the annoyance and abuse of official position.   With great apparent (and I doubt not sincere) earnestness he urged me not to think of leaving.   But there is a time in a man's life when he *must* leave public service, and there is a time when he ought to leave it, and a time when he is entitled to leave it.   I conscientiously think that one of the two latter has very nearly, if not quite, arrived in my case.   If there be no other ground for this opinion, I may honestly say 'the wish is Father to the thought.'   I should be infinitely happier out of office.

" In the evening the President came to see me. . . . Again referring to the difference of views with regard to ' San Domingo,' he expressed regret that Boutwell had not been present on Tuesday when he spoke of his expected assistance from the Members of his Cabinet ; said I had always given him aid with regard to it.   (I have certainly been loyal to a measure of policy which he inaugurated, and after it was entered upon have done what I could to sustain it.   I might have paused before entering upon it, and think it has been embarrassed unnecessarily by the interference of those who were not properly charged with the management of such negotiations, and by the intervention of some persons whose standing had not increased public confidence.)   He also said that Belknap, Robeson and Cresswell had sustained it.   That there was no man whom he loved more than Governor Cox, but regretted he had not given the Treaty his support.   He referred to the newspaper rumors of further changes in the Cabinet, and that reporters had called upon him yesterday to inquire as to them ; said he had given **Mr.** Gobright (Agent of the Associated Press) the correct statement, and asked if I had read it; the New York *Times* of this morning was lying on my table, and I read Gobright's article, and the correspondence between Hoar and him; he says Gobright's article is substantially correct. Taking up the subject of newspaper rumors, and newspaper reporters, I say that I had observed the rumors with respect to myself, and had been visited last evening by many reporters, and I now desired again to repeat what I had more than once before said to him, that I should be glad to withdraw from the Cabinet, and would do so at any moment when he would accept my resignation. He replied, ' I will tell you when I want to do so — don't speak of it until then.' I answered that it was a laborious position, full of responsibilities, and without thanks, exposing one to great abuse and misrepresentation, and I could not stand it much longer. He said that he was aware of the thanklessness of the position, and could understand that nothing, but a sense of duty, would retain a man in the position of a Cabinet Minister. He would not, however, listen to my wish to withdraw. . . .

" I referred to the recent debate and vote in the House on the Cuban question, and remarked in connection therewith, ' I hope that you have no reason to regret sending the Message.' He replied, ' I like the vote very much — the debate was violent, and denunciatory ; it is strange that men cannot allow others to differ with them, without charging corruption as the cause of the difference ; ' pressing the question again as to the Message, he said, ' No — I think it has done good ; ' he continued in deprecation of the personalities and abuse heaped upon public men ; said he had been the subject of investigation (referring to the Davis-Hatch inquiry, now in progress), and alluded to the ' Gold Speculation' investigation of some months back, with a good deal of feeling, and said, ' There is little inducement other than a sense of duty in holding public position in this country — but for that I do not know what there is to induce a man to take either the place I hold, or one in the Cabinet, and were it not for that I would resign immediately.' He seemed very well satisfied with the result of the Cuban discussion, and said that he observed that General Butler had thought proper to disclaim the authorship of the message for Cushing. I said that the papers, especially the New York *Sun*, ascribe every paper officially written to Cushing, but that as to the message on Cuban belligerency, no person whatever had seen a word of it, until I had read it to him on Monday morning, except the Attorney-General, that I wrote it every word with my own hand on Sunday, and went in the afternoon to Judge Hoar's; read it to him, and he suggested the change of some three or four words, only, which change was made."

APPENDIX F[1]

THE expression used in the text that "this premised, the course now pursued in the deposition of Mr. Sumner from the chairmanship of the Committee on Foreign Relations was more than justifiable; it was necessary, as well as right," has, since the publication of this address, been criticised. Friends and admirers of Mr. Sumner, of whom there are many, especially in New England, have taken issue on this point, contending that, under all the circumstances even yet disclosed, the removal was unprecedented, and an arbitrary exercise of power by a partisan majority of Republican Senators, acting in obedience to what was, practically, an executive demand.

By the word "right" in the text, it was meant that the action taken in this matter was taken for good and sufficient reasons, and with due regard to those public interests which should always be the dominating consideration in the minds of legislators, whether members of the United States Senate or any other parliamentary body. This conclusion was reached after a careful examination of the record and the principles involved; nor have I seen any reason why it should be withdrawn, or in any way modified. In reviewing the subject, some repetition of statements made in the text is unavoidable.

The contention on the part of the adherents of Mr.

[1] See *supra*, p. 183.

Sumner appears to be based upon erroneous premises, leading to conclusions which would render parliamentary government in the United States practically impossible. Some confusion of thought, as well as misapprehension of facts, seems also to pervade many of the criticisms. It is, in the first place, tacitly, perhaps unconsciously, assumed that the Senate of the United States is, in some inscrutable way, a judicial rather than a legislative body, and that the chairmen of Senate committees are, by usage and prescription, amounting to an unwritten law, entitled to retain their positions, in any event, until the political complexion of the body is so changed that one party supplants the other as the dominating power. This subject will be discussed presently; here it is only necessary to say that no ground whatever exists on which to rest any such assumption. The United States has a system of parliamentary government; and that term implies a government by party, the executive and the legislative being independent of each other in theory, but, in practice, expected to coöperate and work in party harmony. As a rule, and under normal conditions, it is essential to the proper management of public business that one political party should control both departments of government — the legislative as well as the executive. If a policy is to be carried out, the two cannot be continually at cross-purposes.

In 1871, a large majority of those composing both branches of Congress were friendly to the administration of General Grant. They were what are known, and properly known, as Administration men, occupying, in parliamentary language, the government benches.

In every legislative body, it is well understood that the committees should, for the proper transaction of business, reflect the feelings and sympathies of the whole body, the majority being dominant in them. If they fail so to do, they are, and should be, remodelled so as to bring the desired result about. This is essential to any successful government by party. While the Executive may not interfere in any improper way in the appointment of legislative committees, the Chief Executive has a perfect right, and, indeed, it is his duty, to cause members of Congress, whether in the Senate or the House, to be fully informed as to the policy of the Administration; and it has been the practice that the machinery of each body is so arranged as to work in harmony with that policy, and not in opposition to it. Such has always been the practice. All this is elementary.

This being so, it is now contended that Mr. Sumner was deposed from the chairmanship of his committee, which he held through usage and under prescriptive right, by executive action. In other words, that President Grant brought his influence to bear upon a subservient, not to say servile, majority of the Senate, causing a gross injustice to be done to an eminent leader of his own party. There is no evidence on which to base such a contention. This is apparent from a careful review of the facts as heretofore disclosed, and it is improbable that any new or additional facts will come to light.

It was asserted at the time, and is still asserted, that the removal of Mr. Sumner was due entirely to his course in regard to the San Domingo treaty. Of this, again, there is no evidence. On the contrary, in

voting against the ratification of the San Domingo
treaty Mr. Sumner acted in unison with a majority
of the Senate, and reflected the views of a majority.
That the San Domingo treaty was the remote cause
of Mr. Sumner's displacement is true.   It is not true
that it was the approximate, or moving, cause.   The
quarrel — for in the end it became a personal quarrel, and not a political difference over a specific measure — between Mr. Sumner, General Grant and Mr.
Fish — did, it is true, originate on the San Domingo
question; but, so far as that issue went, it was an
ordinary political difference.   Subsequently, in his
strong desire to secure the ratification of the treaty,
President Grant took the very unusual course of calling upon Mr. Sumner personally at his house on an
evening in January, 1871, under the circumstances
fully described by Mr. Pierce, and in this paper.   What
followed grew out of a difference of recollection between himself and Mr. Sumner as to what then took
place, aggravated by a constitutional incompatibility
in the tempers of the two men.   President Grant
always insisted that Mr. Sumner then promised to
throw his influence in aid of the ratification of the
treaty.   There is no question that General Grant was
here in error.   Mr. Sumner, taken by surprise, naturally spoke in a guarded manner; and the President
misconstrued his words.   Afterwards, the tale-bearers
and gossip-mongers, especially of the White House
military staff, carried to General Grant's ears exag-
gerated reports of indiscreet remarks on the part of
Mr. Sumner, for which, there is no question, there
was more or less basis.   Subsequently, Mr. Sumner
did not go to the President, and frankly explain his

position, — a failure on his part for which he afterwards more than once expressed regret. The breach between the two then rapidly widened, and soon involved Mr. Fish; for Secretary Fish, acting in loyalty to the head of the Administration, endeavored to influence Mr. Sumner. This attempt Mr. Sumner met in a characteristic way; that is, by charging the Secretary with a change of front, and insisting upon it that, under the circumstances, the proper course for him to pursue was to resign. This he did in a way which deeply offended Mr. Fish; and Mr. Fish had not a forgiving disposition. The quarrel thus begun culminated over the papers relating to the dismissal of Mr. Motley, ending in an open affront put upon the Secretary of State by the Senator from Massachusetts, at a dinner given by General Schenck, in January, 1871. At that very time the negotiations leading to the Treaty of Washington were actively going on.

Such was the position of affairs in January, 1871. The Chairman of the Committee on Foreign Relations of the Senate, as it was then constituted, was not on speaking terms with either the President or the Secretary of State. Meanwhile, as stated in the text, the position of the Chairman of the Committee on Foreign Relations of the Senate then was, as it now is, different from that of any other member of the whole legislative body. The Senate participates in executive functions so far as treaties are concerned; hence it is obviously necessary to the proper conduct of any foreign policy that friendly, and even intimate, relations should exist between the executive department and the chairman of that committee; for he of necessity is the spokesman of the Executive on the floor of the Senate, the Senate alone of the legislative department having any immediate connection with foreign policy. All business relating to treaties, nominations, etc., is thus put in the hands of the chairman of the committee. He shapes it, brings it before his committee, and subsequently has charge of it on the floor of the Senate. Under these circumstances, it would seem to be so obvious as to call for no argument that matters relating to the foreign policy of the government cannot be properly handled if the chairman of the Senate committee having them in charge and the two chiefs of the executive department do not act in harmony. When the friends of the Administration, therefore, control the Senate, it is eminently desirable, if the party to which the Administration and they belong is to be responsible for a foreign policy, that the Senate Committee on Foreign Relations should be so composed as to act in perfect accord with the Executive. The friends of Mr. Sumner contend, however, that, in his case, this was unnecessary; that the business of the country could have been conducted without public detriment by a chairman who was in open and avowed hostility to the Executive, and that, in such case, the Executive had no good ground of complaint, and, certainly, would not be justified in urging its friends in the Senate to readjust the committee so as to give the Administration a fair chance both to have a policy, and to carry it into effect. This proposition I do not care to argue. To my mind it is plainly untenable. That the public business, under such circumstances, would go on after a fashion, is probable; that it would go on as it should go on, is out of the question.

Such being the facts, a change of assignments having become expedient, for the proper conduct of public affairs, it would seem unreasonable to expect the President to dismiss from the executive councils the Secretary of State, and then to resign himself, in order to make way for others less personally objectionable to the chairman of a Senate committee. A reorganization of the committee, and the transfer of its chairman to some other field of influence and usefulness, would seem to offer a more practicable solution of the trouble. This obvious fact could hardly fail to suggest itself to the average senatorial mind. It implied no indisputable, or even pronounced, tendency to subserviency. It is a conclusion, on the contrary, which any self-respecting man might so discipline himself as, in time, to reach.

It is obvious that, in the early days of January, 1871, the Executive had not become fully satisfied that a rearrangement of the Senate committee was indispensable. Had such a conclusion been reached, the Secretary of State would not, as he did, have called on the chairman of the Committee on Foreign Relations to get his views on the subject of the proposed negotiation with Great Britain, and, if possible, to gain his support thereto. That proposed negotiation, it must further be borne in mind, was the cardinal feature in the policy of the Administration at that time. As such it took precedence. On it the Administration largely rested its claim for the support of the country in a presidential election then nearly impending. For the Secretary of State thus to seek

the opinion of the chairman of the Committee on
Foreign Relations was unprecedented. Nevertheless,
he did it. Greater deference could not have been
paid.

The result of the interview that followed is set forth
in the text. But it is maintained by the friends of
Mr. Sumner that, when he said, as, in his memorandum to Mr. Fish he did say, that the "withdrawal of
the British flag cannot be abandoned as a condition
or preliminary" to the proposed negotiation, he should
not have been considered as having proposed an ultimatum, as it is called; and it indicated almost a
degree of moral turpitude on the part of the Secretary to suppose that he really meant any such thing.
The Secretary, it is contended, should have assumed
that this utterance was on his part a mere diplomatic
pretence, and that subsequently he would prove amenable to reason, or, at the proper time, change his
mind.

Such a process of convenient and surely foreseeable
change is scarcely in accordance with the general
understanding of Mr. Sumner's public record and
mental attributes. He had no sense of humor; and,
therefore, it was improbable that he could have intended his memorandum as a pleasantry. What he
wrote was written after two days of careful consideration, in the full light of a prolonged oral discussion
with the Secretary. The whole ground had been
gone over. As the result of much meditation, and
acting unquestionably under a grave sense of public
responsibility, he then penned his memorandum, than
which it would seem nothing could be more explicit.
The Secretary certainly was justified in assuming that

the Senator meant what he wrote. Mr. Fish then
found himself in a difficult position. Mr. Sumner
had also said in the memorandum, in a clause not
quoted in the text, that " no proposition [looking to
renewed negotiations] can be accepted unless the
terms of submission are such as to leave no reasonable doubt of a favorable result. There must not be
another failure." In that opinion the Secretary fully
coincided. Mr. Fish, therefore, found himself confronted with this proposition : — He was to begin a
negotiation, — which, on no account, should fail of
success, — in the face of an explicit statement of the
chairman of the Senate Committee on Foreign Relations that the negotiation in question should be
entered upon only upon a condition, or preliminary,
which, if stated, would bring it at once to a close.
The dilemma was obvious; there was but one course
for the Secretary to pursue. If he proposed to deal
honestly by the British government, making no attempt
to inveigle it into a false position, he must explain the
situation to its representatives fairly and openly, and,
if they then expressed a willingness to proceed, it only
remained for him to pledge the Administration to
carry it to a satisfactory result, if it could, over any
opposition which the chairman of the Committee on
Foreign Relations might have it in his power to offer.
To those who knew Mr. Sumner, it needs no argument to prove that, under the circumstances, it would
have been altogether unjustifiable for the Secretary
to enter into a negotiation, leaving Mr. Sumner as an
unknown quantity in position to control the result.
He had to be eliminated. At least, that was a reasonable view to take of the situation ; the only view,

unquestionably, which would commend itself to the military mind of General Grant. He could never have been disposed to leave a formidable enemy intrenched in his rear.

The rest followed, naturally and inevitably. After careful deliberation, Secretary Fish sent for four leaders of the Senate, two of each party, — Messrs. Thurman and Bayard on the part of the Opposition, and Messrs. Conkling and Edmunds representing the friends of the Administration. With them he consulted freely, making plain the situation. They advised together as to the course best to pursue.

All apparently agreed. Naturally, being experienced men, skilful in handling a parliamentary body, the question at once arose, how the issue could best be presented. Mr. Sumner's displacement from his stronghold, the chairmanship of the Committee on Foreign Relations, was the result to be brought about. The fact that he was not friendly to the proposed negotiation could not well be put forward, in view of the grounds upon which he rested his opposition. This was obvious. Under these circumstances, the parliamentary leaders naturally fell back upon the very sufficient difficulty apparent in the attempt properly to conduct a foreign policy under a condition of affairs so wholly unexampled as that then existing. It is said that the removal of Mr. Sumner was unprecedented. So also, it will be agreed, was the situation. An unprecedented situation can only apparently be dealt with through exceptional measures of correction.

Under the rules of that body, and the practice of the government from the beginning, it is customary to revise the committees of the Senate every two years, the terms of one third of the Senators then coming to a close, and the places of that third being filled, either by reëlection or by change of occupant. This periodical rearrangement was to be made in March, 1871, after the Forty-first Congress expired. The matter was considered in a caucus of Republican Senators, and the necessity of reorganizing the Committee on Foreign Relations was discussed, upon the grounds stated. Undoubtedly, the Executive had intimated to its friends in the Senate that such a change was in its judgment necessary to the development of a policy, and the proper conduct of public affairs. Those affairs would sustain detriment by a continuance of existing conditions. It was also right and proper that this argument in favor of a change should be advanced. Furthermore, it was right and proper that Senators should give due consideration to it. To the majority the argument seemed good ; and the change was made.

This is believed to be a fair statement of the case ; and, in the light of such statement, it is difficult to see how any allegation of improper interference of the Executive in legislative action can be sustained. It is futile to argue that the Senate is a quasi-judicial body, and that the Executive has consequently no more right to try to influence its members than it would have to seek to affect the decision of a court of law by representations made to judges out of court. The two cases are in no respect analogous. The issues before the Senate are political ; the issues before the court of law are legal. On political issues — questions of policy — it is the business and duty of the Executive to try by all legitimate means to bring

about harmonious action.   The legislative department
should understand thoroughly the purpose and policy
of the Executive.   In March, 1871, it was notorious
that Mr. Sumner had broken with the Administration.   A year later the break was avowed.   He then
went over to the Opposition.   In 1871 his proper seat
was, so to speak, below the gangway ; in 1872 it was
on the opposition side of the chamber.   Under such
circumstances it is difficult to see how his displacement by the act of a majority with whom he was no
longer in sympathy, and whose views he had ceased to
represent, can be characterized as " among the most
unwarrantable, grossly unjust, and inexcusable acts in
our political history." [1]   Stronger language could not
have been used had Mr. Sumner held his position by
vested right, or judicial tenure.   The logical result of
such a contention would be to insist that the so-called
" courtesy of the Senate " is one of the precious muni-
ments of the Constitution, having no limits and admitting of no exceptions.   The displacement of Mr.
Sumner was in disregard of " the courtesy of the
Senate ; " it was, therefore, equivalent to a wilful
infraction of the fundamental law.

That the contrary view here taken is sustained by
men of experience in public life, and after years of
reflection on the facts of this particular case, admits

[1] D. H. Chamberlain, in the Boston *Herald* and the Springfield
Republican, of Sunday, February 23, 1902.   The paper here referred
to, afterwards published in pamphlet form under the title of " Charles
Sumner and the Treaty of Washington," is by far the most elaborate
and carefully argued discussion of the displacement of Mr. Sumner
from his committee chairmanship which has yet appeared.   It is unnecessary to say that the conclusions reached by Governor Chamberlain
are diametrically opposed to those set forth in this paper.

of proof. George S. Boutwell, for instance, was at the time Secretary of the Treasury. Though a member of Grant's Cabinet, Mr. Boutwell sympathized with Mr. Sumner on the Dominican issue. He has recently expressed himself thus as regards the displacement of Mr. Sumner from his chairmanship : —

" Mr. Sumner's course in regard to the acquisition of San Domingo contributed to the separation between the President and the chairman of the Committee on Foreign Relations, but opposition without personality would not have produced alienation on the part of the President. Other Senators were opposed to the acquisition of San Domingo, and there were members of his Cabinet who did not sympathize with his policy, as the President well knew ; but those facts in themselves did not tend in the least to alienation. . . . As far as I have knowledge, you have stated with accuracy the conditions and circumstances which led to and required the removal of Mr. Sumner from the head of the Committee on Foreign Relations. The time had come when Mr. Sumner limited his conversation with the Secretary of State to official matters. Such are the requirements of administration that it is not possible for the head of a department to conduct the business of his department, unless he can have full and free conversation with the members of committees, not even excluding those who represent a party in Opposition. Inasmuch as the hostility which Mr. Sumner entertained for the Secretary of State extended to the President, it was not possible that any change of intercourse between the department and the head of the Committee on Foreign Relations could be effected by the removal of the Secretary. Hence a change in the chairmanship of the Committee on Foreign Relations became a public necessity, essential to the administration of the government."

George F. Edmunds was, as stated in the text, then a Senator from Vermont. After thirty-one years of reflection, Mr. Edmunds has recently expressed himself as follows. In reading what he says, it is only necessary to bear in mind that many Senators who were satisfied of the propriety of the act on grounds of public policy were opposed to it for reasons of party unity. They felt apprehensive of the ill feeling it would necessarily generate. Mr. Edmunds has said : —

" At the time of the caucus in December, 1870, it was thought by a majority of the Republican Senators that the relations between Mr. Sumner and Mr. Fish had not become so absolutely broken as to prevent the necessary communications between the Secretary of State and the chairman of the Committee on Foreign Relations. When the new Congress came into being, and the Senate committees had all expired, and many changes had taken place in the personnel of the Senate, and the relations between the Secretary of State and Mr. Sumner had become entirely severed, it was thought that the public interest absolutely demanded that the chairman of the committee should be on terms of personal good-will and civility with the Secretary of State, and accordingly, and I think almost unanimously, the Republican caucus determined not to reappoint Mr. Sumner, and this, so far as I recollect, was done without any factional or other inquiry into whether Mr. Sumner or Mr. Fish were in the wrong ; and I believe that at least three fourths if not nine tenths of the gentlemen concerned both respected, and were on personally friendly terms, with Mr. Sumner, as I was myself. The rules of the Senate were framed with the purpose that at the opening of a new Congress the Senate should feel perfectly free to make such changes in the chairmanship and personnel of all her committees as should be deemed expedient, without giving any gentleman a right to complain that he had been dismissed from office."

John Sherman of Ohio was then, as for many years afterwards, a leading member of the Senate. Few were more influential in that body. Writing over twenty years later, Mr. Sherman said : — " Social relations between the Secretary of State and Mr. Sumner had become impossible ; and — considering human passion, prejudice and feeling — anything like frank and confidential communication between the President and Mr. Sumner was out of the question. A majority of the Republican Senators sided with the President. . . . When we met in March it was known that both [the San Domingo and British negotiations] would necessarily be referred to the Committee on Foreign Relations, and that, aside from the hostile personal relations of Mr. Sumner and the Secretary of State, he did not, and could not, and would not, represent the views of a majority of his Republican colleagues in the Senate, and that a majority of his committee agreed with him. Committees are, and ought to be, organized to represent the body, giving a majority of members to the prevailing opinion, but fairly representing the views of the minority. It has been the custom in the Senate to allow each party to choose its own representatives in each committee, and in proportion to its numbers. . . . In deciding Mr. Sum-

ner's case, in view of the facts I have stated, two plans
were urged : —

" First — To place him at the head of the new and
important Committee of Privileges and Elections,
leaving the rest of the Committee on Foreign Relations to stand in the precise order it had been, with
one vacancy to be filled in harmony with the majority.

" Second — To leave Mr. Sumner to stand in his
old place as chairman, and to make a change in the
body of the committee by transferring one of its members to another committee, and fill the vacancy by a
Senator in harmony with the majority.

" My own opinion was that the latter course was the
most polite and just; but the majority decided, after
full consideration and debate, upon the first alternative." [1]

Though Mr. Sherman expressed himself in the
subsequent debate in open Senate in terms of strong
opposition to the course pursued, his objection was
based on party considerations. In his judgment the
situation called for remedial action; but not the action
proposed. He preferred to put Mr. Sumner in a
minority, and under guardianship, in the committee of
which he was to remain the nominal head. If he still
remained chairman, and, as such, the official mouthpiece of the committee and its intermediary with the
Department of State, this position would certainly
have been to him both embarrassing and mortifying.
He would scarcely have submitted to it. It would seem
more kindly, and scarcely less courteous, squarely to
reorganize the committee; which, at least, had the
merit of accomplishing the result in view, and avoid-

[1] *Recollections of Forty Years*, vol. i. pp. 471, 472.

ing unseemly conflicts both in committee and on the floor of the Senate.

The following extracts from the editorial pages of the New York *Nation* — then very critical of the course pursued by the Administration — give a contemporary view of the whole matter, and of the personage chiefly concerned : —

" It seems not improbable that an attempt will be made in the Senate to make the settlement of the *Alabama* case depend on the willingness of Great Britain to abandon all her possessions on this side of the ocean, including her West Indian Islands. The germ of this idea made its appearance in the columns of the *Tribune* about two years ago, in the shape of a hint that nothing short of the cession of Canada would suffice to satisfy the American public for the wrongs it had suffered. The source of this suggestion could hardly have been doubtful, as it was a natural enough deduction from Mr. Sumner's statement of the measure of damages in his famous speech. Under the rule he laid down, the surrender of Canada indeed would have only been a moderate atonement. Since then the conception has grown and expanded until it involves the total retirement of England from the Western continent and the adjacent isles; and Mr. Sumner is apparently as anxious to connect his name with the execution of this great scheme as the President is to connect his with the settlement of the affair in the ordinary way by the payment of pecuniary damages. Of course, the production of the plan by the American commissioners is not at all likely, as they are all rational politicians and men of business; but it is not at all unlikely to find supporters enough in the Senate to secure the rejection of any treaty the commissioners may agree on." (February 23, 1871.)

" The main business of the chairman of the Senate committee is not to negotiate treaties, but to discuss with the Executive such treaties as have been negotiated, and to receive from it explanations about them. His first business, therefore, is to be a good organ of communication on this particular class of subjects between the President and Senate, and nobody can be said to be well fitted for this duty whose personal relations with the President are of an unpleasant nature. In fact, we go so far as to say that a proper sense of his duty, and of the fitness of things, and a proper appreciation of the delicacy of the machinery of such a government as ours, might have suggested to Mr. Sumner the expediency of resigning the chairmanship as soon as he found himself arrayed in open and bitter hostility to General Grant. It must be remembered that his resigning the chairmanship would not deprive the Senate of the benefit of his counsels. It would enable no act of the Administration to escape his supervision. . . .

" We allude to his [Sumner's] want of judgment and want of sense of responsibility in the use of language. He talks sometimes in the wildest way, and apparently without being fully conscious of the force or bearing of what he says. . . . It would not be unnatural that, in view of all these facts, and on the eve of an attempt to settle a most important controversy with England, in which he has taken a most excited part, and has given utterance to most extraordinary views of international law and morality, the Administration should wish for some friendlier, calmer, and more accurate organ of communication with the body which is to ratify any treaty it may enter into." (March 16, 1871.)

"Some fresh light has, however, been thrown on the causes of the great Sumner-Fish quarrel, by the new Washington paper, the *Capital*, whose account is said to be 'semi-official.' It appears to have arisen out of an ill-judged attempt of the foolish Fish to get Sumner to take the English mission and abandon his opposition to the San Domingo scheme. Sumner, of course, refused with a pitying smile. The unhappy Fish 'left the house a baffled and disappointed man,' and then went to work to 'insult' Mr. Motley. After the appearance of his letter to Moran, however, the poor old coward did not dare to go near 'the Old Bay State Lion' for some time, but at last mustered up courage to call at his den to meet Sir John Rose on official business. The evening passed quietly enough, and, we are glad to say, 'intellectually and profitably,' and the Fish doubtless thought he was forgiven and restored to favor. Far from it. After he had gone, Sumner sat down 'after midnight in the quiet of his library,' and considered his case afresh, and came to the conclusion that he ought still further to punish him. This cruel but we presume just decision reached, the house of Mr. Schenck was chosen for the execution of the sentence. The judge and culprit met there at dinner, and in the course of the meal poor Fish, little knowing what was in store for him, 'made a frivolous remark about duck and partridge' across the table to the 'Numidian Lion' — for as such it appears Mr. Sumner figured on this occasion, doubtless having ascertained that an 'Old Bay State Lion'

was, to say the least, an anomaly. ' The Lion ' merely
looked at him, and made no reply. ' Fish's weak
nature,' says the chronicler, ' felt the shock.' Small
blame to him, say we ; whose nature would n't ' feel
the shock ' if a Numidian Lion looked at him in
silence across a small table ?   The effect on American
securities of this dreadful business, we are glad to say,
has not yet been perceptible ; but mighty agencies
work slowly."   (March 23, 1871.)

APPENDIX G [1]

IT is curious, as well as historically interesting, to trace in the correspondence and memoranda of Mr. Fish the gradual change of his tone and feeling towards Mr. Sumner. Their personal as well as social relations, as colleagues in the Senate from 1851 to 1857, have already been referred to.[2] Though taking very different views, politically and morally, of the issues of the day, they were intimate.[3] Indeed, in no house in Washington was Mr. Sumner so intimate or so welcome as in that of Mr. Fish. The single term during which the latter served expired in March, 1857. Twelve years later, in March, 1869, he was unexpectedly called into Grant's cabinet. He then at once wrote to Mr. Sumner, expressing' the earnest hope that he might " rely upon your friendship and your experience and ability, for your support and aid to supply my manifold deficiencies." During the earlier months of Secretary Fish's tenure of office, the relations between the two were of the most friendly character, — official, social and personal. Indeed, officially, no Senator had ever been treated by the head of the State Department in so confidential a way, — it might almost be said, a way so deferential. The first difference arose over the instructions to Mr. Motley, as stated already. Mr. Sumner

---

[1] See *supra*, p. 187. [2] *Supra*, p. 106.

[3] Pierce : *Sumner*, vol. iv. pp. 375–379.

on that occasion was, in his peculiar way, distinctly overbearing; and Mr. Fish did not conceal his sense of the fact. It was on the 15th of May, and at the State Department. After reading the draught of instructions, Mr. Sumner walked up and down the room, talking in a most excited way, and declaring that he would "make Motley resign;" speaking of the Minister to Great Britain as if he was his man, or agent. To this the Secretary replied, — "Let him resign. I will put a better man in his place."

Mr. Bancroft Davis describes another characteristic scene which occurred at about this time. Mr. Sumner one evening had called, this time by appointment, at Mr. Fish's house, to discuss the instructions. When his visitor rose to go, Mr. Fish accompanied him to the door. "It was one of those mild evenings in May which in Washington make the doorsteps so attractive. Standing there, Sumner opened his case. They talked long. Sumner's voice at last became so loud, as his feelings were aroused, that Mr. Fish said, pleasantly: 'Sumner, you roar like the bull of Bashan. The police will be after us. I think we had better adjourn.' Sumner smiled, and bade him good-night." All this occurred in May, nearly eight months before that after-dinner call on Mr. Sumner at which the President tried to secure the Senator's approval of the Babcock Dominican treaty. During that time the friction between the Secretary and the Senator had sensibly increased. Their correspondence was marked by occasional exhibitions of feeling, indicative of less cordiality. From January to June, 1870, this tendency to a separation developed apace, until, in June, the President insisted on the recall of Mr. Motley.

Grant and Sumner had now openly quarrelled. Each denounced the other. E. R. Hoar, up to that time Attorney-General in Grant's cabinet, altogether sympathizing with Sumner in his opposition to the West Indian expansion policy, yet maintained his friendly, as well as official, relations with the President. Judge Hoar was wont in after years to describe with much humor the Washington doorstep interviews he at that time had with Mr. Sumner. Going to the house of that gentleman in the evening, his host would accompany him to the door as he went away, and there, on one side of Lafayette Square, using the Attorney-General as a species of buffer between him and the President, he would, gradually and unconsciously, raise his voice until he roared, as Mr. Fish expressed it, "like a bull of Bashan." He would then, in terms equally unmeasured and stentorian, denounce the man in the White House on the other side of the Square. It would at times seem, as Judge Hoar expressed it, as if all Washington, including Mrs. Grant, must hear him, and the police would have to interfere.

On the issues now raised, the Secretary of State, after much hesitation, sided with the President. He did so with reluctance; but he was a member of the Cabinet, and, moreover, as he wrote to a friend at the time, "I have a very strong affection for the President; he is a very true man, and warm friend, — accustomed to deal with men of more frankness and sincerity, and loyalty to a cause, than many of those whom the business of Washington attracts hither." He then went on in the same letter thus to refer to Mr. Sumner : — " Congress is incapable, — suffering from the want of leadership, and cursed with incapable aspirants to leadership. Jealousies and disappointments develop in old Senators, who exhibit arrogance, the attendant perhaps of long continuance in senatorial position. Clay and Benton, each domineered in their day, but they were men capable of position; the aspirant to their control, in the present day, knows nothing but books, and not over-much of them." This was written on the 23d of June, 1870, fifteen months after Grant's inauguration. Within the ten days preceding or following, the Dominican treaty was rejected by the Senate, and the resignation of the Attorney-General, and the Minister to Great Britain, called for. Though, in the Dominican matter, Judge Hoar had not seen his way to follow the same course of loyalty to the head of the administration which Mr. Fish had pursued, he recognized the fact that grounds might exist for an honest difference of opinion, and retained a warm friendly regard for Mr. Fish personally as well as great respect for his character and ability; a respect which he always afterwards felt, and did not fail freely to express. The evening of the second day after that upon which he had, in response to the President's somewhat curt request, sent in his resignation, Judge Hoar, as elsewhere appears,[1] called on Mr. Fish to explain the reasons thereof, and to urge him " under all circumstances to hold fast; " earnestly adding in language already quoted that in his judgment the Secretary of State was " the bulwark now standing between the Country and its destruction." It was characteristic of the two men that Mr. Sumner was at the same time roughly de-

[1] *Supra*, p. 221.

manding of Mr. Fish why, under the circumstances in which he found himself placed, he did not forthwith resign.

On this point, Mr. Fish, fortunately, hearkened to the appeal of Judge Hoar, disregarding the suggestion of Mr. Sumner. But the breach between him and the latter was now fast widening. Five weeks later, on the 6th of August, Mr. Fish thus wrote to Senator Howe of Wisconsin: —

" Mr. Sumner, I fear, is implacable. I passed an hour in his study the evening before I left Washington. His general tone towards me was very friendly, and my farewell was cordial and kind as ever. But he was very severe towards the President, and in one or two outbursts of rhetorical denunciation he included me and any one connected with the Administration. I am quite convinced that on such occasions, he is not conscious of the extent and violence of his expressions, and is not wholly the master of himself. . . . With large ability, high culture, extended reading, and remarkable power of oratory, he lacks knowledge of men, is overborne by much vanity (much of it quite justifiable), is arrogant and domineering, and these qualities increase with years. He has no one of the peculiar elements essential for leadership, to which he thinks that his long service, and his admitted ability, entitle him. . . . Under the name of Mr. Perley Poore, he has made a publication neither generous nor frank. I should have been quite justified in noticing it and denouncing it, and should have done so but for my desire to avoid anything to confirm him in his estrangement or his antagonism to the Administration, and for my determination to avoid, if practicable, being brought personally into controversy with one with whom for many years I have had such friendly relations, and who has so many very fine qualities. . . . I intend not to lose him as a personal friend. I wish not to lose him as a political associate and coworker."

In the same spirit Mr. Fish some three weeks later (August 25) wrote from his home at Garrison to Senator Morrill of Vermont: —

" I had several very friendly interviews with him [Sumner], and made statements to the very limit that the confidence of my official position would allow, and which ought to satisfy any sensible man.   But on the subject of Mr. Motley's removal, and on his own relations with the President, I cannot regard Mr. S. as either a reasonable or a *reasoning* man. He fell back always from the facts I presented to a severe expression of feeling, and some rhetorical phrase. He seemed to me determined to consider himself the cause and the object of all that had been, or might be, done. . . . I am not insensible of his arrogance and overbearing temper, but I know, too, his extended literary attainments, his power of eloquence, and his many good qualities, and should deeply regret on his own account, and on that of the Republican party, that at this late day he should fall from the faith."

Finally, on the 6th of September following, he wrote again, still to Senator Morrill: —

" He [Sumner] is of great value and importance to us ; but, unfortunately, he thinks that value and importance to embrace the existence of the party. . . . He nourishes his supposed griefs, and seems to take comfort in imagining everything that is done without

him, or contrary to his wishes, as a personal offence."
This letter was probably received by Senator Morrill
on the 7th of September. While it was lying on his
table, there came to him from Mr. Sumner a most
characteristic effusion, dated the 8th, to which, two
days later, he referred, in reply, as follows : — " You
characterize [the President's] acts, and that with
severity — perhaps with greater severity than you are
aware of. Your words must leap out in your conversation, and they will inevitably reach the ears of the
President. 'Brutality,' 'indignity,' 'offensive,' ' utterly
indefensible conduct,' ' excuses, apologies, and reasons
which are obviously pretexts, subterfuges, and after-
thoughts,' would make any man's ears tingle. It may
be too much to ask you to forget and forgive : but I
think it might be wise to let the subject ' alone se-
verely.' " [1]

This excellent advice Mr. Sumner could not follow ; and, in the course of the next few weeks, incidents of personal intercourse apparently occurred which
brought matters to a crisis. Though not a man of
aggressive disposition, Mr. Fish seems, when aroused, to
have had in him a strong infusion of that stubbornness
so characteristic of the Dutch stock. He also was
resentful of what he regarded as affronts ; and of
anything of the nature of personal insult, he was un-
forgiving. In view of past friendly relations he bore
much from Sumner, as being Sumner's way, but,
finally, the limit seems on some occasion to have been
passed. Thereafter, the sense of personal exaspera-
tion on the part of the Secretary of State was not less

[1] " Notable Letters from my Political Friends," by Justin S. Morrill, *The Forum*, vol. xxiv. p. 409 ; December, 1897.

than that felt by the President ; and when Mr. Boutwell, the head of the Treasury, truthfully as well as
charitably, suggested that Mr. Sumner was apt to forget what he said, Mr. Fish sharply replied, — " Sumner is crazy.   He is a monomaniac upon all matters
relating to his own importance, and his relations to
the President."   Mr. Sumner and Roscoe Conkling,
then Senator from New York, were naturally antago-
nistic.   As Rufus Choate would have phrased it, they
disliked each other, not for cause, but peremptorily.
To Conkling, Mr. Fish now said, — " Sumner is partially crazy.   Upon a certain class of questions, and
wherever his own importance or influence are concerned, or anything relating to himself, or his own
views, past or present, or his ambition, he loses the
power of logical reasoning, and becomes contradictory,
violent, and unreasoning.   That is mental derange-
ment."

This evidence of such contemporaries as Mr. Dana
and Mr. Fish, both during long periods warm personal as well as close political friends of Mr. Sumner,
is highly suggestive.   It affords indications of mental
methods and characteristics which, explaining much,
would in no wise be inferred from anything to be
found in the elaborate biography of Mr. Pierce.   Certainly, neither General Grant nor Mr. Fish were
considered among their contemporaries men difficult
to get on with, or prone to take offence.   They were
both, at the outset, most solicitous of Sumner's friendship and support.   They were anxious to conciliate
him.   Grant and Sumner never were on terms of
personal intimacy.   They had little in common.   But
the same is hardly less true of Grant and Fish.   They

saw nothing of each other socially, in later years, when both were residents of the same city. Simply, they were not congenial natures. But, in the early months of his presidency, Grant was sincerely desirous of being on good terms with Sumner. Hence the appointment of Motley; hence the unfortunate after-dinner visit in January, 1870. Yet, all this being unquestionably so as late as January, 1870, in January, 1871, — twelve months afterwards only, — neither President nor Secretary was on speaking terms with the Senator. The differences had become personal and bitter. This was suggestive.

The simple fact was that Mr. Fish, instinctively and unconsciously, knew how to deal with Grant, and how to accomplish results which depended on him. Mr. Sumner did not. He was essentially aggressive; and General Grant resented aggressiveness. His friends, while greatly admiring his strong and brilliant qualities, could not but be conscious of his foibles; they did not, however, state them in the somewhat direct language used by Mr. Fish. On the contrary, they indulged in much circumlocution. For instance, Senator Hoar of Massachusetts, almost a disciple of Mr. Sumner's, once said of him : — " It has always seemed to me as if Mr. Sumner thought the Rebellion was put down by a few speeches he made in the Senate, and that he looked upon the battles fought as the noise of a fire-engine going by while he was talking." Mr. Schurz furnishes a curious illustration of this idiosyncrasy. The renomination of President Grant was, in 1872, a foregone conclusion. Mr. Sumner felt impelled to take ground against it in a speech. Mr. Schurz then says : — " When, shortly before the National Republican Convention of 1872, he had delivered in the Senate that fierce philippic for which he has been censured so much, he turned to me with the question, whether I did not think that the statement and arguments he had produced would certainly exercise a decisive influence on the action of that convention. I replied that I thought it would not. He was greatly astonished — not as if he indulged in the delusion that his personal word would have such authoritative weight, but it seemed impossible to him that opinions which in him had risen to the full strength of overruling convictions . . . should fall powerless at the feet of a party which so long had followed inspirations kindred to his own. Such was the ingenuousness of his nature."

Yet Mr. Sumner was essentially a man of large, kindly nature, and generous impulses. He felt slights keenly, and made personal issues; but he did not bear malice, nor was he small or vindictive. A curious illustration of this occurred in the experience of George F. Edmunds of Vermont, whose first full term in the Senate coincided with Sumner's uncompleted last term. Mr. Edmunds, it will be remembered, was one of those in the confidence of Secretary Fish during the incipient negotiations which led up to the Treaty of Washington. Active in effecting the reorganization of the Committee on Foreign Relations, he had taken part adversely to Mr. Sumner in the debate on that subject. He subsequently, in a familiar letter, thus described what thereupon occurred:— "It is true that I was visited with Mr. Sumner's resentment of my connection with the change, for he absolutely cut my acquaintance ; which was not renewed until some months afterwards, when, in vacation, we suddenly met in a New York omnibus, and he at the moment had forgotten my wickedness, and we cordially shook hands ; and were on the friendliest terms for the rest of his life."

III

A NATIONAL CHANGE OF HEART [1]

A TERRIBLE and tragic episode in our national life has burned itself into history since the last meeting of the Society, — the assassination of President McKinley. Twice before have we, in common with the whole land, been shocked by like occurrences.[2] At the time of both, Mr. Winthrop occupied this chair; [3] and, on each occasion, fitting resolutions, submitted by him and unanimously adopted, were spread upon our records. From the precedents thus established I propose to deviate; not that I have failed to sympathize in the outburst of feeling this truly terrible event has excited, or the expressions elicited by it; but, on now reading the resolutions heretofore passed on similar occasions, they seem to me, though drawn with all Mr. Winthrop's accustomed felicity, unequal to the occasion, — in one word, almost of necessity, formal, conventional, perfunctory. I also feel that I could not express myself more adequately. Of President McKinley all has in this way been said that can be said : —

[1] A paper read before the Massachusetts Historical Society, at its monthly meeting, October 10, 1901.

[2] April 20, 1865, following the death of President Lincoln; and October 13, 1881, following that of President Garfield.

[3] Robert C. Winthrop was President of the Massachusetts Historical Society from 1855 to 1885.

" Duncan is in his grave ;
After life's fitful fever he sleeps well ;
Treason has done his worst ; nor steel, nor poison,
Malice domestic, foreign levy, nothing,
Can touch him further."

He cannot hear ; and, as to her for whom the latter years of the dead President's life were one long record of affectionate, self-sacrificing care, no formally set down words of mine could add one iota to the expression of sympathy — deep and prolonged as sincere — which has already gone forth. This being so, silence seems best.

Still, to one aspect of this awe-impelling tragedy I wish to call attention, for that aspect has to my mind an historic interest. Perhaps, already discussed, it is an old story ; if such is the case I can only excuse myself on the ground that, having been absent from the country, and only just returned to it, I am less informed as to what has been said than I otherwise might have been. But, when some event like this last murder of a high official startles and shocks the whole civilized world, the first impulse always is to attribute its occurrence to present conditions, — moral or material, — to some circumstance or teaching or appliance peculiar to the day, — and to ask in awe-struck tones, — To what are we coming ? Whither do tendencies lead ? In what will they result? So, as of genuine historical interest, in this connection, I want to call attention to the very noticeable fact that this murder of President McKinley by the wretched, half-witted Czolgosz has no significance whatever, as respects either cause or method, in connection with the times in which we live, its destructive appliances, or its moral instruction. This, somewhat curiously, is true not only of President

McKinley's assassination, but of all the assassinations of a like nature, with two exceptions, which have occurred within the last half century. Of such, I easily recall eight : (1) The Orsini attempt on Napoleon III. in 1858, which resulted in numerous deaths, though the person aimed at escaped unharmed ; (2) the slaying of President Lincoln in 1865 ; (3) that of the Czar Alexander II. in 1881 ; (4) that of President Garfield three months later in the same year ; (5) that of President Carnot in 1894 ; (6) that of the Empress Elizabeth of Austria in 1898 ; and (7, 8) those of King Humbert in 1900, and, more recently, of President McKinley.

This is truly enough the age of advance,—scientific and intellectual. Strange doctrines are promulgated, and widely preached. There is a freedom given to utterances, at once wild and subversive, the like of which the world has not known before; we do not believe in the suppression of talk; the press disseminates incendiary doctrines broadcast among the partially educated, and the half, where not wholly, crazed. Then, in its turn, science has put the most deadly and destructive of appliances within easy reach of the irrational or reckless. Yet, of all the attempts I have enumerated, two only have borne an earmark of this age. The Orsini conspiracy of 1858 and the death of the Czar Alexander in 1881 brought into play implements of destruction unknown to former generations ; the other six cases out of the eight had no features in any respect different from similar crimes of the long past. The impulses, the methods, and the weapons of Booth and Guiteau, in 1865 and 1881, were identical in every way with those of Gérard and Ravaillac in

1584 and 1610, three centuries before. They had in them nothing epochal, — nothing peculiar to the dynamitic age. Consider, in the first place, the aim of the assassin, the object of his animosity, — McKinley and Garfield were neither tyrants nor despots ; nor were William the Silent and Henry of Navarre. On the contrary, all those named were men of a merciful, not to say singularly genial disposition. Beneficent as rulers and magistrates, they were in the popular mind connected with no severities towards individuals. In not one of these cases had the assassin, directly or indirectly, immediately or remotely, suffered injury at the hands of his victim. It was the same with Lincoln and Carnot, Humbert and Elizabeth. In all these instances, moreover, the weapons used in killing, if not identical, were common to the earlier and the later period. Henry of Navarre in 1610, President Carnot in 1894, and Elizabeth of Austria in 1898, were murdered by thrusts of a poniard ; William of Orange in 1584, King Humbert in 1900, and Presidents Lincoln, Garfield and McKinley, all within forty years, met their deaths from pistol-shots. In no one of these tragedies did the modern high explosive play any part. They were all ordinary shootings or stabbings of the old style.

Nor was it otherwise as respects motive. The more recent instances developed nothing peculiar to any age or doctrines, except that in the earlier cases the crime originated in a morbid fanaticism born of religious zeal ; whereas, in the later, social and anarchistic teachings had taken the place of theological. In the process of human development, or evolution as we call it, the same character of mind was set in action to a like end by a common diseased impulse, only under another name. There is no new factor at work; merely the teaching of social rights now operates, in a certain order of brooding minds, as the teachings of theology once did on minds of the same temper. So far as these recent murders are concerned, the world and human nature have, therefore, undergone no change. The Czolgosz of 1901 is the Gérard of 1584 reëmbodied, but actuated by the same impulse, and armed with his old weapon! Luccheni is Ravaillac. The three centuries between introduced no element of novelty. Indeed, the thought this recent murder has most forced on me has been one of surprise, on the whole, that such things so rarely happen. Here in America are now seventy millions of people, — gentle and simple, rich and poor, sane and insane, healthy and morbid; of those seventy millions not a few are men who, like Macbeth's hired assassin, might truthfully enough declare themselves of those

> " Whom the vile blows and buffets of the world
> Have so incensed that I am reckless what
> I do to spite the world ; "

and, when thus thought of, it seems cause for genuine surprise that among those seventy millions there do not more frequently develop single individuals — some one person in the half million — who, seized in his brooding moments with the homicidal mania, asserts his equality and his hate by striking at the most shining mark. To my mind, contemplating mankind as an infinitely varied and well-nigh countless mass, it is the rarity of these attempts in our day, not their occasional occurrence, which should excite our special wonder.

At the time of the assassination of the President, I chanced to be in England, having left home on the 10th of August. It was a vacation trip ; and, in the course of it, I thus had some opportunity to witness that singular, and very suggestive, outburst of sympathy and fellow-feeling on the part of our kin beyond the sea, which was so marked a feature of that unhappy episode. On Thursday, September 19, I was in London, and present at the memorial services in Westminster Abbey. Certainly, they were most impressive. Seated in the choir, I was not in position to see the nave of the Abbey, except in part and by glimpses ; but, throughout the solemn observances of that day and place, an atmosphere of genuine sympathy and deep feeling pervaded the great assembly. Every nook and corner was occupied ; a sense of awe was apparent. The day had been dull and obscure, — a September noon in London, — but, towards the close of the ceremonial, as the solemn tones of the great organ, intermingled with the responses of the choir, rolled up through the arches of the vaulted roof, the clouds broke away without, and the sun shone down through the windows of stained glass on the vast congregation below. It was Milton's " dim religious light ; " and the dusky atmosphere seemed laden with the smoke of incense, as the chant of the choir died slowly away.

To me personally, however, this outburst of English sentiment towards the United States and all things American — the demonstration of an undemonstrative people — contained within itself much food for thought. I freely acknowledge I have seen nothing like it. And, as my eyes witnessed the Present,

memory called the Past to mind. What, I could not
but ask myself, did it signify? In what did it originate? Was it merely external? Was it matter of
policy? Or did it indicate a true change of heart?
And if a change of heart, to what was that change
due?

My thoughts then reverted to remote days and
other experiences, now, in Great Britain, quite forgotten, — memories still fresh with me, though a generation has since passed on. I recalled my first
experiences in England far back in the " sixties," —
in the dark and trying days of our Civil War; and
again, more recently, during the commercial depression, and contest over the free coinage of silver, in
1896. Then, especially in the earlier period, nothing
was too opprobrious — nothing too bitter and sting-
ing — for English lips to utter of America, and men
and things American.[1] We were, as the *Times*, echoing the utterances of the governing class, never wearied of telling us, a " dishonest " and a " degenerate "
race, — our only worship was of the Almighty Dollar.
A hearty dislike was openly expressed, in terms of
contempt which a pretence of civility hardly feigned
to veil. They openly exulted in our reverses; our
civilization was, they declared, a thin veneer; democracy, a bursted bubble. In true Pharisaic spirit they
made broad their phylacteries, thanking God that
they were not as we, nor we as they. All this I distinctly recalled; it was the atmosphere — frigid, con-

---

[1] See *supra*, pp. 74–79; also *Life of C. F. Adams*, American
Statesmen Series, pp. 291–305; for a collection of parliamentary
utterances from the pages of Hansard, see Blaine: *Twenty Years of
Congress*, vol. ii. pp. 478–481.

temptuous, condescending — in which I had first lived and moved in London. And now what a change ! — and so very sudden ! Nothing was too good or too complimentary to say of America. Our representatives were cheered to the echo. In the language of Lord Rosebery, at the King Alfred millenary celebration at Winchester, on the day following the McKinley observances, the branches of the great Anglo-Saxon stock were clasping hands across the centuries and across the sea ; and the audience applauded him loudly as he spoke.[1]

The heartiness was all there. That at least admitted of no question. But what did it mean ? Why had this people so suddenly awakened to a kinship, in which formerly they had felt something in no way akin to pride ? It was over this I pondered. At last I evolved an explanation, mistaken, perhaps, — I may say probably mistaken, — but still plausible, and to me satisfactory. At the risk, perchance, of seeming ungracious, — of appearing to respond somewhat unfeelingly to an outburst of genuine sympathy on the part

[1] Mr. E. L. Godkin, formerly editor of the *Nation*, called attention to this great change of tone in the very last published communication from his pen, dated Lyndhurst, England, July 31, 1901, printed in the New York *Evening Post* of the 10th of the following month. Mr. Godkin is peculiarly qualified to speak on this point. A Briton by birth, he has, after long residence in this country, been a frequent visitor in England during recent years, returning there recently in failing health. " The American," he wrote in the letter referred to, " who in any profession enjoys ever so slight a distinction at home, has little idea what a great man he is until he comes to England. It is, however, just as well for him in this respect that he comes now instead of ten years earlier. . . . At the present time American fortunes, and freedom in distributing them, and wide financial operations generally, have so captured the English imagination that they now hasten to embrace indiscriminately the cousins whom they snubbed for a century, and to pronounce them and their works good, one and all."

of a kindred people, calling on us to forgive and forget the ill-considered utterances and unwise policy of another time, I purpose here to put my much pondered explanation coldly on record.

In the first place let me premise, and, in so doing, emphasize, my sense of the little worth of the judgment of an individual, and that individual an alien, on what may be the feeling of any community, taken in the aggregate, on a question which does not at once absorb and concentrate attention. Even in our own country, except when deeply stirred by some outburst of patriotism or sympathy,—a common impulse sweeping over the land, and bending minds as a strong gust inclines one way a field of ripening grain, — except on occasions such as this, we know how little real insight the average man has into what is passing in the minds of those among whom he has from his birth lived and moved. We all are conscious of that sense of weariness which almost daily comes over us when we read, in editorial parlance, what the American People have made up their minds to do or not to do, — to have or not to have. On this point the average journalist is always fully advised. His insight is infallible. To his conclusions, knowing by long experience their utter worthlessness, we pay no attention. Yet not an American goes to Europe for a vacation trip, but he comes home fully convinced that he knows more or less of the tendencies of foreign thought. Yet all the insight he has, has been picked up from newspapers and conversations in the railway carriage or the smoking-room. It is true that, in the case of Great Britain, descended from one parent stock, we speak the same language. None the less, an American in Great Britain must almost of necessity draw his inferences as to Great Britain as a community from casual sources and a narrow range of observation. He may read the *Times* and the *Saturday Review*, or the *News* and the *Spectator;* he may have an introduction into English domestic and social life, passing as a guest from one great house to another; he may mix in business or financial circles, and be familiar with "the city;" he may belong to the church, and breathe the atmosphere of the close or the university; he may be a non-conformist, and so frequent the conventicle: — and yet, when all is said and done, he is still a stranger in a strange land. In spite of himself, except it be as the result of a long and varied sojourn, he necessarily draws his conclusions largely from matters of accident, — chance conversations overheard or participated in at hotels and in clubs, in waiting-rooms and in railway carriages, — unsigned communications in copies of papers he may pick up, — or even from talking with bagmen, waiters, cab-drivers, and casual travelling companions. In this way what may be called the general drift of public opinion, so far as it reaches him, finds its expression. Much undoubtedly in such cases depends, also, on the individual; for, though every one is apt to generalize from his individual experience, not all men are either sympathetic or approachable. Yet, allowing for all these peculiarities of the individual, — these kaleidoscopic chances of travel, — certain large features stand forth and impress themselves; some general inferences may at times not unsafely be drawn.

I think I know the Englishman fairly well; at any rate, I have known him through personal contact for over thirty years. I may add that I like him; and, individually, I think he does not dislike me. We certainly get on fairly well together. About him and her there is a downrightness, sometimes, it is true, bordering on brutality, which commands my respect. He does not conceal his feelings. He is not good at playing policy. But, high or low, gentle or simple, rich or poor, the Englishman and the Englishwoman respect and admire the wealthy, the successful, the masterful. This is natural, for the English themselves are essentially masterful. They are also a commercial people. Of late years the struggle for life in Great Britain, as elsewhere, has become more intense, — the cost of living higher, — the social scales more exacting. There, as in America, wealth, and the possession of wealth, has become a larger and larger factor in the common existence; and the newspaper, with its elaborate daily accounts of what is taking place among the rich and the fashionable, has distorted ideals. Now, of recent years, — since, we will say, the close of our Civil War, or 1870, — no people on earth have been comparably so successful as the Americans in the rapid accumulation of wealth, none have shown themselves more masterful; and, as he has more and more so shown himself, the Englishman has undergone a change of feeling towards him, — and this change is, I believe, real. Whether real or not, it certainly is sudden. The outward expression is of recent date; but the influences which have gradually brought it about have been a good while at work. The change, as now witnessed, may, I think, be traced to one remote and several immediate causes. I will enumerate some of the more prominent.

The first was the outcome of our gigantic, prolonged Civil War. At one stage of that struggle, America — loyal America, I mean — touched its lowest estate in the estimation of those called, and in Great Britain considered, the ruling class, — the aristocracy, the men of business and finance, the army and navy, the members of the learned professions.[1] None the less, they then saw us accomplish what they had in every conceivable form of speech pronounced " impossible." We put down the Rebellion with a strong hand ; and then, peacefully disbanding our victorious army, made good our every promise to pay. We accomplished our results in a way they could not understand, — a way for which experience yielded no precedent. None the less, the dislike, not unalloyed by contempt, was too deep-rooted to disappear at once, much more to be immediately transmuted into admiration and cordiality. They waited. Then several striking events occurred in rapid succession, — all within ten years.

I am no admirer of President Cleveland's Venezuela diplomacy. I do not like brutality in public any more than in private dealings. Good manners and courtesy can always be observed, even when firmness of bearing is desirable. None the less, bad for us as the precedent then established was, and yet will prove, there can be no question that, so far as Great Britain was concerned, the tone and attitude on that occasion adopted were productive of results at once profound and, in some ways, beneficial. The average Englishman from the very bottom of his heart respects a man who asserts himself, — provided always he has the will, as well as the power, to make the self-assertion good.

---

[1] *Supra*, pp. 62, 63.

This, as a result of our Civil War, they felt we had. We had done what they had most confidently proclaimed we could not do, and what they, in their hearts, feel they have failed to do. Throughout our Rebellion they had insisted that, even if the conquest of the Confederacy was possible, — which they declared it manifestly was not, — the pacification of the Confederates was out of the question. They thought, also, they knew what they were talking about. Had they not for centuries had Ireland on their hands? Was it not there now? Were they not perpetually floundering in a bottomless bog of Hibernian discontent? Would not our experience be the same, except on a larger scale and in more aggravated form? The result worked out by us wholly belied their predictions. Not only was the rebellion suppressed, but the Confederates were quickly conciliated. The British could not understand it; in the case of the Transvaal they do not understand it now. They merely see that we actually did what they had been unable to do, and are still trying to do. The Spanish war showed that our work of domestic conciliation was as complete as had been that of conquest.

Then came the commercial depression of 1893, and the silver issue. Again they predicted all possible disaster. I was in London in the summers of 1896 and 1897, in close touch with financial circles. The tone and atmosphere at that time prevalent reminded me forcibly of the dark days of the Rebellion. Even as recently as four years back, nothing was too bad for the Englishman " on 'Change " to say or to predict of America, or " Americans," as our securities were called. Suddenly, and in our own way, we emerged from under the cloud, and, again erect and defiant, challenged British commercial supremacy. That they understood ; while they feared, in their hearts they admired. Then came our Spanish war ; and at Manila and Santiago they saw us crush a European navy, such as it was, much as the lion they have taken for their emblem might crush some captive jackal of the desert. This they understood best, and most admired. The rest naturally followed. We were unquestionably rich, unmistakably powerful ; that we too were a masterful race was evident ; we fearlessly challenged supremacy ; we had a way of somehow accomplishing results which they had been at much pains vociferously to pronounce altogether out of the question. So they respected and feared us ; then they began, in a way, to feel proud of us. Were we, after all, not flesh of their flesh, — bone of their bone ?.

Finally came their own war in the Transvaal. Among the nations of Europe, Great Britain found itself in a state of extreme isolation. We ourselves know from recent experience to what this is due. Under some law of development as yet only partially understood, the leading nations of the earth have, especially within the last quarter of a century, been reaching out for dominion in every direction. In this process Great Britain, for reasons plain to every observer, took the lead. In so doing, she had a century's start ; but, none the less, she came in necessary but sharp contact with others, all bent on the same work. The result was logical. A few years ago we suddenly entered on the same path, — Imperialism, it is called. We all know what followed. We came in conflict with a nation belonging to Latin Europe. Immediately, all the Latin communities were in sympathy with Spain, and looked loweringly upon us. The English, at about the same time, came in conflict with an offshoot of the Germanic stock; and instantly all those of German blood scowled upon her. France, she had offended in Africa; Russia was traditionally a rival, and an enemy in Asia. It so chanced that a fellow feeling then brought the United States and Great Britain together. We were in a not dissimilar situation. As Mr. Richard Cobden observed long ago of his countrymen, — " We generally sympathize with everybody's rebels but our own." [1] This is not a peculiarly British characteristic. We, in America, were inclined to sympathize strongly with the rebels of South Africa; but we now have rebels of our own. Rebels, therefore, are with us not in such high favor as they were, — temporarily, of course. Thus, instinctively and insensibly, Great Britain and the United States, each being to a degree isolated, drew together in face of the Germanic and the Latin races. Especially was this so with Great Britain; for her isolation and consequent unpopularity were much the more pronounced of the two. It thus became, to a certain extent, those of the English-speaking race against the world. Blood, speech, descent, told; and it told more plainly with them than with us.

Thus, as I more and more reflected upon it, I began to realize that the change in the English heart was not only real, but altogether human, as well as eminently characteristic. I saw, also, or thought I saw, just how it came about. The mass of the English

[1] *Speeches*, vol. ii. p. 88.

people — the great wage-earning class, the toiling millions — never had shared in the fear and dislike, so long and loudly proclaimed, of America and Democracy. They, on the contrary, throughout the slaveholders' rebellion, and during our time of greatest stress, as a whole, sympathized with the national spirit and the Union cause. They instinctively felt that we somehow were fighting their battle with privilege and aristocracy. Their hearts, therefore, were true; in them no change had to take place. The governing or influential classes, on the other hand, though prejudiced, were quick, in their way, to learn. They now felt British isolation; they feared for their trade; they found themselves in trouble in Ireland and in Africa. So their hearts turned towards their kin beyond the sea; and they turned in good earnest. The new-born sympathy was real; its expression genuine. They themselves did not analyze the motive. Perhaps it was as well they did not, for that adulation which goes forth to those whom success has crowned savors of the Philistine, rather than of the disciples of sweetness and light. None the less it is human; and, moreover, there is much to urge in extenuation of it. But, in this case, the worship of success was but one of the factors which entered into the situation. We ourselves, it must not be forgotten, had, in the years that had passed and the bitter experiences through which we had gone, been largely transmuted. More assured of our position, we had that increased confidence in ourselves which relieved us in a degree of self-consciousness. We had a record, and a future. The national crudeness, so conspicuous in the past, was largely of the past. It was no longer necessary to assert our equality, for our equality was no longer challenged. Thus the change was as much in ourselves as in the estimate held of us by others.

All this we only partially appreciate. In my own case, remembering the situation of a generation back, while I saw how differently they regarded us, I could but be to some extent conscious of a failure to realize how different we had ourselves become. In reality it was much as if, from under the parental roof, a father had watched some rebellious, self-assertive youth, who had gone forth into the world to work out his destiny in his own way and on his own account, not over and above respectful, and setting all precept and experience at defiance. At first, and for a good while, he would be looked at askance; failure would be pronounced his predestined fate. Then, by degrees, as, always asserting his equality, he overcame difficulties, — as he acquired wealth, power, fame, — the father would begin to look with pride on the stalwart, broad-shouldered, big-boned youth, moving on from success to success, achieving victory after victory, ever accomplishing results before pronounced impossible, by processes peculiarly his own working out a great destiny in defiance of rule, but ever changing, developing, ripening as he did so. And gradually that father, however set in his ideas, would undergo a change of heart, not the less real because unconfessed, saying to himself: " This is my offspring, — bone of my bone, flesh of my flesh! And what an extraordinary fellow he is, — and enormously rich withal! "

And this, unless I greatly err, is the process through which Great Britain has gone, — is going; we have gone, and are going. In any event, I now submit it as a tentative explanation of an extremely noticeable recent something, — a manifestation no less unmistakable than suggestive. As a change of demeanor, too, it was not otherwise than agreeable to some of us, as, last month, we sat in quiet reminiscent mood during the ringing plaudits. The " Old Home " had not always welcomed us back in just that way ; we probably were other than we had been ; they certainly looked upon us with more kindly eyes.

IV

AN UNDEVELOPED FUNCTION [1]

"History is past Politics, and Politics are present History." — ED-
WARD A. FREEMAN.
"Politics are vulgar when they are not liberalized by history, and
history fades into mere literature when it loses sight of its relation to
practical politics." — SIR JOHN SEELEY.

HERE are aphorisms from two writers, both justly
distinguished in the field of modern historical research.
Sententious utterances, they would probably, like most
sententious utterances, go to pieces to a greater or less
extent under the test of severe analysis. They will,
however, now serve me sufficiently well as texts.

That politics should find no place at its meetings
is, I believe, the unwritten law of this Association;
and, by politics, I refer to the discussion of those questions of public conduct and policy for the time being
uppermost in the mind of the community. Taking
into consideration the character and purpose of our
body, and the broad basis on which its somewhat loose
membership rests, the rule may be salutary. But
there are not many general propositions not open to
debate; and so I propose on this occasion to call this

---

[1] Address as President of the American Historical Association, delivered at the Annual Meeting of the Association, in Washington,
December 27, 1901. Owing to its length, this address was compressed
in delivery, occupying forty-five minutes only; it was printed, in
part, in the *American Historical Review* for January, 1902, vol. vii.
pp. 203-232.

unwritten law of ours in question. While so doing, moreover, I shall distinctly impinge upon it.

Let us come at once to the point. May it not be possible that the unwritten law, — perhaps it would be better to speak of it as the tacit understanding, — I have referred to, admits of limitations and exceptions both useful and desirable? Is it, after all, necessary, or even, from a point of large view, well considered, thus to exclude from the list of topics to be discussed at meetings of historical associations, and especially of this Association, the problems at the time uppermost in man's thoughts? Do we not, indeed, by so doing abdicate a useful public function, — surrender an educational office; practically admitting by our act that we cannot trust ourselves to discuss political issues in a scholarly and historical spirit? In one word, are not those composing a body of this sort under a species of obligation, in a community like ours, to contribute their share, from the point of view they occupy, to the better understanding of the questions in active political debate? This proposition, as I have said, I now propose to discuss; and, in so doing, I shall, for purposes of illustration, draw freely on present practical politics, — using as object lessons the issues now, or very recently, agitating the minds of not a few of those composing this audience, — indeed, I hope, of all.

I start from a fundamental proposition. The American Historical Association, like all other associations, whether similar in character or not, either exists for a purpose, or it had better cease to be. That purpose is, presumably, to do the best and most effective work in its power in the historical field. I then further,

and with much confidence, submit that the standard
of American political discussion is not now so high as
not to admit of elevation.   On the contrary, while,
comparatively speaking, it ranks well both in tone and
conduct, yet its deficiencies are many and obvious.
That, taken as a whole, it is of a lower grade now
than formerly, I do not assert; though I do assert,
and propose presently to show, that in recent years it
has been markedly lower than it was in some periods
of the past, and periods within my own recollection.
That, however, it is not so high as it should be, —
that it is by no manner of means ideal, — all will, I
think, admit.   If so, that admission suffices for present
purposes.

My next contention is perhaps more open to dispute.   It is a favorite theory now with a certain class
of philosophers, somewhat inclined to the happy-go-
lucky school, that in all things every community gets
about what it asks for, and is qualified to appreciate.
In political discussion — as in railroad or hotel service, and in literature or religion — the supply, as
respects both quality and quantity, responds with sufficient closeness to the demand.   There is, however,
good reason for thinking that, with the American
community which to-day is, or at least with some
sections and elements thereof, this at best specious
theory does not at the present time hold true.   Our
recent political debates have, I submit, been conducted
on a level distinctly below the intelligence of the
constituency; the participants in the debate have not
been equal to the occasion offered them.   Evidence
of this is found in the absence of response.   I think I
am justified in the assertion that no recent political

utterance has produced a real echo, much less a reverberation; and it would not probably be rash to challenge an immediate reference to a single speech, or pointed expression even, which during the last presidential campaign, for instance, impressed itself on the public memory. That campaign, seen through the vista of a twelve-month, was, on the contrary, from beginning to end, with a single exception, creditable neither to the parties conducting it, nor to the audience to whose level it was presumably gauged.

Recall, I pray you, its incidents; already almost forgotten, they come back, when revived by an effort of memory, with a remote, far away echo, as of mockery. In the first place, on neither side were the issues of 1900 clearly defined or well presented; indeed, the long indecision as to what should be accepted as the "paramount issue" was, not remotely, suggestive of a certain very memorable "Hunting of the Snark." Ignoring the personal element which entered so largely into it, as it enters into all canvasses, the favorite argument with one set of orators was the *post ergo propter*, as illustrated in " the Full Dinner Pail; " which argument those of the other side met by fierce denunciation of " Department Stores," and the manifestly pertinent inquiry, addressed to the general auditory, as to what they proposed to do with their sons. The fate in store for their daughters, it was gloomily intimated, would admit of little question, should the opposing candidate. be chosen. So far as what is known as " Labor " is concerned, one candidate posed as the prescriptive protector of American Industry, while the other warmly declared himself in favor of " The Man against the Dollar." The talk from the hustings under this head was irresistibly suggestive of the scene in Dickens's *Old Curiosity Shop*, — the adherents of both candidates stoutly maintained that Codlin was the Workingman's friend, not Short; Short might be very well as far as he went, but the real friend was Codlin.

But, apart from this, the one noticeable feature, possibly the single significant feature of the canvass, was that it distinctly deteriorated as it progressed. It was opened by Mr. Bryan, on the 8th of August, with a speech at Indianapolis which struck a lofty note, promising a high level of discussion. That speech fairly startled the reflecting portion of the community. It seemed for the moment as if the party in power would be forced to reckon seriously with the opposition throughout a sustained debate. How completely this promise failed of realization is fresh in memory. No subsequent utterance on either side made any impression on the public mind. Mr. Bryan, using his audience as a sounding-board, seemed thereafter to bid continually down; and, finally, the contest degenerated into a mere trial of endurance between himself and the talking candidate of the other side, the telegraph day by day recording the number of speeches made by each. A less inspiring competition could hardly be imagined; and, as the papers in flaring, modern-time head-lines declared that Mr. Roosevelt had the previous day broken all records by making eighteen speeches, they went on gravely to announce that Mr. Bryan had arranged a programme for the morrow under which he would " see " his opponent and " go him two better," orating to a square score of distinct audiences between 10 A. M. and midnight.

But was this all the occasion called for? Did our much vaunted American intelligence demand nothing better? *Credat Judæus!* Not for a moment do I believe it. To that canvass, then, I propose presently to return, using it as an object lesson. I shall seek to revive the memory of its issues, — for already they are far advanced on the road to oblivion, — and I shall contrast what I have described as actually occurring with what was easily possible, had that same debate been actively participated in by organizations such as this of ours; organizations whose representative spokesmen would have at least approached the discussion, not in a partisan, but in a scientific spirit. For even active political issues, I contend, freed from the deflection always incident to party prejudice and personal feeling, may be viewed in the light of principle, precedent and experience.

Perhaps, however, I can best illustrate what I have to say, — enforce the lesson I would fain this evening teach, — by approaching it through retrospect. So doing, also, if there is any skill in my treatment, cannot well be otherwise than interesting, for I shall deal with events almost all within the recollection of those yet in middle life. But while those events are sufficiently removed from us to admit of the necessary perspective, having assumed their true proportions to what preceded and has followed, they have an advantage over the occurrences of a year ago; for the controversial embers of 1900 may still be glowing in 1901, — though, I must say, to me the ashes seem white and cold and dead enough. Still, I do not propose to go back to any very remote period, and I shall confine myself to my own recollection, speaking

of that only of which I know, and in which I took
part. My review will begin with the year 1856,
— the year of my graduation, and that in which I
cast my first vote; also one in which a President
was chosen, James Buchanan being the successful candidate.

Under the provisions of our Constitution, a great
national debate is preordained for every fourth year.
The whole policy of the government is thus at fixed
periods challenged and reviewed. Whether, as the
country has expanded and its population multiplied,
while the questions involved in material interests of
ever growing volume have become more complex and
difficult of comprehension, this fixed Olympic period
is wise, or, if wise, that assigned is not too short, are
open questions. I think the period at any rate too
short. Large bodies proverbially move slowly, and
considerable stages of fixity are necessary to adjustment. In the case of so large and complex a body
politic as the United States has now become, four
years are manifestly insufficient for that purpose.
Recent experience has shown such to be the case.
But this is not now to be discussed. For our present
purpose we must take things as they are; and the
fundamental law imposes on us a national political
debate every fourth year, wholly irrespective of circumstance. As 1856 was one of the years thus in
advance assigned, I have now taken part in no less
than twelve presidential canvasses. Approaching them
in a spirit strictly historical, these I propose briefly to
review.

Yet it must be premised that each election does not
represent a debate, — not infrequently it is merely a

stage in a debate. It was so in 1856; it has been so several times since. Indeed, since 1840, — the famous " Log Cabin and Hard Cider " campaign of " Coon-Skin Caps," and " Tippecanoe and Tyler, too," — probably the most humorous, not to say grotesque, episode in our whole national history, that in which the plane of discussion reached its lowest recorded level, — since 1840 there have been only six real debates; the average period of a debate being, therefore, ten years. These debates were (1) that over Slavery, from 1844 to 1864; (2) that over Reconstruction, from 1868 to 1872; (3) Legal Tenders, or " Fiat Money," and Resumption of Specie Payments were the issues in 1876 and 1880; (4) the issue of 1888 and 1892 was over Protection and Free Trade; (5) the debate over Bimetallism and the Demonetization of Silver occurred in 1896; and, finally, (6) Imperialism, as it is called, came to the front in 1900. Since 1856, therefore, the field of discussion has been wide and diversified, — presenting several issues of great moment. Of necessity, also, the debates have assumed many and diverse aspects, — ethical, ethnological, legal, military, economical, financial, historical. The last-named aspect is that which interests us.

In every one of these debates, — and it goes almost without saying, — the historical aspect has been prominent, — it is, indeed, the one aspect which is all-pervasive. And this must be the case just so long as men, yielding respect to precedent, seek guidance from the experience of the past. My purpose is, briefly passing these debates in review, to measure the degree to which the trained historical element in the American community entered into them as an influencing factor, and to estimate the extent to which such an element might have entered into them, with results manifestly beneficial. I shall endeavor to show the great benefit, the elevating influence, which in all these debates, though far more in some than in others, would have been derived from the active participation therein of such an organization as this, — an organization wholly free from party lines, but divided in opinion, which would approach the questions at issue from a point of view distinctly scholarly and scientific. In doing this, let it be always borne in mind that, in scholarship and in science also, unanimity is not to be expected, scarcely to be desired. In the study of history, as in religion and in science, schools differ. The record is voluminous and full of precedents from which very contradictory conclusions, all more or less plausible, may be drawn. In this field, as in others, the great desideratum is to have every side fully and vigorously presented, with a full assurance that the soundest conclusions will survive as being, here also, always the most fit.

The first of these debates, that involving the slavery issue, is now far removed. We can pass upon it historically; for the young man who threw his maiden vote in 1860, when it came to its close, is now nearing his grand climacteric. Of all the debates in our national history that was the longest, the most elevated, the most momentous and the best sustained. It looms up in memory; it projects itself from history. As a whole, it was immensely creditable to the people, — the community at large, — for whose instruction it was conducted. It has left a literature of its own, — economical, legal, moral, political, imaginative. In fiction it produced *Uncle Tom' s Cabin*, still, if one can judge by the test of demand at the desks of our public libraries, one of the most popular books in the English tongue. In the law, it rose to the height of the Dred Scott decision; and, while the rulings in that case laid down have since been reversed, it will not be denied that the discussion of constitutional principles involved, whether at the bar, in the halls of legislatures, in the columns of the press or on the rostrum, was intelligent, of an order extraordinarily high, and of a very sustained interest. It was to the utmost degree educational.

So far as the historical aspect of that great debate is concerned, two things are to be specially noted. In the first place, the moral and economical aspects predominated; and, in the second place, what may be called the historical element as an influencing factor was then in its infancy. Neither in this country nor in Europe had that factor been organized, as it now is. The slavery debate was so long and intense that all the forces then existing were drawn into it. The pulpit, for instance, participated actively. The physiologist was much concerned over ethnological problems, trying to decide whether the African was a human being or an animal; and, if the former, was he of the family of Cain. Thus, all contributed to the discussion; and yet I am unable to point out any distinctly historical contribution of a high order; though, on both sides, the issue was discussed historically with intelligence and research. Especially was this the case in the arguments made before the courts and in the scriptural dissertations; while, on the political side, the speeches of Seward and Sumner, of Jefferson

Davis and A. H. Stephens, leave little to be desired. The climax was, perhaps, reached in the memorable joint debate between Lincoln and Douglas, of which it is not too much to say the country was the auditory. The whole constituted a fit prologue to the great tragedy which ensued.

Beginning, in its closing stage, in January, 1854, when the measure repealing the Missouri Compromise of 1820 was introduced into the Senate of the United States, and closing in December, 1860, with the passage of its ordinance of secession by South Carolina, this debate was continuous for seven years, covering two presidential elections, those of 1856 and 1860. So far as I know, it was *sui generis ;* for it would, I fancy, be useless to look for anything with which to institute a comparison, except in the history of Great Britain. Even there, the discussion which preceded the passage of the Reform Bill of 1832, or that which led up to the repeal of the Corn Laws in 1846, or, finally, the Irish Home Rule agitation between 1871 and 1893, — one and all sink into insignificance beside it. Of the great slavery debate it may then in fine be said that, while the study of history and the lessons to be deduced from history contributed not much to it, it made history, and on history has left a permanent mark.

Of the canvass of 1864, from our point of view little need be said. There was in it no field fruitful for the historical investigator, the issue then presented to the people being of a character altogether exceptional. The result depended less on argument than on the outcome of operations in the field. There was, I presume, during August and September of that year, a wordy debate; but the people were too intent on Sherman as he circumvented Atlanta, and on Sheridan as he sent Early whirling up the valley of the Shenandoah, to give much ear to it. Had this Association then been in existence, and devoted all its energies to elucidating the questions at issue, I cannot pretend to think it would perceptibly have affected the result.

Nor was it greatly otherwise in the canvass of 1868. The country was then stirred to its very depths over the questions growing out of the war. The shattered Union was to be reconstructed; the slave system was to be eradicated. These were great political problems; problems as pressing as they were momentous. For their proper solution it was above all else necessary that they should be approached in a calm, scholarly spirit, observant of the teachings of history. Never was there a greater occasion; rarely has one been so completely lost. The assassination of Lincoln silenced reason; and to reason, and to reason only, does history make its appeal. The unfortunate personality of Andrew Johnson now intruded itself; and, almost at once, what should have been a calm debate degenerated into a furious wrangle. Looking back over the canvass of 1868, and excepting General Grant's singularly felicitous closing of his brief letter of acceptance, — " Let us have peace! " — I think it would be difficult for any one to recall a single utterance of that campaign which produced any lasting impression. The name even of the candidate nominated in opposition to Grant is not readily recalled. In that canvass, as in the preceding one, I should say there was no room for the economist, the philosopher, or the historian. The country had, for the time being, cut loose from both principle and precedent.

The debate over Reconstruction, begun in 1865, did not wear itself out until 1876. In no respect will it bear comparison with that debate over slavery which preceded it. Sufficiently momentous, it was less sustained, less thorough, far less judicial. Towards its close, moreover, as the country wearied, it was gravely complicated by a new issue; for, in 1867, began that currency discussion, destined to last in its various phases through the lifetime of a generation. It thereafter entered, in greater or less degree, into no less than nine consecutive presidential elections, two of which, those of 1876 and 1896, actually turned upon it.

The currency debate presented three distinct phases; first, the proposition, broached in 1867, known as the Greenback theory, under which the interest-bearing bonds of the United States, issued during the Rebellion, were to be paid at maturity in United States legal tender notes, bearing no interest at all. This somewhat amazing proposition was speedily disposed of; for, early in 1869, an act was passed declaring the bonds payable "in coin." But, as was sure to be the case, the so-called "Fiat Money" delusion had obtained a firm lodgment in the minds of a large part of the community, and to drive it out was the work of time. It assumed, too, all sorts of aspects. Dispelled in one form, it reappeared in another. When, for instance, the act of 1869 settled the question as respects the redemption of the bonds, the financial crisis of 1873 reopened it by creating an almost irresistible popular demand for a government paper currency as a permanent substitute for specie. Finally, when, seven years later, this issue was put to rest by a return to specie payments, the over-production of silver, as compared with gold, already foreshadowed the rise of one of the most serious and far-reaching questions which has perplexed modern times. Thus, as the ethical and legal issues, which were the staples of public discussion from 1844 to 1872, were disposed of, or by degrees settled them-selves, a series of monetary questions arose, destined, even if at times in a somewhat languid way, to occupy public attention through thirty years.

Yet there is, in connection with the canvasses of 1876, 1880 and 1884, a suggestive reflection, which, if laid properly to heart, ought to bear fruit in future quadrennials. It is not now easy for those who took part — perhaps an eager and interested part — in those elections, to name off-hand the opposing candi-dates, much less to state the issues upon which the country then divided. It is very suggestive how much less momentous the average presidential choice becomes, the further we get away from it. Finally, we come to realize that, in world development, and even in national life, it would have been very much the same whichever candidate was chosen. Perhaps, after all, this lesson is that of not least historical value to be deduced from the study of well-nigh for-gotten presidential campaigns.

It is difficult to say what the dividing issue of 1876 really was. The country was then slowly re-covering from the business prostration which followed the collapse of 1873. The issues involved in recon-struction, if not disposed of, were clearly worn out.

The country, weary of them, would not respond, turning impatiently from further discussion. Those issues might now settle themselves, or go unsettled; and, though that conclusion was reached thirty years ago, they are not settled yet. The living debate was over material questions, — the cause of the prolonged business depression, and the remedy for it. The favorite specific was, at first, a recourse to paper money : the government printing-press was to set it in motion ; and even hard-money Democrats of the Jacksonian school united with radical Republicans of the Reconstruction period in guaranteeing a resultant prosperity. Again, the teachings of history were ignored. What, it was contemptuously exclaimed in the Senate, do we care for " abroad " ? From this calamity the country had been saved by the veto of President Grant in 1874 ; and, the following year, an act was passed looking to the resumption of specie payments on the 1st of January, 1879. Seventeen years of suspension were then to close. Over this measure, the parties nominally joined issue in 1876. The Republicans, nominating Governor Hayes of Ohio, demanded the fulfilment of the promise ; the Democrats, nominating Governor Tilden of New York, insisted on the repeal of the law. Yet it was well understood that the candidate of the Democracy favored the policy of which the law in debate was the concrete expression. The contest was thus in reality one between the " ins " and the " outs." We all remember how it resulted, and the terrible strain to which our machinery of government was in consequence subjected. In the wrangle which ensued, the material and business interests of the country recuperated in a natural way, just as had repeatedly been the case before, and more than once since ; and the United States then entered on a new era of increased prosperity. This brought the paper money debate to a close. The issues presented had, in the course of events, settled themselves.

But, not the less for that, in the canvass of 1876 a field of great political usefulness was opened up to the historical investigator ; a field which, I submit, he failed adequately to develop. A public duty was left unperformed. It was in connection with what John Stuart Mill has in one of his *Dissertations and Discussions* happily denominated "The Currency Juggle." From time immemorial, to tamper with the established measures of value has been the constant practice of men of restless and unstable mind, honest or dishonest, whether rulers or aspirants to rule. History is replete with instances. To cite them was the function of the historical investigator ; to marshal them, and bring them to bear on the sophistries of the day, was the business of the politician. A professorial discussion in a meeting of such an organization as this would then have been much to the point ; and yet, curiously enough, a new historical precedent was about to be worked out. That was then to be done which had never been done before, — a country which had gone to the length the United States had gone in the direction of "fiat money" — two thirds of the way to repudiation — was actually to retrace its steps, and resume payments in specie at the former standards of value. History would have been searched in vain for a parallel experience.

The administration of President Hayes was curiously epochal. During it the so-called " carpet-bag governments " disappeared from the southern states; the country resumed payments in specie ; and, on the 28th of February, 1878, Congress passed, over the veto of the President, an act renewing the coinage of silver dollars, the stoppage of which, five years before, constituted what was destined thereafter to be referred to as " the crime of 1873." This issue, however, matured slowly. Public men, having recourse to palliatives, temporized with it ; and, through four presidential elections it lay dormant, except in so far as parties pledged themselves to action calculated, in the well-nigh idiotic formula of politicians, to " do something for silver." The canvasses of 1880 and 1884 are, therefore, devoid of historical interest. The first turned largely on the tariff ; and yet, curiously enough, the single utterance in that debate which has left a mark on the public memory was the wonderful dictum of General Hancock, the candidate of the defeated opposition, that the tariff was a local issue, which, a number of years before, had excited a good deal of interest in his native state of Pennsylvania. The gallant and picturesque soldier, metamorphosed into a political leader *pro hac vice*, simply harked back to the " Log Cabin " and "Coon-Skin " campaign of 1840, when, a youth of sixteen, he was on his way to West Point.

Nor is the recollection of the debate of 1884 much more inspiring. It was a lively contest enough, under Grover Cleveland and James G. Blaine as opposing candidates ; — a struggle between the " outs " to get in, and the " ins " not to go out. But a single formula connected with it comes echoing down the corridors of time, the alliterative "Rum, Romanism, and Rebellion" of the unfortunate Burchard. An interlude in the succession of great national debates, the canvass of 1884 called for no application of the lessons of history.

That of 1888, presenting at last an issue, rose to the dignity of debate. In his annual message of the previous December, the President, in disregard of all precedent, had confined his attention not only to the tariff, but to a single feature in the tariff, the duty on wool. In so doing he had, as the well-understood candidate of his party for reëlection, flung down the gauntlet ; for, only three years before, the Republican party, in its quadrennial declaration of articles of cardinal political faith, had laid heavy emphasis on "the importance of sheep industry," and "the danger threatening its future prosperity." The opposition had thus pledged itself to "do something" for wool, as well as for silver ; and the President now struck at wool as "the Tariff-arch Keystone." But, while in this debate the economist came to the front, there was no pronounced call and, indeed, small opportunity for the historian. The silver issue was in abeyance ; the pension list and civil service were not calculated to incite to investigation ; nor had history much to say on either topic. As to the "sheep industry," now so much in evidence, the British woolsack might afford a text suggestive of curious learning in connection with England's once greatest staple, — how, for instance, as a protective measure, it was by one Parliament solemnly ordained that the dead should be buried in woollens ; but it will readily be admitted that the historic spirit does not kindle over tariff schedules. The lessons of experience to be drawn from revenue tables appeal rather to the school of Adam Smith than to the disciples of Gibbon.

Returning to the review of our national debates, in that of 1892 the shadow of coming events was plainly perceptible. The tariff issue had now lost its old significance; for the infant industries had developed into trade and legislation-compelling trusts. These were suggestive of new and, as yet, inchoate problems; but to them the constituency was not yet prepared intelligently to address itself. Populism was rife, with its crude and restless theories; a crisis in the history of the precious metals was clearly impending, with the outcome in doubt; indiscriminate and unprecedented pension-giving had reduced an overflowing exchequer to the verge of bankruptcy. The debate of 1892 accordingly dropped back to the politician's level, — that of 1876, 1880 and 1884. In it there was nothing of any educational value; nothing that history will dwell upon. The " ins " pointed with pride; the " outs " sternly arraigned the " ins; " while the student, whether of economics or history, there found small place and a listless audience. The memory of the canvass which resulted in the second administration of Cleveland is quite obliterated by the issues, altogether unexpected, which the ensuing years precipitated.

Of quite another character were the two canvasses of 1896 and 1900. Still fresh in memory, the echoes of these have indeed not yet ceased to reverberate; — and I assert without hesitation that, not since 1856 and 1860, has this people passed through two such wholesome and educational experiences. In 1896 and in 1900, as in the debates of forty years previous, there was a place, and a large place, for the student, whether investigator or philosopher. Great problems, — problems of law, of economics and ethics, problems involving peace and war, and the course of development in the oldest as in the newest civilizations, — had to be discussed, on the way to a solution. That the prolonged debate running through those eight years was at all equal to the occasion, I do not think can be claimed. Even his most ardent admirers will hardly claim that Mr. Bryan in 1896 and 1900 rose to the level reached by Lincoln forty years before ; nor do the utterances of Mr. Roosevelt, Mr. Depew, or Mr. Hanna bear well a comparison with those of Seward, Trumbull and Sumner. And that this momentous, many-sided debate failed to rise to the proper height was due, I now unhesitatingly submit, to the predominance in it of the political " Boss," and the absence from it of the scholar. In it, those belonging to this association, and to other associations similar in character to this, did not play their proper part, — they proved themselves unequal to the occasion. Indeed, in the whole wordy canvass of 1896, I now recall but two instances of the professor or philosopher distinctively taking the floor ; but both of those were memorable. They imparted an elevation of tone to discussion, immediately and distinctly perceptible, in the press and on the platform. I refer to the single utterance of Carl Schurz, before a small audience at Chicago, on the 5th of September, and to the subsequent publications of President Andrew D. White, in which, from his library at Ithaca, he drew freely on the stores of historical experience in crushing refutation of demagogical campaign sophistry. Amid the petulant chat-

tering of the political magpies, it was refreshing to
hear those clear-cut, incisive utterances, — calm,
thoughtful, well-reasoned. I have been told that in
its various forms of republication, no less than five
millions, and some authorities say ten millions, of copies
of that Chicago speech of Mr. Schurz were then put
in circulation. It was indeed a masterly production,
— a production in which a high keynote was struck,
and sustained. But the suggestive and extremely encouraging fact in connection with it was the response
it elicited. Delivering himself at the highest level to
which he could attain, Mr. Schurz was only on a level
with his audience. To the political optimist that fact
spoke volumes ; it revealed infinite possibilities.

Twelve presidential canvasses and six great national
debates have thus been passed in rapid review. It is
as if, in the earlier history of the country, we had run
the gamut from Washington to Van Buren. Taken as
a whole, — viewed in gross and perspective, the retrospect leaves much to be desired. That the debates
held in Ireland and France during the same time have
been on a distinctly lower level, I at once concede.
Those held in Great Britain and Germany have not
been on a higher. Yet ours have at best been only rela-
tively educational ; as a rule extremely partisan, they
have been personal, often scurrilous, and more frequently still, I regret greatly to find myself compelled
to say, intentionally deceptive. A singular feature
in them has been the noticeable fact that where,
from time to time, the clergy have intervened, their
so doing has not tended to elevate. They have been
conspicuous neither for moderation nor for charity,

while they actually seemed to revel in their ignorance of the teachings of the past. One fact in the
review is, however, salient. With the exception of
the first, — that of 1856–60, — not one of the debates reviewed has left an utterance which, were it
to die from human memory, would by posterity be
accounted a loss. This, I am aware, is a sweeping
allegation ; in itself almost an indictment. Yet, with
some confidence, I challenge a denial. Those here are
not, as a rule, in their first youth, and they have all
of them been more or less students of history. Let
each pass in rapid mental review the presidential canvasses in which he has in any degree participated, and
endeavor to recall a single utterance which has stood
the test of time, as marking a distinct addition to mankind's intellectual belongings, — the classics of the
race. It has been at best a babel of the commonplace.
I do not believe one utterance can be named for which
a life of ten years will be predicted. Such a record
undeniably admits of improvement. Two questions,
then, naturally suggest themselves : — To what has
this shortcoming been due ? — Wherein lies the
remedy for it ?

The shortcoming, I submit, is in greatest part due
to the fact that the work of discussion has been left
almost wholly to the journalist and the politician, —
the professional journalist and the professional politician. And in the case of both, there has in this
country, during the last forty years, been, so far as
grasp of principle is concerned, a marked tendency to
deterioration. Nor, I fancy, is the cause of this far to
seek. It is found in the growth, increased complexity,
and irresistible power of organization as opposed to

individuality, — in the parlance of the day, it is the all-potency of the machine over the man; equally noticeable whether by that word, "machine," we refer to the political organization or to the newspaper.

Let the last be considered first. The daily journal — the newspaper — is indisputably the one far-reaching organ of popular political education. Through its columns, as a medium, the teachings of those who think on all subjects — educational, religious, moral, political — percolate slowly, and, as a rule, in a very diluted form, finding thus at last lodgment and acceptance in the public thought. They are slowly assimilated. But the newspaper of to-day is altogether the product of the last century — almost of the last half of the century. Practically brought into being by James Gordon Bennett and Horace Greeley during "the forties," it then, and for nearly thirty years after, represented an editorial individuality, of which Greeley was the highest type. From 1841 to 1872, Horace Greeley was the New York *Tribune;* and the New York *Tribune* during those years was the greatest educational factor — economically and morally — this country has ever known. The protective tariff is its monument, *ære perennius.* The *Tribune* still exists; but the *Tribune* of to-day is no longer the organ of one man. A news medium, owned by a syndicate, its utterances shaped by a business management — an editorial Aulic Council — are turned out by the yard by salaried ready writers, — quill-drivers of fortune, — whose necessary fate it is always to strive to reduce superficiality to a system. "By journalism," a modern writer of much acumen says, " is to be understood, I suppose, writing for pay on matters of which you are ignorant;" [1]

[1] Leslie Stephen, *Letters of John Richard Green,* p. 66.

and, as an evolution, the modern newspaper is the necessary outcome of existing conditions. A financial combination controls a most intricate, costly and influential machine. Since 1872 the intense, widely pervasive personality of Horace Greeley has given place to the ordered and stereotyped utterances of the *Tribune's* editorial staff.

Mutatis mutandis, it is the same in politics. As Tennyson wrote two generations ago : —

" The individual withers, and the world is more and more."

The intricacy of modern political life, the magnitude of interests and expenditure, the cohesive power of plunder, the number of those who make of political life a breadwinning trade, the size of the constituency, — all these concurring conditions have resulted in a state of affairs in which " the machine," of necessity, predominates. Among the qualities which go to constitute that natural aptitude calculated to win success in public life, — to secure office and retention in office, — grasp of principle, or a philosophical or statesmanlike turn of mind, no longer find a place. What is needed is the faculty of managing men, combining interests, or conforming to tendencies. In a word, what is vulgarly but most expressively known as the " Boss " is, in our American public life, the logical outcome of the syndicate and machine principle applied to existing political conditions. The " Boss " is, in fact, to America what the Imperator was to Rome. It is the master mechanic with his hand on the lever ; but, as the machine responds to his touch, the individual is eliminated.

This tendency of the day, few, I think, deny. Indeed, all must recognize the growth of combination.

It can be studied everywhere, save in the highest forms of art and thought. Syndicates cannot turn out great poems, or noble statues, or attain to a deep insight. In letters, their power is confined to the profuse manufacture of printed matter, — dictionaries, blue-books, coöperative histories, and the like. But we have now to do only with the political life, and the higher educational forces there in action, or possible to bring into action in any emergency; and the increased power of the machine in that field, I take to be one of the indications of the time, not less unmistakable than significant. Machine work always has a degenerating tendency. The more powerful the machine, the more it inclines to self-aggrandization and the perpetuation of abuse. A perfect machine is as nearly soulless as may be. Such a machine was the Church of Rome in the days of Voltaire and the Calas tragedy; such a machine is the French army now, as exemplified in the Dreyfus affair, and the experience therein of Zola. The tendency from the individual towards the machine, in American journalism and public life, cannot be denied. It distinctly does not promote a loftier, a more liberal and scholarly tone of discussion; on the contrary, it works always in the opposite way.

This being so, in what direction may we look for the corrective agency? In a body politic, so full of vitality, so instinct with life, as that of ours, each evil works its own cure. The remedial action is apt to reveal itself in unexpected quarters, and in shapes not at once recognized; but, unless the body politic is decadent, it is as sure to assert itself as it is in the case of disease in a physical organization not moribund.

That those who philosophize and prescribe in this

and kindred cases generally reach wrong conclusions
is quite indisputable; it is safe, indeed, to say that
they do so in more than nine cases out of ten. As
Mr. Disraeli long since sagely observed, "It is the
unexpected which is apt to occur." In the present
case I wish, therefore, in advance, to acknowledge that
I am probably quite wide of the mark in both my
diagnosis of the disease and my forecast of the remedy.
That remedy, moreover, when it comes, will, I am
confident, not be in the nature of some ingenious discovery, — an invention which might admit of letters
patent. On the contrary, it will be an evolution, — the
natural development of internal healing force asserting
itself to meet a pathological condition. Not posing
here, therefore, as a physician prescribing a sure cure
of his own devising, but as an observer of conditions
and symptoms, I propose to point out, so far as my
observation and insight enable me so to do, the indications of a self-curative process already asserting itself.

The source of trouble being located in the tendency
to excessive organization, it would seem natural that
the counteracting agency should be looked for in an
exactly opposite direction; that is, in the increased
efficacy of individualism. Of this, I submit, it is not
necessary to go far in search of indications. Take, for
instance, the examples already referred to, of Mr.
Schurz and President White, in the canvass of 1896;
and suppose, for a moment, efforts such as theirs then
were, made more effective as resulting from the organized action of an association like this. Our platform
at once becomes a rostrum, — and a rostrum from
which a speaker of reputation and character is insured
a wide hearing. His audience, too, is present to listen

and repeat. From such a rostrum, the observer, the professor, the student — be it of economy, of history, or of philosophy — might readily be brought into immediate contact with the issues of the day. So bringing him is but a step. He would appear, also, in his proper character and place, — the scholar having his say in politics; but always as a scholar, not as an office-holder, nor an aspirant for office. His appeal would be to intelligence and judgment, not to passion or self-interest, or even to patriotism. The elements are all there; the question is only as to a method of effective concentration. It must, I submit, be sought for here on the floor of the academy, and not in the confusion of the caucus.

A due sense of political proportion might then become possible. Heretofore, the view customarily taken has been too narrow and too close. The continuity of movement has been ignored, and the true relation of things intentionally distorted. The effort has uniformly been to give each contest, in so far as possible, a crucial aspect. All has been made to depend on that particular cast of the dice. The future of the race, one would suppose, rests on the outcome of some struggle, in which, in fact, those immediately participating are alone concerned. The retrospect I have just invited you to tells a very different story. Sixteen presidential elections, and only six national debates in sixty years! The issues, moreover, involved in those debates have in most cases been settled, not on the hustings or in Congress, but by the course of events, — the logic of the philosopher, the scientist, or the economist. Illustrations of this, also, are not far to seek. In the journal of the day on which I am writing these words, I find, for instance, a confession of faith by a United States Senator, in which he indulges in this, for a politician, refreshing form of speech, — " In 1896 we had a campaign on the money question. Everything was depressed, — idleness, discontent, distrust and misery, everywhere. We were told that the salvation of the country depended upon the free coinage of silver. I believed then, and I believe now, that theoretically we were right; but new and unforeseen forces came into play, and I have enough sense to recognize the fact that the restoration of confidence about which Mr. Cleveland talked, and about which I did not know enough at the time to understand, the discovery of gold in the Klondike, the influx of money seeking investment from abroad, and the increase of banking facilities, have, for the time being at least, settled the money question, and nobody but a fool would make a ' free silver' speech now." What did the politicians have to do with the restoration of confidence? It was the work of time, and of the producing and business community. What did they have to do with the discoveries in the Klondike? or with the cyanide treatment of refractory ores? or with the increase of capital, seeking employment itself and giving employment to labor? Throughout that long and momentous debate, I submit, so far as the result was concerned and the record shows, our statesmen and journalists remind us only of Burke's famous metaphor of the dozen grasshoppers making the field ring with their importunate chink, while thousands of great cattle, chewing the cud, silently repose under the shadow of the British oak. Looking back over the whole period that is gone since that

April day thirty-six years ago, when Grant and Lee, at Appomattox, brought the conflict in the field to a close, and speaking in perfect moderation, I cannot point to one single beneficial result of a positive character which can properly be classed as political. As a species of safety-valve, political debate has, I admit, been of infinite service. Unending, and mostly idle in character, it has prevented ill-considered and precipitate action, and given natural influences time in which to work out their results. Beyond this, what can be put to its credit? Take the debates in their order. The political Congressional reconstruction of the slaveholding and rebellious South has certainly failed to bear the test of time. What was then done has since been undone, and the section concerned is even now groping its way, painfully, and with no excess of intelligence and humanity, towards a more practical and better-considered solution. Thanks to a providential veto, the great currency debate ended in an absolutely do-nothing policy. Of the tariff debate I will not speak. Stretching through a whole century, it once brought the country to the verge of civil war, and its history is read in a vast literature of its own, — a veritable Serbonian bog of sophistry, saturated with bad rhetoric. The practical outcome, as studied in our last general tariff revision, has not been deemed specially creditable to American political disinterestedness or scientific fiscal thought. Our pension list is, indeed, a monument, but scarcely of public liberality judiciously exercised. Finally, the advocates of free-silver coinage, having erased from the statute-book that "Sherman-bill" which they themselves had inscribed there, confess that "a fool" only would be guilty of " a silver speech " now. Congress has all along been but a clumsy recording machine of conclusions worked out in the laboratory and machine-shop; and yet the idea is still deeply seated in the minds of men, otherwise intelligent, that, to effect political results, it is necessary to hold office, or at least to be a politician, and to be heard from the hustings. Is not the exact reverse more truly the case? The situation may not be, indeed it certainly is not, as it should be; it may be, I hold that it is, unfortunate that the scholar and investigator are finding themselves more and more excluded from public life by the professional with an aptitude for the machine: but the result is none the less patent. On all issues of real moment, — issues affecting anything more than a division of the spoils, or the concession of some privilege of exaction from the community, — it is the student, the man of affairs and the scientist who, to-day, in last resort, closes debate and shapes public policy. His, the last word. How to organize and develop his means of influence is the question.

> " Here 's what should strike, could one handle it cunningly :
> Help the axe, give it a helve ! "

So far as the historian is concerned, this association is, I submit, the helve to the axe.

Of this the presidential election which closed just a year ago affords an apt illustration, ready at hand. No better could be asked for. What might then well have been? The American Historical Association, as I have already said, is composed of those who have felt a call for the investigation and treatment of historical problems. Its members — largely instructors in our advanced education — feel that keen interest in the issues of the day, natural and proper in all good citizens, irrespective of calling. They want to contribute their share to discussion ; and, in that way, to influence results, so far as in them lies. From every conceivable point of view it is most desirable that they should have facilities for so doing. I hold, therefore, that, in the last presidential canvass, a special meeting of this association, called to discuss the issues then pending, might well have tended to the better general and popular comprehension of those issues, and to the elevation of that debate. Conducted on academic principles, and looking to no formal expression of results in any enunciated platform of principles, such a gathering would have exercised an influence, as perceptible as beneficial, in lifting the discussion up into the domain of philosophy and research. It would have brought to bear the lessons of the past on the questions of the day. In any event, it would certainly not have descended to that contemptible *post ergo propter* formula, which, on the one side or the other, has in every presidential canvass been the main staple of argument.

What were the issues of the last presidential canvass ? — on what questions did its debate turn ? Three in number, they were, I think, singularly inviting to those historically minded. To the reflecting man the matter first in importance was what is known as " Imperialism," — the problem forced upon our consideration by the outcome of the war with Spain. Next I should place the questions of public policy involved in the rapid agglomerations of capital, popularly denominated " Trusts." Finally, the silver issue still lingered at the front, a legacy from the canvass of four years previous. The debate of 1900 is a thing of the past. Each of those issues can now be discussed, as it might well then have been discussed, in the pure historical spirit. Let us take them up in their inverse order.

Historically speaking, I hold there were two distinct sides to the silver question ; and, moreover, on the face of the record, the advocates of bimetallism, as it was called, had in 1896 the weight of the argument wholly in their favor. In his very suggestive work entitled *Democracy and Liberty*, Mr. Lecky referred to the discovery of America as producing, among other far-reaching effects, one which he considers most momentous of all. To quote his words : — " The produce of the American mines created, in the most extreme form ever known in Europe, the change which beyond all others affects most deeply and universally the material well-being of man : it revolutionized the value of the precious metals, and, in consequence, the price of all articles, the effects of all contracts, the burden of all debts." This was during the sixteenth century, — the years following the great event of 1492. Again, the world went through a similar experience within our own memories, in consequence of the California and Australia gold-finds, between 1848 and 1852. These revolutions were due to natural causes, and came about gradually. They were also of a stimulating character. From the beginning of modern commercial times, however, to the close of the last century, the exchanges of all civilized communities had been based on the precious metals ; and silver had been quite as much as gold a precious metal for monetary purposes. Shortly after 1870 the policy of demonetizing silver was entered upon; and, in 1873, the United States gave in its adhesion to that policy. Thereafter, in the great system of international exchanges, silver ceased to be counted a part of that specie reserve on which draughts were made. Thenceforth, the drain, as among the financial centres, was to be on gold alone. In the whole history of man, no precedent for such a step was to be found. So far as the United States was concerned, the basis on which its complex and delicate financial fabric rested was weakened by one half; and the cheaper and more accessible metal, that to which the debtor would naturally have recourse in discharge of his obligations, was made unavailable. It could further be demonstrated that, without a complete readjustment of currencies and values, the world's accumulated stock and annual production of gold could not, as a monetary basis, be made to suffice for its needs. A continually recurring contest for gold among the great financial centres was inevitable. A change which, in the language of Lecky, "beyond all others affects most deeply and universally the material well-being of man," had been unwittingly challenged. The only question was, — Would the unexpected occur? — Then, if it did occur, what might be anticipated? Such was the silver issue, as it presented itself in 1896. On the facts, the weight of argument was clearly with the advocates of the continued use of silver.

Four years later, in 1900, the unexpected had occurred. As then resumed, the debate was replete with interest. The lessons of 1492 and 1848 had a direct bearing on the present, and, in the light by them shed, the outcome could be forecast almost with certainty; but it was a world-question. Japan, China, Hindostan entered into the problem, in which also both Americas were factors. It was a theme to inspire Burke, stretching back, as it did, from this latter day light to the middle age darkness, and involving the whole circling globe. Rarely has any subject called for more intelligent and comprehensive investigation; rarely has one been more confused and befogged by a denser misinformation. The discoverer and scientist, moving hand in hand, had, during the remission of the debate, been getting in their work, and, under the magic touch of their silent influence, the world's gold production rose by leaps and bounds. Less than ten millions of ounces in 1896, in 1899 it had nearly touched fifteen millions; and, in money value, it alone then exceeded the combined value of the gold and silver production of the earlier period. What did this signify? — History was only repeating itself. The experiences of the first half of the sixteenth century and the middle decennaries of the nineteenth century were to be emphasized on the threshold of the twentieth.

So much for the silver question and its possible treatment. In the discussion of 1900, the last word in the debate of 1896 remained to be uttered. A page in history, both memorable and instructive, was to be turned. Next trusts, — those vast aggregations of capital in the hands of private combinations, constituting practical monopolies of whole branches of industry, and of commodities necessary to man. Was the world to be subject to taxation at the will of a moneyed syndicate? The debate of a year ago over this issue, if debate it may be called, is still very recent. In it the lessons of history were effectually ignored ; and yet, if applied, they would have been sufficiently suggestive. The historian was as conspicuous for his absence as the demagogue was in evidence.

The cry was against monopoly and the monopolist, — a cry which, as it has been ringing through all recorded times, suggests for the historical investigator a wide and fruitful field. Curiously enough, the first lesson to be derived from labor in that field is a paradox. Practically, so far as extortion is concerned, there is almost nothing in common between the old-time monopoly and the modern trust. Of examples of the first, the record is monotonously full. Mere agents of the government, sometimes the favorites of the Crown, the whole machinery of the state has time out of mind been put at the service of monopolists to enable them to exact tribute from all. To the student of English history the names and misdeeds of Sir Francis Michell and Sir Giles Mompesson at once suggest themselves ; while others, more familiar with the drama, recall Sir Giles Overreach, or that powerful scene in Ruy Blas in which the Spanish courtiers wrangle together, coming almost to blows, over a partition among themselves of the right to extort. The old system still survives. For example, in France to-day the manufacture and sale of salt is a government monopoly. A prime necessity of life, no person not specially authorized may engage in the production of salt, or import it into France. If a peasant woman, living on the sea-coast of Brittany or Normandy, endeavors to procure salt for her family by the slow process of evaporating a pailful of sea-water in the sun, she is engaged in an illicit trade, and becomes amenable to law. Her salt will certainly, if found, be confiscate. So of improved pocket matches. In France, their manufacture is a government revenue monopoly. They are notoriously bad. Those made and sold in Great Britain are, on the contrary, noted for excellence. If, however, passing from England to France, a box of British matches is found in the pocket of a traveller, it is taken from him and the contents are destroyed at once ; indeed, he is fortunate if he escapes the payment of a fine. This is monopoly ; the whole strength of a government being put forth to exact an artificial profit on the sale of a commodity in general use. There is a historical literature pertaining to the subject, — a lamentation, and an ancient tale of wrong.

Into that literature I do not propose to enter. It is familiar ; and fully explains the deadly effect of the word " Monopoly " to-day, or of the opprobrious term " Monopolist," when flung as a missile from the hustings. It is an epithet suggestive of a branding-iron, and of the scars of burns, the recollection of which is imbedded in the popular mind.

The curious feature in the present discussion — that which in the thought of the student of things as opposed to words imparts a special interest to it — is that, while the trust, or vast aggregation of capital and machinery of production in the hands of individuals designed to the end that competition may be brought under control, is in fact the modern form of monopoly, it is in its methods and results the direct opposite of the old-time monopoly ; for, whereas the purpose and practice of that was to extort from all purchasers an artificial price for an inferior article through the suppression of competitors, the first law of its existence for the modern trust is, through economies and magnitude of production, to supply to all buyers a better article at a price so low that other producers are driven from the market. The ground of popular complaint against the trust is, not that it exacts an inordinate profit on what it sells, but that it sells so low that the small manufacturer or merchant is deprived of his trade. This distinction, with a difference, explains at once the wholly futile character of the politician's outcry against trusts. It is easy, for instance, to denounce from the platform the magnates of the Sugar Trust to a sympathizing audience ; and yet not one human being in that audience, his sympathies to the contrary notwithstanding, will the next morning pay a fraction of a cent more per pound for his sugar, that, by so doing, he may help to keep alive some struggling manufacturer, who advertises that his product does not bear the trust stamp.

As to the outcome of conflicts of this character, history is a monotony. They can have but one result, — an industrial readjustment. A single familiar illustration will suffice. Any one who chooses to turn back to it can read the story of the long conflict between the spinning-wheel and the loom. Formerly, and not so very far back, the distaff and spinning-wheel were to be seen in every house ; homespun was the common wear. To-day, the average man or woman has never seen a distaff, nor heard the hum of a spinning-wheel. Ceasing long since to be a commodity, homespun would be sought for in vain. Yet the struggle between the loom of the manufacturing trust and the old dame's spinning-wheel was, literally, for the latter, a fight to the death; for, in that case, the livelihood of the operator was at stake. Her time was worth absolutely nothing, except at the wheel. She must needs work for any wage; on it depended her bread. A vast domestic, industrial readjustment was involved; one implying untold human suffering. The result was, however, never for an instant in doubt. The trust of that day was left in undisputed control of the field; and it always must, and always will be, just so long as it supplies purchasers with a better article, at a lower price than they had to pay before. The process does not vary; the only difference is that each succeeding readjustment is on a larger scale, and more far-reaching in its effects.

Such, stripped of its verbiage and appeals to sympathy, is the trust proposition. But the popular apprehension always has been, as it now is, that this supply of the better article at a lower price will continue only until the producer — the monopolist — has secured a complete mastery of the situation. Capital, it is argued, is selfish and greedy; corporations are proverbially soulless and insatiable; and, as soon as competition is eliminated, nature will assert itself. Prices will then be raised so as to assure inordinate gains; and when, in consequence of such profits, fresh competitors enter the field, they will either be crushed out of existence by a temporary reduction in price, or absorbed in the trust.

All this has a plausible sound; and of it, as a theory of practical outcome, the politician can be relied upon to make the most. On this head, however, what has the historical investigator to say? His will be the last word in that debate also; his, the verdict which will be final. The lessons bearing on this contention to be drawn from the record cover a wide field of both time and space; they also silence discussion. They tend indisputably to show that the dangers depicted are imaginary. The subject must, of course, be approached in an unprejudiced spirit, and studied in a large, comprehensive way. Permanent tendencies are to be dealt with; and exceptional cases must be instanced, classified, and allowed for. Attempts, more or less successful, at extortion, in a confidence of mastery, can unquestionably be pointed out; but, in the history of economical development, it is no less unquestionable that, on the large scale and in the long run, every new concentration has been followed by a permanent reduction of price in the commodity affected thereby. The world's needs are continually supplied at a lower cost to the world. Again, the larger the concentration, the cheaper the product; until now a new truth of the market-place has become established and obtained general acceptance, — a truth of the most far-reaching consequence, — the truth that the largest returns are found in quick sales at small profits. To manage successfully one of those great and complex industrial combinations calls for exceptional administrative capacity in individuals, — for men of quick perception, and masterful tempers. These men must be able correctly to read the lessons of experience, and, accepting the facts of the situation, they must find out how most exactly to adapt themselves to those facts. No theorist, be he politician or philosopher, appreciates so clearly as does the successful trust executive the fundamental laws of being of the interests he has in charge. Such have good cause to know that, under conditions now prevailing, competition is the sure corollary of the attempted abuse of control; and, moreover, that the largest ultimate returns on capital, as well as the ónly real security from competition, are found, not in the disposal of a small product at a large profit, but in a large output at prices which encourage consumption. Throwing exceptional cases and temporary conditions out of consideration, as not affecting final results, the historical investigator will probably on this subject find himself much at variance with the political canvasser. That the last will get worsted in the argument hardly need be said.

Does history furnish any instance of a financial, an industrial, or a commercial enterprise — a bank, a factory, or an importing company — ever having been powerful enough long to regulate the price of any commodity regardless of competition, except when acting in harmony with and supported by governmental power? Is not the monopolist practically impotent, unless he has the constable at his call? To answer this question absolutely would be to deduce a law of the first importance from the general experience of mankind. So doing would call for a far more careful examination than is now in my power to make, were it even within the scope of my ability; but, if my supposition prove correct, the corollary to be drawn therefrom is to us as a body politic, and at just this juncture, one of the first and most far-reaching import. In such case, the modern American trust, also, so far as it enjoys any power as a monopoly, or admits of abuse as such, must depend for that power, and the opportunity of abuse, solely on governmental support and coöperation. Its citadel is then the custom-house. The moment the aid of the United States revenue officer is withheld, the American monopolist would cease to monopolize except in so far as he could defy competition by always supplying a better article at a price lower than any other producer in the whole world. And here, having deduced and formulated this law, the purely historical investigator would find himself trenching on the province of the economist. The so-called protective system would now be in question. Thus again, as so often before, the tariff would become the paramount issue. But the tariff would no longer stand in the popular mind as the beneficent protector of domestic enterprise; it would on the contrary be there closely associated with the idea of monopoly, it would be assailed as the stronghold of the trust. From the historical and economical point of view, however, the debate would not because of that undergo any diminution of interest. Whatever the politician might in the course of that debate assert, or the opportunist incorporate into legislation, we may rest assured that this issue will ultimately settle itself in accordance with those irresistible underlying influences which result in what we know as natural evolution. History is but the record of the adjustment of mankind in the past to the outcome of those influences; and, in this respect, when all is said and done, it is tolerably safe to predict that the future will present no features of novelty. If, then, we can measure correctly the nature of the influences at work, the character, as well as the extent, of the impending readjustment may be surmised. For such a diagnosis the historian and economist must furnish the data.

It remains to pass on to the third and last of the matters in debate during 1900 — that known as Imperialism. This was the really great issue before the American people then, and, I submit, it is the really great issue before them now. That issue, moreover, I with confidence submit, can be intelligently considered only from the historical standpoint. Indeed, unless approached through the avenues of human experience, it is not even at once apparent how the question, as it now confronts us, arose, and injected itself into our political action ; and, accordingly, it is in some quarters even currently assumed that it is there only fortuitously, — a feature in the great chapter of accidents, — a passing incident, which may well disappear as mysteriously and as suddenly as it came. Studied historically, I do not think this view of the situation will bear examination. On the contrary, I fancy even the most superficial investigator, if actuated in his inquiry by the true historical spirit, would soon reach the conclusion that the issue so recently forced upon us had been long in preparation, was logical and inevitable, and, for our good or our evil, must be decided, rightly or wrongly, on a large view of great and complex conditions. In other words, there may be reason to conclude that an inscrutable law of nature, at last involving us, has long been, and now is, evolving results. It is one more phase of natural evolution, working itself out, as in the case of Rome twenty-five centuries ago, through the survival and supremacy of the fittest.

I need hardly say, I feel myself now venturing on a dangerous generalization ; and yet I do not see how the American investigator, who endeavors to draw his conclusions from history, can recoil from the venture. His deductions will probably be erroneous, — indeed, they are sure to be so to some extent ; — and, in making them, he is more than likely to make a not inconsiderable display of superficial knowledge. None the less, even if it be of small value, he is bound to offer what he has. If the seed that sower sows bears no fruit, it can do small harm.

Mr. Leslie Stephen, in one of his essays, truly enough says, " The Catholic and the Protestant, the Conservative and the Radical, the Individualist and the Socialist, have equal facility in proving their own doctrines with arguments, which habitually begin, ' All history shows.' Printers should be instructed always to strike out that phrase as an erratum; and to substitute, ' I choose to take for granted.' " And elsewhere the same writer lays it down as a general proposition that " Arguments beginning ' All history shows' are always sophistical." [1] What is by some known as the doctrine of Manifest Destiny is, I take it, identical with what others, more piously minded, refer to as the Will, or Call, of God. The Mohammedan and the modern Christian gospel-monger say, " God clearly calls us " to this or that work ; and with a conscience perfectly clear, they then proceed to rob, oppress and slay. In like manner, the political buccaneer and land-pirate proclaims that the possession of his neighbor's territory is rightfully his

[1] *Social Rights and Duties,* vol. i. p. 129; *An Agnostic's Apology,* p. 260.

by Manifest Destiny. The philosophical politician next drugs the conscience of his fellow men by declaring solemnly that " all history shows " that might is right ; and with time, the court of last appeal, it must be admitted possession is nine points in the law's ten. It cannot be denied, also, that quite as many crimes have been perpetrated in the name of God and of Manifest Destiny as in that of Liberty ; and that, at least, " all history shows ; " but, all the same, just as Liberty is a good and desirable thing, so God does live, and there is something in Manifest Destiny. As applied to the development of the races inhabiting the earth, it is, I take it, merely an unscientific form of speech, — the word now in vogue is evolution, — the phrase " survival of the fittest." When all is said and done, that unreasoning instinct of a people which carries it forward in spite of and over theories to its Manifest Destiny, amid the despairing outcries and long-drawn protestations of theorists and ethical philosophers, is a very considerable factor in making history ; and, consequently, one to be reckoned with.

In plain words, then, and Mr. Stephen to the contrary notwithstanding, "all history shows " that every great, aggressive and masterful race tends at times irresistibly towards the practical assertion of its supremacy, usually at the cost of those not so well adapted to existing conditions. In his great work, Mommsen formulates the law with a brutal directness distinctly Germanic. " By virtue of the law, that a people which has grown into a state absorbs its neighbors who are in political nonage, and a civilized people absorbs its neighbors who are in intellectual nonage, — by virtue of this law, which is as universally valid

and as much a law of nature as the law of gravity, —
the Italian nation (the only one in antiquity which was
able to combine a superior political development and
a superior civilization, though it presented the latter
only in an imperfect and external manner) was entitled to reduce to subjection the Greek states of the
East which were ripe for destruction, and to dispossess
the peoples of lower grades of culture in the West —
Libyans, Iberians, Celts, Germans — by means of its
settlers ; just as England, with equal right, has in Asia
reduced to subjection a civilization of rival standing,
but politically impotent, and in America and Australia has marked and ennobled, and still continues to
mark and ennoble, extensive barbarian countries with
the impress of its nationality." [1]   Professor von Holst
again states a corollary from the law thus laid down
in terms scarcely less explicit, in connection with a
well-known and much discussed act of foreign spolia-
tion in our own comparatively recent history.   " It is
as easy to bid a ball that has flown from the mouth of
the gun to stop in its flight, and return on its path, as
to terminate a successful war of conquest by a voluntary surrender of all conquests, because it has been
found out that the spoil will be a source of dissension
at home." [2]   And then von Holst quotes a very significant as well as philosophical utterance of William H.
Seward's, which a portion of our earnest protestants of
to-day would do well to ponder.   " I abhor war, as I
detest slavery.   I would not give one human life for
all the continent that remains to be annexed.   But I
cannot exclude the conviction that the popular passion

[1] *History of Rome*, Book v. chap. 7.
[2] *History of the United States*, vol. iii. p. 304.

for territorial aggrandizement is irresistible. Prudence, justice, cowardice, may check it for a season, but it will gain strength by its subjugation. . . . It behooves us then to qualify ourselves for our mission. We must dare our destiny." [1]   One more, and I have done with quotations.   The last I just now commended to the thoughtful consideration of those classified in the political nomenclature of the day as Anti-Imperialists.   A most conscientious and high-minded class, — possessed with the full courage of their convictions, —the efforts of the Anti-Imperialists will not fail, we and they may rest assured, to make themselves felt as they enter into the grand result.   Nevertheless, for them also there is food for thought, perhaps for consolation, in this other general law, laid down in 1862 by Richard Cobden, than whose, in my judgment, the utterances of no English-speaking man in the nineteenth century were more replete with shrewd sense expressed in plain, terse English : " From the moment the first shot is fired, or the first blow is struck, in a dispute, then farewell to all reason and argument ; you might as well attempt to reason with mad dogs as with men when they have begun to spill each other's blood in mortal combat.   I was so convinced of the fact during the Crimean war, which, you know, I opposed, — I was so convinced of the utter uselessness of raising one's voice in opposition to war when it has once begun, that I made up my mind that as long as I was in political life, should a war again break out between England and a great Power, I would never open my mouth upon the subject from the time the first gun was fired until the peace was made, because,

[1] *Works*, vol. iii. p. 409.

when a war is once commenced, it will only be by the exhaustion of one party that a termination will be arrived at. If you look back at our history, what did eloquence, in the persons of Chatham or Burke, do to prevent a war with our first American colonies? What did eloquence, in the persons of Fox and his friends, do to prevent the French Revolution, or bring it to a close? And there was a man who, at the commencement of the Crimean war, in terms of eloquence, in power, and pathos, and argument equal — in terms, I believe, fit to compare with anything that fell from the lips of Chatham and Burke — I mean your distinguished townsman, my friend Mr. Bright — and what was his success? Why, they burnt him in effigy for his pains." [1]

Turning from the authorities, and the lessons by them deduced from the record called History, let us now consider the problem precipitated on the American people by the Spanish war of 1898. There has of late been much talk of the sudden development of the United States as a " World Power," and of the new and prominent part it henceforth has to play, — talk, as I hold it, empty, idle and wearisome, — closely bordering on cant. The United States without question is a world power; but, that it has been such a power hard upon a century, I hold not more open to denial. The United States became a world power in the eyes of all nations between five minutes after 6 o'clock P. M. of the 19th of August, 1812, and the following half hour; the frigate Constitution, within those twenty-five minutes, having by her broadsides put the frigate Guerrière in such a position that the

---

[1] *Speeches*, vol. ii. p. 314.

British flag had to come down. Since the hands of the Constitution's chronometer marked the half hour after 6 o'clock of that eventful afternoon, there has been, I hold, no room for debate as to the United States as a world power.

For more than eighty years afterwards, the efforts of that power at supremacy were, in obedience to the law of its being and subject to the conditions of its environment, confined to filling up the waste spaces in its immediate neighborhood or to aggressive attitude, sometimes resulting in action, towards the less well adapted who chanced to find themselves in its path. But, as the world's solidarity increased, and trade and intercourse, assuming new forms, forced their way into fresh fields, it became inevitable, as the prescriptive barriers, one by one, gave way, that a new and larger policy would evolve itself for the United States also. That policy, moreover, would not fail to find expression soon or late in some assertion of supremacy. It was only a question of place, time and degree.

We all know how it came about. It is needless for me here and now to refer in detail to the war with Spain, and the fight in Manila Bay. Suffice it to say that, if human experience goes for anything in such cases, what has since resulted was in its larger scope inevitable, — in the nature of a logical outcome. Nor in thus stating a conclusion do I imply a spirit of fatalism, or say anything calculated to disparage opposition at the beginning, or discourage discussion now. On the contrary, " all history shows " — and this time, I submit, shows indisputably and conclusively — that final results are the outcome, not of some of the antecedent influences, or even of those among them most preponderating, but of all of them, combined and forever interacting. Every ingredient goes into the grand total, there making its presence felt. This being premised, it must next be admitted that there are few things which, when they first confront perplexed mankind, call more emphatically for challenge than the apparitions of manifest destiny. Such invariably come in questionable shapes. As our own experience teaches, — " as all history shows," — not one time in ten that manifest destiny is heralded does the thing so confidently pronounced as destined come to pass. How many times within our own memories it has been appealed to, and in behalf of what causes, — Ostend manifestoes, Fenian raids, servile insurrections, " Naboth's vineyard," miscegenation, and the like, — the record indicates. It cannot, therefore, and should not even for an instant be assumed that the appeal to God's Will, or Manifest Destiny, is entitled to consideration until it has so proved itself by actually overcoming the most strenuous opposition. That puts its reality to the test. Nor, when, in the matter of so-called expansion, the given manifestation has in the outcome proved itself genuine, and remains an established fact, — as, citing our own experience, in the cases of Texas, California, Alaska, Porto Rico and Hawaii, — a condition, and no longer a theory, — not then even is the struggle necessarily over. The details remain to be settled ; and the details, including all questions of form, involve the whole final character of the development. It is then to be decided whether the inevitable is to assume shape in harmony with our traditions, or in defiance of them. This is the final outcome of conflicting views and opposing forces. In the case now under discussion, therefore, while the battle of Manila Bay and the Treaty of Paris did, as is now apparent, settle the main issue, and finally committed the United States to a new phase and sphere of expansion, — a peopled, trans-Pacific acquisition, — to that expansion a shape was, and is yet to be given. It was in debate during the last presidential canvass ; it is in debate now.

That question — the burning political issue of the hour — I propose here and now to discuss. I propose to discuss it, however, from the purely historical stand-point, and not at all in its moral or economical aspects. So far, then, as this question is concerned, the last pre-sidential vote — that of 1900 — settled nothing, except that the policy which had assumed a certain degree of form in the Treaty of Paris should not be reversed. All else was left for debate and ulterior settlement. Certain lessons, calculated greatly to influence the character of that settlement, can, I submit, now be most advantageously drawn from history. At formu-lating those lessons, I propose here to try my hand.

The first and most important lesson is one which, in theory at least, is undisputed; though to live up to it practically calls for a courage of conviction not yet in evidence. That a dependency is not merely a possession, but a trust — a trust for the future, for itself and for humanity — is accepted ; — accordingly it is in no wise to be exploited for the general benefit of the alien owner, or that of individual components of that owner, but it is to be dealt with in a large and altruistic spirit, with an unselfish view to its own utmost development, materially, morally, and politically. And, through a process of negatives, "all his. tory shows" that only when this course is hereafter wisely and consecutively pursued — should that blessed consummation ever be attained — will the dominating power itself derive the largest and truest benefit from its possession.

As yet no American of any character, much less of authority, has come forward to controvert this proposition. That it will be controverted, and attempts made by interested parties to sophisticate it away through the cunningly arranged display of exceptional circumstances, can with safety be predicted. In this respect, to use a cant phrase, "we know how it is ourselves." We all remember, for instance, the unspeakable code of factitious morals and deceptive philosophy manufactured to order in these United States as a " Gospel of Niggerdom " less than half a century ago. Coming down to more recent times, we can, none of us, yet have forgotten the wretched sophistry ignorantly resurrected from French Revolution and assignat days in glorification of " Fiat Money," and a business world emancipated at last from any heretofore accepted measures of value. The leopard, rest assured, has not changed its spots since either 1860 or 1876. The New Gospel phase of the debate now on is, however, yet to develop itself. But, assuming the correctness of the proposition I have just formulated, a corollary follows from it. A formidable proposition, I state it without limitations, meaning to challenge contradiction. I submit that there is not an instance in all recorded history, from the earliest precedent to that now making, where a so-called inferior race or community has been elevated in its character, or made

self-sustaining and self-governing, — or even put on
the way to that result, — through a condition of
dependency or tutelage. I say "inferior race;" but,
I fancy, I might state the proposition even more
broadly. I might, without much danger, assert that
the condition of dependency, even for communities of
the same race and blood, always exercises an emasculating and deteriorating influence. I would undertake,
if called upon, to show also that the rule is invariable,
— that, from the inherent and fundamental conditions
of human nature it has known, and can know, no
exceptions. Of this history affords well-nigh innumerable examples, — ourselves among them. In our
case, it required a century to do away in our minds
and hearts with our colonial traditions. The Civil
War, and not what we call the Revolution, was our
real war of Independence. And yet in our dependency days you will remember we were not emasculated
into a resigned and even cheerful self-incapacity as
the natural result of a kindly, paternal and protective policy; but, as Burke, with profound insight,
expressed it, with us the spirit of independence and
self-support was fostered " through a wise and salutary
neglect." But, for present purposes, all this is unnecessary, and could lead but to a poor display of commonplace learning. The problem to-day engaging the
attention of the American people is more limited. It
relates solely to what are called "inferior races;"
those of the same race, or of cognate races, we as yet
do not propose to hold in a condition of permanent
dependency; those we absorb, or assimilate. Only
those of "inferior race" — the less developed or decadent — do we propose to hold in subjection, — dealing

with them, in theory at least, as a guardian deals with a family of wards.

My proposition then broadens. If history teaches anything in this regard, it is that race elevation, the capacity in a word of political self-support, cannot be imparted through tutelage. Moreover, the milder, the more paternal, kindly and protective the guardianship, the more emasculating it will prove. A " wise and salutary neglect " is in the end the more beneficent policy; for, with races as with individuals, a state of dependency breeds the spirit of dependency. Take Great Britain, for instance. That people, — working at it now consecutively through three whole centuries, — after well-nigh innumerable experiences and as many costly blunders, — Great Britain has, I say, developed a genius for dealing with dependencies, — for the government of " inferior races ; " — a genius far in advance of anything the world has seen before. Yet my contention is that, to-day, after three rounded centuries of British rule, the Hindostanese, — the natives of India, — in spite of all material, industrial and educational improvements, — roads, schools, justice and peace, — are in 1900 less capable of independent and ordered self-government than they were in the year 1600, — the year when the East India Company was incorporated under a patent of Elizabeth. The native Indian dynasties — those natural to the Hindoos — have disappeared ; accustomed to foreign rule, the people have no rulers of their own, nor could they rule themselves. The rule of aliens has with Hindostan thus become a domestic necessity. Remove it, — and the highest and most recent authorities declare it surely will some day be removed, —

chaos would inevitably ensue. What is true of India is true of Egypt. That, under British rule, Egypt is to-day in better material and political case than ever before in its history — modern, biblical, hieroglyphic or legendary — scarcely admits of dispute. Schools, roads, irrigation, law and order, and protection from attack, she has them all; —

> " But what avail the plough or sail,
> Or land or life, if freedom fail ? "

The capacity for self-government is not acquired in that school.

This fact is to-day more than ever before forcing itself on the attention and engaging the anxious thought of those Englishmen most familiar with the imperial system. " As yet there is no sign that the British are accomplishing [in Hindostan] more than the Romans accomplished in Britain, that they will spread any permanently successful ideas, or that they will found anything whatever. It is still true that if they departed, or were driven out, they would leave behind them, as the Romans did in Britain, splendid roads, many useless buildings, an increased weakness in the subject people, and a memory which in a century of new events would be extinct. . . . So far as one can see, not a European idea, not a European habit, not a distinctively European branch of knowledge, ever penetrated into Asia. . . . We are told every day how Europe has influenced Japan, and forget that the change in those islands was entirely self-generated, that Europeans did not teach Japan, but that Japan of herself chose to learn from Europe methods of organization, civil and military, which have so far proved successful." [1]

[1] Meredith Townsend: *Asia and Europe*, pp. 25, 27, 28.

Such is the recent testimony of one closely observing Englishman, the larger portion of whose life has been passed in Asia. Another says, to the same effect, " The very peace and security which a great Empire establishes may prove a deadening influence. . . . In India peace reigns to-day, and order, but there is certainly less scope for the Eastern patriotism of race and class, less romance and food for poetry, less motive for heroic self-sacrifice, less to stir the heart and imagination of Rajput and Sikh, of Mahratta and Pathan, than there was in those years of glorious turbulence in the breaking up of the Mogul empire. British rule tends to destroy native originality, vigor and initiative. How to replace that which our rule takes away is the great Indian problem." [1]   Evidence on this head might be accumulated to any desired extent; and yet to-day a vague idea, almost an aspiration, is floating through our American popular mind that a single generation of our beneficent rule will suffice to convert Malays into self-governing communities of the Anglo-Saxon type.

But England, in its own two thousand years of history, furnishes an example of what I have been asserting, — an example well-nigh forgotten. In fundamentals human nature is much the same now as twenty centuries back. During the first century of the present era, the Romans, acting in obedience to the law laid down by Mommsen, — the law quoted by me in full, and of which Thomas Carlyle is the latest and most eloquent exponent, — the law known as the Divine Right of the most Masterful, — acting in obedience to that law, the Romans in the year of Grace

[1] Bernard Holland : *Imperium et Libertas*, p. 12.

43 crossed the British Channel, overthrew the Celts and Gauls gathered in defence of what they mistakenly deemed their own, and, after reducing them to subjection, permanently occupied the land. They remained there four centuries — a hundred years longer than the English have been in Calcutta. During that period they introduced civilization, established Christianity, constructed roads, dwellings and fortifications. Materially, the condition of the country vastly improved. The Romans protected the inhabitants against their enemies; also against themselves. During four hundred years they benevolently assimilated them. Doubtless, on the banks of the Tiber, the inhabitants of what is now England were deemed incapable of self-government. Probably they were; unquestionably they became so. When the legions were at last withdrawn, the results of a kindly paternalism, secure protection and intelligent tutelage became apparent. The race was wholly emasculate. It cursed its independence; it deplored its lost dependency. As the English historian now records the result, " crushing all local independence, crushed all local vigor. Men forgot how to fight for their country when they forgot how to govern it." [1]

There is a familiar saying to the effect that, while Man is always in a hurry, God never is. Certainly, Nature works with a discouraging indifference to time. Each passing generation of reformers does love to witness some results of its efforts; but, in the case of England, in consequence of the emasculation incident to tutelage, and dependency on a powerful, a benevolent and beneficent foreign rule, after that rule

[1] Green: *Short History of the English People*, vol. i. p. 9.

ended, — as soon or late such rule always must end, — throughout the lives of eighteen successive generations emasculated England was overrun. At last, with some half dozen intermediate rulers, the Normans succeeded the Romans. They were conquering masters; but they domesticated themselves in the British Islands, and in time assimilated the inhabitants thereof, — Britons, Picts and Celts, — benevolently, or otherwise. But, as nearly as the historian can fix it, it required eight centuries of direst tribulation to educate the people of England out of that spirit of self-distrust and dependency into which they had been reduced by four centuries of paternalism, at once Roman and temporarily beneficent. Twelve centuries is certainly a discouraging term to which to look forward. But steam and electricity have since then been developed to a manifest quickening of results. Even the pace of Nature was in the nineteenth century vastly accelerated.

Briefly stated, then, the historical deduction would seem to be somewhat as follows : Where a race has in itself, whether implanted there by nature or as the result of education, the elevating instinct and energy, — the capacity of mastership, — a state of dependency will tend to educate that capacity out of existence; and the more beneficent, paternal and protecting the guardian power is, the more pernicious its influence becomes. In such cases, the course most beneficial in the end to the dependency, now as a century ago, would be that characterized by " a wise and salutary neglect." Where, however, a race is for any cause not possessed of the self-innate saving capacity, — being stationary or decadent, — a state of dependency, while it may improve material conditions, tends yet further to deteriorate the spirit and to diminish the capacity of self-government : if severe, it brutalizes ; if kindly, it enervates. History records no instance in which it develops and strengthens.

Following yet further the teachings of experience, we are thus brought to a parting of the ways, — a parting distinct, unmistakable. Heretofore the policy of the United States, as a nationality, has, so far as the so-called inferior races are concerned, been confined in its operation to the North American continent; but, as a whole and in its large aspects, it has been well defined and consistent. We have proceeded on the theory that all government should in the end rest on the consent of the governed ; that any given people is competent to govern itself in some fashion ; and that, in the long run, any fashion of self-imposed government works better results than will probably be worked by a government imposed from without. In other words, the American theory has been that, in the process of Nature and looking to ultimate, perhaps remote, conditions, any given people, not admitting of assimilation, will best work out its destiny when left free to work it out in its own way. Moreover, so far as outside influence is concerned, it could, in the grand result, be more effectively exercised through example than by means of active intervention. Where we have not therefore forcibly absorbed into our system foreign and inferior races alien in character and more or less completely assimilated them, we have, up to very recently, adopted and applied what may perhaps in homely speech best be described as a " Hands-off and Walk-alone " doctrine, relying in our policy toward others on the theory practised at our private firesides, — the theory that self-government results from example, and is self-taught.

I have already quoted Richard Cobden in this connection; I will quote him again. Referring, in 1864, to the British foreign policy, then by him as by us denounced, though by us now imitated, Cobden said, — " I maintain that a man is best doing his duty at home in striving to extend the sphere of liberty — commercial, literary, political, religious, and in all directions; for if he is working for liberty at home, he is working for the advancement of the principles of liberty all over the world." [1]

Mexico and Hayti afford striking illustrations of a long and rigid adherence to this policy on our part, and of the results of that adherence. Conquering and dismembering Mexico in 1847, we, in 1848, left it to its own devices. So completely had the work of subjugation been done that our representatives had actually to call into being a Mexican government with which to arrange terms of peace. With that simulacrum of a national authority we made a solemn treaty, and, after so doing, left the Aztec land to work out its destiny, if it could, as it could.[2] In spite of numerous domestic convulsions and much internal anarchy, from that day to this we have neither ourselves intervened in the internal affairs of our southern continental neighbor, nor long permitted such interference by others. To Mexico, we have said, " Walk alone; "

[1] *Speeches*, vol. ii. p. 353.

[2] See the very suggestive paper entitled " The Proposed Absorption of Mexico in 1847-1848," by Professor E. G. Bourne: *Essays in Historical Criticism*, pp. 227-242.

to France, " Hands off." The result we all know. It has gone far to justify our theory of the true path of human advancement. Forty years is, in matters of race development, a short time. A period much too short to admit of drawing positive, or final, inferences. Dr. Holmes was once asked by an anxious mother when the education of a child should begin; his prompt, if perhaps unexpected, reply was, — " Not less than two hundred and fifty years before it is born." To-day, and under existing conditions, Mexico, though republican in name and form only, is self-governing in reality. It is manifestly working its problem out in its own way. The statement carries with it implications hardly consistent with the Might-is-Right, latter-day dispensation voiced by Mommsen and Carlyle.

Hayti presents another case in point, with results far more trying to our theory. We have toward Hayti pursued exactly the policy pursued by us with Mexico. Not interfering ourselves in the internal affairs of the island, we have not permitted interference by others. Occupied by an inferior race, apparently lapsing steadily toward barbarism, for the condition of affairs prevailing in Hayti the United States is morally responsible. Acting on the law laid down in the extract I have given from the pages of Mommsen, we might at any time during the last quarter of a century have intervened in the name of humanity, and to the great temporary advantage of the inhabitants of the one region " Where Black rules White." The United States, in pursuance of its theories, has abstained from so doing. It has abstained in the belief that, in the long run and grand result, the inhabitants of Hayti will best work out their problem, if left to work it out themselves. In any event, however, exceptional cases are the rocks on which sound principles come to wreck; and, so far as the race of man on earth is concerned, it is better that Hayti should suffer self-caused misfortune for centuries, as did England before, than that a precedent should be created for the frequent violation of a great principle of natural development. Yet the case of Hayti is crucial. Persistently to apply our policy there evinces, it must be admitted, a robust faith in the wisdom of its universal application. The logical inference, so far as the Philippine Islands are concerned, is obvious.

The rule guiding, or that should guide, the United States in its dealings with alien races, probably inferior, as being either as yet undeveloped or else in a state of arrested development, is simple. The capacity for self-government, and, consequently, the consent of the governed, should be assumed, until, as the result of experience, a negative is proved; the interference should then be the least necessary to arrest decay or secure stability. The assumption should ever be in favor of a tendency to progressive self-development. The British rule is the reverse. Incapacity is assumed, until capacity is proved.

Historically speaking, those now referred to are the only two theories of a national policy to be pursued in dealing with practical dependencies, which challenge consideration, — the American and the British. The others, whether ancient and abandoned, or modern and in use, — Phœnician, Roman, Spanish, French, Dutch, German, or Russian, — may be dismissed from the discussion. They none of them ever did, nor do any of them now, look to an altruistic result. In all, the dependency is confessedly exploited on business principles, with an eye to the trade development of the alien proprietor. Setting these aside, there remain only the American, or " Walk-alone and Hands-off " theory ; and the British, or " Ward-in-Chancery " theory. The first is exemplified in Mexico and Hayti ; the last in Hindostan and Egypt. The question now in debate for the United States may, therefore, be concisely stated, thus : Taking the Philippine Islands as a subject for treatment, and the ultimate elevation of the inhabitants of those islands to self-government as the end in view, which is the policy best calculated to lead to the result desired, — the traditional and distinctively American system, as exemplified in the cases of Mexico and Hayti, or the modern and improved British system, to be studied in Hindostan and Egypt ?

Subject to limitations of time and space I have now passed in review the great political debates which have occupied the attention of the American public during the last half century. I have endeavored to call attention to the plane on which those debates have been conducted, and to the noticeable absence from them of a scholarly spirit. The judicial temper and the patience necessary to any thorough investigation have in them, I submit, been conspicuously lacking. Then, starting from the point of view peculiar to this Association, I have examined the issues presented to the country in the last presidential canvass, and, for purposes of illustration, I have discussed them, always in a purely historical temper.

While the result of my experiment is for others to pass upon, my own judgment is clear and decided. I hold that the time has now come when organizations such as this of ours, instead of, as heretofore, scrupulously standing aloof from the political debate, are under obligation to participate in it. As citizens, we most assuredly should, in so far as we may properly so do, contribute to results, whether immediate, or more or less remote. As scholars and students, the conclusions we have to present should be deserving of thoughtful consideration. The historical point of view, moreover, is, politically, an important point of view; for only when approached historically — by one looking before, as well as after — can any issue be understood in its manifold relations with a complex civilization. Indeed, the moral point of view can in its importance alone compare with the historical. The economical, vital as it unquestionably often is, comes much lower in the scale; for, while an approach through both these avenues is not infrequently necessary to the intelligent comprehension of questions of a certain class, — such, for instance, as the tariff or currency, — it is very noticeable that, though many issues present themselves, — slavery or imperialism, for example, — into which economical considerations do not enter as controlling factors, there is scarcely any matter of political debate which does not to some extent at least have to be discussed historically. Still, though our retrospect has proven this to be the case, the scarcely less significant fact also appears that not more than one presidential canvass in two involves any real issue at all, — moral or economical. Of the last twelve elections, covering the half century, — six were mere struggles for political control; and so far as can now be seen, the course of subsequent events would have been in no material respect other than it was, whichever party prevailed. Judging by experience, therefore, in only one future canvass out of two will any occasion arise for a careful historical presentation of facts. The investigator will not be called upon; and, if he rises to take part in the discussion, he will do no harm, for the excellent reason that no one will listen to him. In the other of each two canvasses it is not so. There is then apt to be a real debate over a paramount issue; and, in all such, the strong searchlight of experience should be thrown, clearly and fully, over the road we are called upon to traverse. In every such case, the presentation, provided always it be made in the true historical spirit, should by no means be of one side only. On the contrary, every phase of the record should have its advocate; every plausible lesson should be drawn. The facts are many, complicated and open to a varied construction; and it is only through the clash of opposing views that they can be reduced to comparative system, and compelled to yield their lessons for guidance.

As I have also, more than once already, observed, this Association is largely made up of those occupying the chairs of instruction in our seminaries of the higher education. From their lecture-rooms the discussion of current political issues is of necessity excluded. There it is manifestly out of place. Others here are scholars, for whom no place exists on the political platform. Still others are historical investigators and writers, interested only incidentally in political discussion. Finally, some are merely public-spirited citizens, on whom the oratory of the stump palls. They crave discussion of another order. They are the men whose faces are seen only at those gatherings which some one eminent for thought or in character is invited to address. To all these, the suggestion I now make cannot but be grateful. It is that, in future, this Association, as such, shall so arrange its meetings that one at least shall be held in the month of July preceding each presidential election. The issues of that election will then have been presented, and the opposing candidates named. It should be understood that the meeting is held for the purpose of discussing those issues from the historical point of view, and in their historical connection. Absolute freedom of debate should be insisted on, and the participation of those best qualified to deal with the particular class of problems under discussion should be solicited. Such authorities, speaking from so lofty a rostrum to a select audience of appreciative men and women, could, I confidently submit, hardly fail to elevate the standard of discussion, bringing the calm lessons of history to bear on the angry wrangles and distorted presentations of those whose chief, if not only, aim is a mere party supremacy.

V

A PLEA FOR MILITARY HISTORY [1]

I AM to contribute to this occasion a paper under the title of " A Plea for Military History." To this subject I have already — more than six months ago — elsewhere alluded, — in the course of an address to the Massachusetts Historical Society, on taking for the fifth time the chair as its president.

" It is scarcely an exaggeration to say that there are not many considerable branches of human knowledge concerning which the historian of the future must not in some degree inform himself. Somewhere and somehow his researches will touch upon them, remotely, perhaps, but still as factors in his problem. . . . Formerly all necessary information, it was supposed, could be acquired from books ; manuscripts were better yet, for those were, without any question, what are termed ' original sources.' But the old-fashioned historian, rarely, if ever, hesitating, flies boldly at every kind of game — all are fish that come to his net. For instance, history is largely made up of accounts of operations and battles on land and on sea. Weary of threading his way through a long period of most unpicturesque peace, trying to make that interesting

[1] A paper read, in part, at the Annual Meeting of the American Historical Association, held in Boston, December 28, 1899. Printed in the *Annual Report of the American Historical Association for* 1900, vol. i. pp. 193–218. Revised and corrected.

which was at best commonplace, the historian draws a
breath of relief when at length he comes to a tumult
of war.   Here are pride, pomp, and circumstance, —
a chance for descriptive power.

" The historian of the future seems now likely to
pursue a different method.   Recognizing the fact that
he probably is not at once a littérateur, a soldier, a
statesman, a lawyer, a theologian, a physician, and a
biologist ; that he certainly will not live forever ; that
he has not the cosmogony at his fingers' ends, and
that to ransack every repository of information on all
possible subjects transcends the powers of even the
most industrious ; recognizing in this degree the limits
of possibility, he will be content to avail himself of
the labors of others, better advised on many subjects
than himself, and, becoming the student of monographs, derive the great body of his information, not,
as the expression now goes, from ' original sources,' or
even from personal observation, but, as we all in the
end must, at secondhand.   His insight will be largely
into the knowledge and judgment of others, and the
degree of reliance to be placed in them.

" I know of but one writer who has described military operations and battles, — those intricate movements of human pawns on a chessboard of much topo-
graphical uncertainty, and those scientific mêlées in
which skill, luck, preparation, superiority of weapons,
human endurance, and racial characteristics decide the
question of mastery as between two marshalled mobs,
— I know, I was saying, of but one writer who has
described battles and military operations in that real-
istic way which impresses me with a sense of both
personal experience and literary skill.   That one is

Tolstoi, the Russian philosopher and novelist. His Austerlitz and Russian campaigns of Napoleon and his Sebastopol are masterpieces. A man of imagination and consummate literary capacity, he had himself served ; and, curiously enough, in the same way, his compatriot, Verestchagin, has put upon canvas the sickening realism of war with a degree of force which could come only from familiarity with the cumbered field, and could by no possibility be worked up in the studio through the study of photographs, no matter how numerous, or the perusal of the accounts 'from our special correspondent,' no matter how graphic and detailed.

" I once, in a very subordinate capacity, though for a considerable period of time, was brought into close contact with warfare and saw much of military operations from within, or, as I may say, on the seamy side. Since then I have read in books of history, and other works more avowedly of fiction, many accounts of campaigns and battles ; and in so doing I have been most deeply impressed with the audacity, not of soldiers, but of authors. Usually, bookish men who had passed their lives in libraries, often clergymen — knowing absolutely nothing of the principles of strategy or of the details of camp life and military organization, never having seen a column on the march, or a regiment in line, or heard a hostile shot, — not taking the trouble even to visit the scene of operations or to study its topography, wholly unacquainted with the national characteristics of the combatants, — these 'bookish theoricks' substitute their imaginings for realities, and in the result display much the same real acquaintance with the subject which would be expected

from a physician or an artist who undertook to treat
of difficult problems in astronomy or mechanics. They
are strongly suggestive of the good Dr. Goldsmith
and his ' Animated Nature.' Once or twice I have
had occasion to follow these authorities, — authors of
standard historical works, — and in so doing have
familiarized myself with the topography of the scenes
they described, and worked down, as best I could, into
the characters of those in command, and what are
known as the ' original sources' of information as to
their plans and the course of operations. The result
has uniformly been a distinct accession of historical
scepticism." [1]

I come now to the true occasion of my being here
to-day. Having a year ago passed this general censure upon " bookish theoricks," I happily bethought
me of a friend of a lifetime to whom it was possible
what I had said might be assumed to apply. I refer
to the late John Codman Ropes. I therefore added
this qualifying sentence, and I now greatly rejoice
that it occurred to me so to do; for Mr. Ropes was
present when I spoke the words I have quoted, having
done me the compliment that day to leave his office
that he might listen to me. The qualifying sentence
was as follows : —

" That among men of the closet and the historical
laboratory are to be found military students of profound, detailed knowledge and great critical acumen,
no one would dispute ; least of all we, with at least
one brilliant and recognized exemplar in our own

---

[1] " Historians and Historical Societies," *Proceedings of the Massachusetts Historical Society* (April, 1899), Second Series, vol. xiii. pp.
81–119.

ranks, — a man who never saw an army in movement or a stricken field, and yet whom I once heard referred to by one who had borne a part in fifty fights, the general then commanding our army, as the first among living military critics."

The hearty applause with which the audience received these words showed that the allusion was understood, and Mr. Ropes did not fail, later on, to express the gratification the incident afforded him. Not yet a month ago, at midnight on the 29th–30th of November last, he died. As I have already said, the friendship which existed between us was almost lifelong. Nearly fifty years ago we were students together at Harvard, though not classmates, and my intimacy with him and my feeling of high regard for him had increased with each passing year. In my existence his death has left a void not to be filled. That is a small matter and personal only ; but, so far as the study of military history is concerned, especially in connection with our Civil War, the loss occasioned by his death is scarcely less great. The work Mr. Ropes was engaged on must remain unfinished ; for the second of his four volumes was published less than a year ago, and of the third volume the beginning only had been prepared. He had brought down his narrative to the battle of Fredericksburg on one side and that of Murfreesboro on the other, following, as he did, the large strategic lines of the conflict only, and paying little attention to those minor operations, almost innumerable, which did not greatly affect the grand result. It was General Schofield, then commanding the armies of the United States, who, in a conversation I had with him more than ten years ago, referred to Mr. Ropes in the language I have quoted, as the first of living military critics. And now, standing here among historical writers, scholars and investigators, speaking over the scarcely closed grave of the man, the student and the friend, I bear such witness as I may to the fact that in my judgment General Schofield in this remark was not guilty of exaggeration. And further let me add that, in my judgment also, so far as the history of the great struggle hereafter to be known as the American Confederate Rebellion is concerned, the death of Mr. Ropes, leaving his work unfinished, is to the highest class of historical research an irreparable loss. As a student of military historical problems he was, so far as my knowledge of such goes, almost unique. Combined with a sufficient literary skill, he had a grasp of the great principles of strategy which could hardly be bettered. His knowledge of tactics, and of the details of the march and of the battlefield, was of course defective. He, too, had never seen a column on the road or a battery in action. Accordingly, when it came to this portion of his subject he could not speak as a man can speak who has himself shared in the prolonged weariness of the march or the sharp stress of conflict. He knew as little of campaign variety as he did of camp tedium. As respects all these elements of warfare — and they have much to do with the evolution of military results; far more than most writers are apt to realize — he was obliged to have recourse to his imagination ; and, while imagination is in good historical writing a most important factor, yet when imagination deals with topics of which the writer has had no practical experience, it is a dangerous guide.

Nevertheless, allowing for these limitations under which Mr. Ropes necessarily labored, I am free to say that, in my estimation, he has contributed more than any other one writer has done, or any other one writer is likely to do, to a correct historical understanding of the great military operations and strategic results of the first two years of the Rebellion. I felt, therefore, that it would not have been well had this meeting of the American Historical Association gone by, the first held since his death, without bearing in its record something indicative of the high appreciation in which he and his work are by us held. But for that feeling I should not trespass on your patience to-day. I am well aware that our president has already fittingly forestalled me in this grateful task, and that mine is but a concurrent testimony on a subject concerning which little new remains to be said. That little, however, is very appropriate to my theme, for it would not be possible on this occasion to enter " A Plea for Military History," and not to feel that in doing so the name and thought of our best exponent of " military history " — he who, in fact, had with us identified himself with it — at once suggested themselves. In all that our president has said of Mr. Ropes I concur, and to it I have sought to add what I might.

Having thus rendered my tribute, I recur to my allotted theme, and I propose to illustrate the criticism I last spring ventured upon by references to a few of the great military operations which have left distinct marks upon American history ; and, in so doing, I shall endeavor to point out how inadequately they have been treated, having, as a rule, been treated by investigators who failed to combine technical knowledge and a professional experience with literary skill. Indeed, among writers who have undertaken to deal with problems of this class we number in the whole record of the United States, so far as I know, but one striking instance to whom this criticism plainly fails to apply, and that exceptional instance is outside the field of military operations. Captain Mahan has recently shown us what naval history becomes when handled by one who had himself sailed the ocean and had thoroughly familiarized himself with maritime conditions. In this I think all will agree. His work constitutes, indeed, a veritable addition to naval historical lore. It marks a new departure ; and it does so for the simple reason that he did combine the two qualities I have referred to, — literary skill with professional knowledge. I think it hardly less safe to say that, so far as strictly military operations are concerned, no similar American writer has yet come forward. These operations, past and present, recent and remote, have been very copiously described and almost lovingly, as altogether too patriotically, dwelt upon ; they have been analyzed on paper, and fought over in print more than enough, but it has been either by military men who failed to possess Captain Mahan's literary gift, or by literary men who had not shared in his professional work. The result, except in the case of Mr. Ropes, has been an inadequate and more or less unsatisfactory treatment, and even his conclusions are to a degree affected by his lack of that personal observation and familiarity bred of contact which was an essential element in the success of Captain Mahan. As Gibbon, referring to his own experience, observed in a well-remembered passage of his autobiography,

" The captain of the Hampshire Grenadiers has not been useless to the historian of the Roman Empire."

Coming to my first illustration, I propose to submit a few words concerning what was the most memorable incident in American military annals prior to the struggle we know as the Revolution, more properly called the War of American Independence. I refer, of course, to Wolfe's capture of Quebec. It is not too much to say that the fall of Quebec led to results which have affected the whole subsequent history of the American continent and of civilization. Though not included in his selection by Professor Creasey, the short struggle on the Plains of Abraham must, therefore, unquestionably be classed among the decisive battles of the world.

In common with every boy who was taught in an American school during the first half of the century, the story of Wolfe's victory and death had been familiar to me from childhood. None the less, though I believe I have been in every other considerable city on the North American continent, with the exception, possibly, of Vera Cruz, Quebec had until last summer unaccountably escaped me. Putting a copy of Parkman's *Montcalm and Wolfe* in my bag, I went there in September last ; and, while there, of course examined with no little interest the scene of the great exploit in that work described. The defects in Parkman's narrative, when studied on the spot, became at once apparent. Written by a scholar who spared no pains in preparation, the result yet showed on its face that it was the work of one who had never himself participated in military operations. It was deficient in precision ; inferences were not drawn ; technical expressions were incorrectly used; it lacked firmness of touch.

I was, in the first place, much surprised on examining the ground over which Wolfe's force reached the Plains of Abraham. All my preconceptions, derived from tradition and confirmed by Parkman's narrative, were at variance with the actual topography. From the descriptions, I had assumed that the path by which Wolfe's forces made their ascent was narrow and very steep, winding along the face of the cliff, and one by which men could go up only in single file, or at most by twos; or, as I have seen it described within a few days in the report of a discourse delivered here in Boston, it was an "ascent up precipitous cliffs, by means of overhanging boughs and projecting crags." [1] On examination, I found it quite another thing. In 1759 the legendary "narrow path" must have been,

[1] " He [Wolfe] was the first to leap on shore and to scale the narrow path where no two men could go abreast. His men followed, pulling themselves to the top by the help of bushes and the crags." (Green: A Short History of the English People, vol. iii. p. 1655.) There has been no more careful and contained British historian than J. R. Green. His name can never be mentioned otherwise than with respect. But Green had no military experience, and this quotation from his work illustrates the difficulties under which merely bookish men write. There is no reason to suppose that Wolfe "was the first to leap ashore." In practical warfare, the General in command does not act as a boatman holding a painter, or fending off with an oar. He was not the first "to scale the narrow path." There was no "narrow path," and he, very properly and in accordance with the necessities of actual field service, immediately sent a reconnoitring party up the gorge to secure the outlet at its summit. He followed, in his proper place, with the main command. The men of the main command did not "pull themselves to the top by the help of bushes and the crags," but tramped up in tolerably solid column, and deployed in the regular way when they debouched at the summit. The accounts given by Lord Mahon and in Knight's Popular History of England are open to similar criticisms.

as it now is, up an acclivity, steep, it is true, but not difficult, and nowhere narrow. A somewhat precipitous gorge, it then was, as it still is, wide and well wooded, — a bit of rough hillside breaking a palisade, up which any group of athletic young men could in ten minutes easily clamber. Especially would this be true of Scotch Highlanders, of whom Wolfe's command was largely made up.

It is here, and in connection with this legendary scaling of the heights, that the technical deficiencies of Parkman's narrative become apparent. Though he had himself, unquestionably, time and again gone over the ground, yet his account fails, as that of no trained military historian would have failed, to give the exact time of the ascent. His narrative is indeed on this important point exasperatingly vague. He says: " Towards two o'clock the boats cast off and fell down with the current." He then adds that " for full two hours the procession of boats steered silently down the St. Lawrence." It must, therefore, have been four o'clock in the morning when the landing was effected, and a small scaling party climbed the heights, " closely followed by a much larger party." Meeting with no resistance, those in the advance, the escaladers, surprised, and captured or routed, a small French outpost at the head of the ravine. Its commanding officer was in bed, and, wounded while trying to escape, was taken prisoner. The shots and shouts of those composing the scaling party notified their comrades below of their success, and the advance of the main body was at once ordered. Apparently this could not have really begun until 4.30 at least; and yet before 6 o'clock 5000 men were in line of battle

on the Plains of Abraham. Before 9 o'clock, moreover, they had also hauled up by hand at least two
pieces of artillery, besides more or less camp equipage.
These facts speak for themselves. Any one who has
ever participated in military movements knows that
for 5000 men, carrying their arms, ammunition, knap-
sacks and rations, to scale a steep ascent of at least
half a mile in the short space of ninety minutes,
they must have been able to swarm up, not in file,
nor by twos and threes, but in a tolerably solid mass.
No one, viewing the locality, would seek to detract
from Wolfe's achievement, — daring in conception, it
was firmly executed. Throughout, it showed the hand
of a true soldier.[1] But that is not in question. The
point is that it was a boldly desperate, rather than a
physically difficult, undertaking. Like the night assault of any place rendered by nature or art hard of
access, the success of the attempt was purely a matter
of surprise and defence ; and at Quebec, the surprise

[1] The last word in the Quebec campaign of 1759 is to be found in
the recently published volume of Colonel Townshend, *The Military
Life of Field-Marshal George, First Marquess Townshend*, 1724-1807
(pp. 142-251). From this it appears that the famous operation, which
resulted in the fall of Quebec, was not designed by Wolfe, but was
adopted by him, contrary to his own judgment, on the formal recommendation of his subordinates in command. From a purely military
point of view, this should not detract from Wolfe's fame. He was
then a very sick man, probably dying ; a physical wreck, in consequence of the fatigues and anxieties he had undergone. None the
less, so to speak, game to the last, he, by adoption, made the plan his
own, and carried it out with spirit and determination. He then had
the great good fortune to be killed in the hour of victory. The problem of the Quebec campaign was, on a very small scale, the same as
that which confronted Grant in his Vicksburg campaign, more than
a century later. It was solved by precisely the same strategic movement. Grant's campaign was, however, of a far higher and more
difficult strategic order than Wolfe's venturesome escalade.

of the defenders being perfect, the ascent presented no great obstacle. It was neither narrow nor precipitous, as was proved by the fact that within two hours artillery and munitions were dragged up, following 5000 men. Provided, therefore, the much-discussed gorge was undefended, as was the case, Wolfe's famous escalade was a by no means unprecedented military operation. Even had the gorge been defended, and by a fairly adequate force, the very steepness of the ascent, as any experienced military authority would appreciate, and as we repeatedly found in our Civil War, would have enabled those composing the attacking party to scale the cliff with no great degree of personal danger. The enemy from far above would almost inevitably have fired over the heads of their assailants. In such case, the resistance to be effective must be determined and by an adequate force; a force, moreover, which does not await attack at the summit, but stubbornly contests every foot of ground from bottom to top.

Having now got Wolfe, with 5000 men in battle array, upon the Plains of Abraham, only ninety minutes after leaving their boats, the thing which next bewildered me was why Montcalm played into his opponent's hands as he did, by hastily attacking him the next morning, — risking the fate of Quebec and of Canada, not upon the result of protracted military operations, but on the cast of sudden battle. What in Montcalm's mind led to this decision? Here again the judgment of the skilful military historian would be of great value. On the face of things, I was unable, as I stood on the Plains of Abraham, to see how Wolfe had greatly bettered his situation by getting there instead of remaining in his camp on the other side of the river, provided always his opponent availed himself to the uttermost of his advantages. The escalade was effected on the morning of September 13. Three days before, on the 10th, the uneasy British naval commanders had held a council, and decided that the lateness of the season required the fleet to leave the St. Lawrence without delay. Among the experienced French authorities some would hardly allow their opponents a week longer of campaigning weather, while Montcalm conceded them only a month. It was merely a question of a few days more or a few days less, and the French could count on the Canadian winter as a grim and irresistible ally, just as surely as did the Russians half a century later. As a matter of fact, the British fleet, delaying to the last moment in view of the success of Wolfe's operations, did not leave Quebec until " it was past the middle of October," as Parkman again expresses it, about five weeks after the escalade. It was, therefore, a question of prolonging the defence that amount of time only.

When the breaking of an equinoctial day revealed Wolfe securely planted on the heights west of Quebec, the outlook for him was, consequently, far from clear. It is true he had with him a force of 5000 very reliable troops, drawn up within striking distance of the land-side defences of Quebec ; but, on the other hand, provided he was not attacked by the covering army, the lateness of the season left one course, and one only, open to him. He must endeavor to storm those defences. And not only must he endeavor to storm fortifications in his front, but, in so doing, he must prepare to be attacked both on his flank and rear by an enemy who, when his detachments were all concentrated, numbered nearly double his own force, though greatly inferior to it in fighting qualities on an open field. Thus, without any sufficient artillery, Wolfe was confronted with the difficult problem of immediately capturing a stronghold, while subject to attack by a numerous covering force, much better supplied than he with artillery. So far as I can yet see, the only thing his opponent had to do was to wait until Wolfe began his necessary assault. It would have involved for him great risk.

Under these circumstances, why did Montcalm decide to take the immediate initiative? Without artillery, without even waiting until his entire force had been concentrated, he made a noisy, futile rush at the British, as if for him there was no other course open. Yet his so doing was exactly what Wolfe must most have hoped for. The result we all know. On this most interesting point, however, Parkman is curiously vague. He is even contradictory; thus betraying the lack of professional insight. At first he says of Montcalm, when the French commander saw the English army in line of battle behind Quebec, — "He could not choose. Fight he must, for Wolfe was now in position to cut off all his supplies" (p. 293). Leaving the imminence of winter out of consideration, this is, in a way, plausible; but a little farther on Parkman says of Montcalm's immediate successor in command of the beaten Canadian army: — "There was no need to fight at once. . . . By a march of a few miles he could have [concentrated the covering force], and by then intrenching himself he would have placed a greatly superior force in the English rear, where his position might have been made impregnable.   Here he might be easily furnished with provisions, and from hence he could readily throw men and supplies into Quebec, which the English were too few to invest " (p. 306). If this was the situation the day after Montcalm suffered defeat, why was it that officer had " no choice " but to fight at once, thirty-six hours before?

Parkman fails to tell us.

To supply the tantalizing omission, even were I competent so to do, is no part of my present plan.   The omission amounts, none the less, in itself, to a " Plea for Military History ; " for I submit that a trained military historian, after a careful examination of the locality and every record of the battle, could form a presumably correct estimate of the considerations which acted on Montcalm, and thus caused France the loss of the key to a continent.

Coming now to a later period and events nearer home, I propose to illustrate my thesis by a brief reference to four battles in our own history, two from the War of Independence and two from that of 1812–15, — the engagements at Bunker Hill and Long Island in the one case, and those of Bladensburg and New Orleans in the other.   None of these incidents in our history have, so far as I know, been treated by any writer competent to handle them from a distinctively military point of view, as, for instance, Captain Mahan has handled the naval operations of Nelson.

Recurring to Bunker Hill, the mistakes and controversies which have arisen among historians and critics in regard to that engagement have well-nigh partaken of the ludicrous.   There has, in the first place, been an almost endless discussion as to who was in command, — a discussion which would have caused no man of military training a moment's pause. It has been elaborately contended that General Putnam must have been in command, because he was the officer of the highest grade upon the ground, obviously outranking Colonel Prescott. The proposition is simply absurd, as being contrary to the first and elementary principles of military subordination. General Putnam was, it is true, on the ground ; but he was on the ground as an officer having a Connecticut commission only, and in command of a detachment from that province. He held no commission from Massachusetts, much less any Continental commission. Colonel Prescott, commanding a Massachusetts regiment, had received his orders from his military superior, Major-General Ward, an officer also in the Massachusetts service. Ward thus was Prescott's superior officer ; Putnam was not. During the operations which ensued, it was open for Putnam to make to Prescott any suggestion he saw fit ; and Prescott, acting always on his own responsibility, might give to such suggestions the degree of weight he deemed proper ; but he could report only to his superior in the same service as himself, — his military commander. Prescott, therefore, showed perfectly well that he knew what he was about when he offered the command to Warren, who had been commissioned by the Massachusetts authorities as a major-general, when Warren appeared upon the field. Warren, very properly, declined the command, remaining purely as a volunteer. But, so far as Putnam was concerned, he was in command merely of such Connecticut troops as were coöperating with the Massachusetts

detachment ; and for a Massachusetts officer to have
received an order as such from him would have subjected that officer to a court-martial.   All this is elementary, — the very alphabet of the military organization, — and yet the lay historians who have written
upon that battle have contended over the question for
years.

The extraordinarily bad tactics of both sides in the
affair of Bunker Hill I have dealt with elsewhere,[1] —
the opportunity which the British lost, the accidental
advantage which the Americans gained.   Luck, combined with good marksmanship, on the one side, and
blundering, bull-headed persistence on the other, were
the predominating elements of the occasion ; and to
those features of it the historians have given scant
consideration.   The cause of American independence
owed much that day to Yankee pluck and straight
shooting ; but more yet to genuine British bulldog
stupidity.   The race learns slowly.   Its representatives then did just what they have recently attempted
in South Africa.

Nevertheless, the effect of the battle of Bunker Hill
upon that on Long Island fourteen months later is,
from a military point of view, interesting and very
worthy of study.   It is not too much to say that the
experience of the earlier absolutely changed the fate
of the subsequent day ; and, on the 17th of June, 1775,
Colonel Prescott not only saved from destruction General Washington and the American army on the 27th
of August, 1776, but he saved the cause of American
independence itself.   Sir William Howe commanded
at Bunker Hill ; he also commanded at Long Island.

[1] *American Historical Review*, vol. i. pp. 401-413 ; April, 1896.

Upon the latter field of operations his movements, though slow, were skilfully planned and well carried out. For a wonder, he had recourse to a flanking movement, which was successfully executed by Clinton; and, as the result of it, Howe found himself in the early hours of that August day in an admirable position to deliver an assault, with the chances at least four out of five in his favor. But the bloody experience at Bunker Hill was fresh in his mind; and so, having his enemy completely in his grasp, he hesitated. He allowed his opponent to elude him; and that opponent chanced to be Washington.

When, some years ago, I had occasion to make a study of operations about New York in August, 1776, I was amazed at the mistakes, from a military point of view, of which Washington was then guilty. Even more amazing, however, was the partisanship of the American historians. In their unwillingness to see any blemish in the career of Washington, their narratives amounted to little less than a falsification of history, — a literary misdemeanor, not to say crime, for which the only plea in justification possible for them to enter would be lack of technical knowledge. Suppressing incontrovertible facts, they gave credence to absurd stories. So much was I at the time surprised at the conclusions to which I found myself compelled that I took my narrative in the manuscript to Mr. Ropes, told him of my perplexity, and asked him to read my paper and give me the benefit of an outspoken criticism. I found him singularly well informed on the subject in a general way, and he readily assumed the task. A few days later he returned me my manuscript with an emphatic written indorsement of the conclusions I had reached. Subsequently the paper was printed in the *American Historical Review*,[1] and may there be consulted.

Time and space do not permit of my now entering again upon this subject, nor would it be worth your or my while were I so to do. Suffice it to say that during the latter part of August, 1776, Washington appears to have disregarded almost every known principle of strategy or rule of tactics, some of them in a way almost grotesque. For instance, while lying on Long and Manhattan islands awaiting the sluggish movements of Howe, a body of Connecticut cavalry appeared, volunteering their services. Substantial, well-mounted men, they were some 400 in number. Washington declined to accept their services as mounted men, on the extraordinary ground that operations being then conducted on islands, there could be no occasion for cavalry. Men, however, were greatly needed, and he suggested that members of the troop should send back their horses, and agree to serve as infantry. When they declined so to do, he roughly dismissed them. In reaching this decision it is not too much to say that Washington betrayed a truly singular ignorance of what cannot be regarded otherwise than as the elementary principles of military movements. It was true the operations then in hand were necessarily conducted on islands; but, as it subsequently appeared, the American army did not have the necessary mounted men to do orderly and courier duty. More than that, the disaster of the 27th of August on Long Island, involving, as it did, the needless destruction of the very flower of the American

[1] Vol. i. pp. 650–670; July, 1896.

army, was wholly due to the lack of a small mounted force. There were on that occasion three roads which led from Gravesend, whence the British began their movement, to Brooklyn, where Washington was intrenched. We will call these the eastern, the middle, and the western roads. Of these three roads, two, the western and the middle, the Americans had occupied in force. The eastern road they wholly neglected. It was assumed, apparently, that the enemy would never go so far out of the direct way. There is unquestionably a well-developed propensity in British commanders to butt their own heads and those of their soldiers directly against any obstacle their enemies may see fit to put in their front. They can generally be counted on so to do. Unfortunately for the American army, it so chanced, as I have already said, that for once a flanking movement suggested itself to some one in the British army at Gravesend, probably not Sir William Howe. Accordingly, having reconnoitred their front, a British division, under the command of Clinton, made a night move on Brooklyn by the easternmost of the three roads. That road, under any known rules of warfare, even the most elementary, should have been picketed, and watched by a mounted patrol. Twenty-five men would have sufficed ; fifty would have been ample. Four hundred men could have picketed the whole of Washington's front, and, holding the enemy in check, have given ample notice of his approach. To neglect such an obvious precaution was so unpardonable as not to admit of explanation. As a matter of fact, the road in question was left not only uncovered, but it was not even observed. The American army had no cavalry, its commander having sent the mounted men offered him home on the curiously suggestive ground that they could be of no possible service, as on islands "horses cannot be brought into action." By this unconsciously innocent remark the trained military expert learns that, at the time it was made, Washington had no conception of the duties and functions of a mounted force in connection with any extended military operations; and, accordingly, the fact, not otherwise comprehensible, is explained that during the short summer night of August 26–27, 1776, Clinton moved forward not only unopposed but actually unobserved, until, in the early morning, he had got himself between the defences at Brooklyn and the right wing of Washington's army under Stirling and Sullivan, thrown forward to cover the western and the middle roads. As a result, that whole wing of the army, its flower, was crushed between Howe, advancing directly from Gravesend, and Clinton, who, by a slightly circuitous night march to the eastward, had got in its rear. The disaster was, as I have said, wholly due to the lack of cavalry on Long Island, and a consequent defective outpost service. Yet these facts, so pregnant with both inferences and consequences, are not even alluded to by any general historian of the operations. The writers of so-called history did not in their turn realize the functions of cavalry in warfare, or observe that the American army in and before New York had no mounted service, or why it had none. The disaster of August 27 on Long Island just failed to bring irretrievable ruin on the cause of American independence. Even as it was, gravely compromising Washington, its influence was perceptible on the whole course of military operations during the succeeding three years. To Washington it was a lesson from which he learned much. Thenceforth he adopted Fabian tactics.

Turning now to the war of 1812–15, the influence of the battle of Bladensburg, and the consequent capture of the city of Washington, is not less apparent in the operations which resulted in the defeat of Pakenham before New Orleans and the failure of the British expedition against Louisiana than was the sharp lesson of Bunker Hill in Howe's cautious movement against the American lines at Brooklyn. The affair at Bladensburg occurred on the 24th of August; the assault on Jackson's lines before New Orleans was delivered on the 8th of January following. Those engagements, and the tactics pursued in them, are, moreover, of peculiar interest just at this time in connection with what is taking place in South Africa. A recurrence to the events of eighty-five years ago will show how very tenacious are military traditions, with the British at least, and how racial characteristics assert themselves, no matter how much conditions change, and in spite of experience. It also, if taken in connection with the other and earlier operations I have referred to, illustrates very curiously the slight degree of reliance which can be placed on the fundamental rules of strategy when it comes to their practical application. They are, in fact, about as dangerous to apply as they are to disregard; for, when all is done and written, in warfare almost everything depends on the character of the man at the head — on his insight into the real facts of the situation, including the topography of the country, and the quality of the material at his command and of that opposed to him. The really great military commander, as in the case of Napoleon in his earlier days, effects his results quite as much by ignoring all recognized rules and principles as by acting in obedience to them. New Orleans was a case in point. At New Orleans, Jackson had no right to succeed; Pakenham had no excuse for failure. The last brought defeat on his army, and lost his own life, while proceeding in the way of tradition and in obedience to accepted principles of strategy; the former achieved a brilliant success by taking risks from which any reasonably cautious commander would have recoiled.

In the first place, however, to understand the why and the wherefore of what took place at New Orleans eighty-five years ago in January, it is necessary to recall to mind what occurred at Bladensburg and in Washington eighty-five years ago last August. The general in command of the British army had been changed, for Ross was killed before Baltimore, and Pakenham, fresh from the battlefields of the Peninsula, had succeeded him; but the regiments which had simply, with a volley, a shout and a rush, walked over the American line at Bladensburg, all took part in the attempt to walk over a similar line before New Orleans. The tactics, if such they deserve to be called, were the same in each case — those of the football field. In other words, at Bladensburg the British officers, proceeding in conformity with their simple traditions and good old rules, endeavored to do, and succeeded in doing, exactly what they intended to do and failed in doing at Bunker Hill; that is, they marched directly up in front of the defending force, carried the position with little loss, routed their opponents, and then, as a matter of course in the case of Washington, captured the city those opponents were there to cover. The proceeding was perfectly simple, — very much, in fact, what we have seen recently in the Philippines, — a body of superior troops carrying by front assault weakly defended defensive points, and this with insignificant loss to themselves. At both Bladensburg and New Orleans the attempt indicated an overweening self-confidence in the attacking party, due to a dangerous contempt for their opponents. The veterans of Wellington's Peninsular campaigns had to do with raw American levies. They regarded them very much as our own volunteers have recently regarded the Filipinos.

Thus New Orleans was the sequel of Bladensburg; it goes far also to explain the recent battle on the Tugela. Thirty-four years after New Orleans, Charles James Napier, brother of the historian of the Peninsular war, writing in a reminiscent mood of the Spanish battle of Busaco, said of Pakenham, — and he and Pakenham had both been wounded at Busaco, — " Poor fellow! He was a heroic man, that Edward Pakenham, and it was a thousand pities he died in defeat; it was not his fault, that defeat." This may possibly be, and Napier was unquestionably a high authority on such a point. None the less there is a large class of military commanders commonly known in camp parlance as " butt-heads," and it is not at once apparent why Major-General Sir Edward Pakenham should not be included therein.[1] James

---

[1] See, also, *Proceedings of the Massachusetts Historical Society,* Second Series, vol. xiii. pp. 412–423.

Parton was, by birth, English, and in his life of Jackson — one of the most picturesque and vivid biographies, be it said, in the language — Parton speaks thus of Pakenham, using forty years ago language curiously applicable to operations in South Africa eighty-five years after those I am criticising : " The British service seems to develop every high and noble quality of man and soldier except generalship. Up to the hour when the British soldier holds an independent command, he is the most assured and competent of men. Give him a plain, unconditional order, — ' Go and do that ! ' — and he will go and do it with a cool, self-forgetting pertinacity of daring that can scarcely be too much admired. All of the man below the eyebrows is perfect. The stout heart, the high purpose, the dextrous hand, the enduring frame, are his. But the work of a general in command demands head — a cool, calculating head, fertile in expedients ; a head that is the controlling power of the man. And this article of head, which is the rarest production of nature everywhere, is one which the brave British soldier is apt to be signally wanting in ; and never so much so as when responsibility rests upon him." For the intelligent student of military operations it is not any easier now than it was for Parton half a century ago to advance any sufficient reasons for the tactics pursued by the British commander when, on the 8th of January, 1815, he went to his own death while thrusting his storming columns against breastworks bristling with artillery and swarming with riflemen. It was simply the wanton throwing away of life to accomplish a result which could have been accomplished in another and more scientific way absolutely without loss ; for New Orleans was then within the easy grasp of the British.

Had Pakenham, as he perfectly well could have done, passed a division of his army over to the western bank of the Mississippi, and then threatened New Orleans from that side of the river, operating upon Jackson's flank and rear, Jackson would have had no choice but to vacate his lines and allow New Orleans to fall. This, when too late, Jackson himself perfectly appreciated ; but the British commander preferred the desperate chance of an assault. The recollection of Bladensburg lured him to destruction.

In reading the literature of that campaign, it is curious to come across the footprints of this fact. Pakenham joined the army before New Orleans on the morning of Christmas-day, 1814, only two weeks before the battle. The English had then already met with much stiffer resistance than they had anticipated, and those whom Pakenham relieved of command recognized the difficulty of the problem before them to solve. Nevertheless, as the reinforcements the new commander-in-chief brought with him stepped on shore, not a few of them expressed their fears lest they should be too late to take part in the advance, as they thought New Orleans would be captured before they could get into line. On the 7th of January, the day before the fight, as one of the Bladensburg regiments was somewhat sulkily moving to the rear for the less valued service across the river, several of its officers grumbled in passing, a new arrival wrote, that " it would be now our turn to get into New Orleans, as they had done at Washington." Among those who had been at Washington, not one had been more conspicuous than Admiral Cochrane, as, a naval officer, mounted on a brood mare, white, uncurried, with a black foal trotting by her side, he rode around personally superintending the work of destruction. And now, when the brave and unfortunate Pakenham hesitated in face of the obstacles in front of him, Cochrane, so the story goes, egged him on with a taunt, telling him, with Bladensburg fresh in mind, that " if the army could not take those mud-banks, defended by ragged militia, he would do it with 2000 sailors, armed only with cutlasses and pistols."

On the other hand, Jackson on this occasion evinced one of the highest and rarest attributes of a great commander ; he read correctly the mind of his opponent — divined his course of action.   The British commander, not wholly impervious to reason, had planned a diversion to the west bank of the river, with a view to enfilading Jackson's lines, and so aiding the proposed assault in front.   As this movement assumed shape, it naturally caused Jackson much anxiety.   All depended on its magnitude.   If it was the operation in chief of the British army, New Orleans could hardly be saved.   Enfiladed, and threatened in his rear, Jackson must fall back.   If, however, it was only a diversion in favor of a main assault planned on his front, the movement across the river might be checked, or prove immaterial.   As the thing developed during the night preceding the battle, Commodore Patterson, who commanded the American naval contingent on the river, became alarmed, and hurried a despatch across to Jackson, advising him of what was taking place, and begging immediate reinforcement.   At one o'clock in the morning the messenger roused Jackson from sleep, stating his errand. Jackson listened to the despatch, and at once said : — " Hurry back and tell Commodore Patterson that he is mistaken. The main attack will be on this side, and I have no men to spare. General Morgan must maintain his position at all hazards." To use a vernacular but expressive term, Jackson had " sized " Pakenham correctly, — the British commander could be depended on not to do what a true insight would have dictated, and the occasion called for. He would not throw the main body of his army across the river and move on his objective point by a practically undefended road, merely holding his enemy in check on the east bank. Had he done so, he would have acted in disregard of that first principle both of tactics and strategy which forbids the division of a force in presence of an enemy in such a way that the two parts are not in position to support each other ; but, not the less for that, he would have taken New Orleans. An attack in front was, on the contrary, in accordance with British military traditions, and the recent experience of Bladensburg. He acted, accordingly, as Jackson was satisfied he would act. In his main assault he sacrificed his army and lost his own life, sustaining an almost unexampled defeat ; while his partial movement across the river was completely successful, so far as it was pressed, opening wide the road to New Orleans. A mere diversion, or auxiliary operation, it was not persisted in, the principal attack having failed.

Possibly it might by some now be argued that, had Pakenham thus weakened his force on the east side of the river by operating, in the way suggested, on New Orleans and Jackson's flank and rear on its west side, a vigorous, fighting opponent, such as Jackson unquestionably was, might have turned the tables on him for thus violating an elementary rule of warfare — the very rule, by the way, so dangerously ignored by Washington at Brooklyn. Leaving his lines and boldly taking the aggressive, Jackson, it will then be argued, might have overwhelmed the British force in his front, thus cutting the column operating west of the river from the fleet and its base of supplies — in fact, destroying the expedition. Not improbably Pakenham argued in this way; if he did, however, he simply demonstrated his incompetence for high command. Failing to grasp the situation, he put a wrong estimate on its conditions. It is the part of a skilful commander to know when to secure results by making exceptions to even the most general and the soundest rules. Pakenham at New Orleans had under his command a force much larger, in fact nearly double that confronting him. While, moreover, his soldiers were veterans, the Americans were hardly more than raw recruits; but, like the Boers of to-day, they had in them good material, and were individually accustomed to handling rifles. As one of the best of Jackson's brigadiers, General Adair, afterwards expressed it, — " Our men were militia without discipline, and if once beaten, they could not be relied on again." They were, in fact, of exactly the same temper and stuff as those who were stampeded by a volley and a shout at Bladensburg; and the principle of military morale thus stated by General Adair was that learned by Washington on Long Island. Troops of a certain class, when once beaten, cannot be relied on again. They are not seasoned soldiers. The force Pakenham had under his command before New Orleans was, on the other hand, composed of seasoned soldiers of the best class. In the open field, and on anything approaching equality of position, he had absolutely nothing to fear. He might safely provoke attack ; indeed, all he ought to have asked was to tempt Jackson out from behind his breastworks on almost any terms. So fully, moreover, did he realize all this that it inspired him to his assault. It is useless, therefore, to suggest that he hesitated to divide his command, overestimating Jackson's numbers and aggressive capacity. Had he done so, he would hardly have ventured to assail Jackson in front. On the contrary, Pakenham's trouble lay not in overestimating, but in underestimating his adversary. He failed to operate on what were correct principles for the conditions which confronted him, not because he was afraid so to do, but because he did not grasp the situation.

In case, then, dividing his command, Pakenham had thrown one half of it across the river to assail New Orleans in force, so turning Jackson's rear, and then with the other half held his position on the east bank, keeping open his communications with the British fleet, the only possible way in which Jackson could have taken advantage of the situation would have been by leaving his lines, and attacking.

Now, it so happens that resisting attack under just such circumstances is the position in which the British soldier has always developed his best staying qualities. Quebec was a case directly in point. Again, the men under Pakenham before New Orleans were even more reliable than those who only five months later at Waterloo, after the auxiliary troops had been swept from the field by the fury of the French attack, held their position from noon to a June sunset against an assaulting force of nearly twice their number commanded by the Emperor himself. Indeed, the tenacity of the English infantry under such circumstances is well known, — it is even now receiving new illustration. But concerning it there is a statement of the French marshal Bugeaud which is so curious, and which bears upon its face such evidence that it was written by a military man of practical experience, that I cannot refrain from quoting it. It is not the utterance of a " bookish theorick," but of one who knew of that whereof he spoke. Marshal Bugeaud, in making this statement, referred not to Waterloo, but to the operations in the Peninsular war, — that school in which the soldiers under Pakenham had learned their business. What he says reveals, moreover, a curious insight into the characteristics of the French and English infantry : —

" The English generally occupied well-chosen defensive positions, having a certain command, and they showed only a portion of their force. The usual artillery action first took place. Soon, in great haste, without studying the position, without taking time to examine if there were means to make a flank attack, we marched straight on, taking the bull by the horns. About one thousand yards from the English line the men became excited, spoke to one another, and hurried their march ; the column began to be a little confused.

" The English remained quite silent, with ordered arms, and from their steadiness appeared to be a long red wall. This steadiness invariably produced an effect on the young soldiers.

" Very soon we got nearer, shouting, ' Vive l'Empereur, en avant! à la bayonette!' Shakos were raised on the muzzles of the muskets; the column began to double, the ranks got into confusion, the agitation produced a tumult; shots were fired as we advanced.

" The English line remained still, silent and immovable, with ordered arms, even when we were only three hundred paces distant, and it appeared to ignore the storm about to break.

" The contrast was striking; in our inmost thoughts each felt that the enemy was a long time in firing, and that this fire, reserved for so long, would be very unpleasant when it did come. Our ardor cooled. The moral power of steadiness, which nothing shakes (even if it be only in appearance) over disorder which stupefies itself with noise, overcame our minds. At this moment of intense excitement the English wall shouldered arms, an indescribable feeling rooted many of our men to the ground — they began to fire. The enemy's steady concentrated volleys swept our ranks; decimated, we turned round, seeking to recover our equilibrium; then three deafening cheers broke the silence of our opponents; at the third they were on us, pushing our disorganized flight. But, to our great surprise, they did not push their advantage beyond a hundred yards, retiring calmly to their lines to await a second attack."

Those thus vividly described by an hereditary race opponent, who had himself confronted them, were the identical men Jackson would have had to attack on their own ground had he found himself compelled on the 8th of January to leave his lines and assume the aggressive, as the only possible alternative to a precipitate retreat and the abandonment of New Orleans. Certainly, that day Andrew Jackson was under great obligations to Edward Pakenham.

I have referred to Washington's operations on Long Island and the short Bladensburg campaign as interesting military studies in connection with New Orleans, or as directly influencing the course of events there. But there is another and far more memorable and momentous American campaign which is deserving of mention in the same connection. I refer to our own army movements on the Mississippi nearly half a century later. I have in this paper contended that at New Orleans one half of the British force there assembled would have been fully equal to holding its own against an assault in front from any force Jackson could have brought against it. Pakenham's flank operations in front of New Orleans could, therefore, in 1815 have been conducted with quite as much safety as were those of Grant before Vicksburg in May and June, 1863. In fact, the positions in the two cases were much the same. Like Pakenham at New Orleans, Sherman, it will be remembered, before Grant's flanking operations began, assailed the works at Vicksburg in front, meeting with a disastrous repulse. Subsequently, Grant devised his brilliant, scientific movement by Grand Gulf and the Big Black, crossing the Mississippi twice and taking his opponents in the rear, exactly as Pakenham could have done from below New Orleans, though on a much larger scale and incurring far greater risks. He thus forced Pemberton to come out from behind his works, to take the chance of even battle, in order to preserve his line of communication. He then whipped him.

And this brings us face to face with what is, after all, the fundamental condition behind all principles and theories of warfare, the individuality and tactical or strategic aptitudes — for they are very different things — of commanders. It was the Confederate general Forrest, I believe, one of the born fighters developed in our Civil War, who defined strategy as the art in warfare of "getting there first with most men." The definition is rather general ; but in it there is much native shrewdness, and, moreover, it smacks strongly of practical experience. Grant illustrated its truth in one way in 1863, just as poor Pakenham illustrated its obverse in 1815. The trouble, however, with most books of so-called history is that the industrious, but, as a rule, quite inexperienced, writers thereof, fail conspicuously to get at what may be called, for want of a better term, the true inwardness of any given situation. They tell of what occurred, after a fashion ; they fail to show why it occurred. The sequence is not revealed. So, where such are not written with a distinct bias of patriotism or hero worship, they are apt to repeat in a stereotyped sort of way accepted traditions or conventional theories; and when, with this, is combined a lack of familiarity and practical experience, the result is apt to be what we are very familiar with when a clergyman sets out to explain difficult problems of constitutional law, or some excellent man of affairs feels impelled to impart in some public way his views upon art.

As I have sought to show, Wolfe at Quebec, Washington on Long Island, Jackson at New Orleans, are

all still interesting studies, studies than which few
are more interesting. But as chance and occasion
have led me to look into them, the result has been, in
the first place, as I stated when I began, a distinct
access of historical scepticism, followed by grave
doubts as to the real value of what are known as general histories, written on the plan heretofore in vogue.
They fail to bear the test of rigid special analysis.
Accordingly, I cannot help fancying that in some
future, not now very remote, a new historical method
must be developed, a method the general character of
which I have this evening illustrated from a special
point of view. Pursuing in other fields of knowledge
the line of thought I have tried to develop in connection with a few familiar military episodes, the general
historian on a large scale will seek to draw his narrative not from his inner consciousness, or his assumed
personal knowledge of military operations as of everything else, or from any supposed natural aptitudes
which he may infer exist in himself. On the contrary,
he will turn to others, and, like some good occupant
of the judicial chair, he will bring his judgment to
bear, not upon the problems themselves, but upon the
degree of reliability to be placed on the conclusions
reached by those specially qualified for the task, who
have undertaken to speak on the problems, — the
laborious writers of scientific monographs. In military affairs as in others, the day of the historian of
the Oliver Goldsmith type, — the facile writer who
knows it all, who is at once a statesman, a diplomat, a
parliamentarian, a lawyer, a theologian, a physician,
a biologist, a mechanician, an architect, a linguist, and,
though neither last nor least, a military and naval

strategist, — the day of the historian of this class is practically a thing of the past; for even historical writers begin to realize that no man can be a specialist in everything; neither is it any longer given to one of finite powers to take all knowledge for his province, and to be a generalizer besides.

VI

"SHALL CROMWELL HAVE A STATUE?"[1]

"Whom doth the king delight to honour? that is the question of questions concerning the king's own honour. Show me the man you honour; I know by that symptom, better than by any other, what kind of man you yourself are. For you show me there what your ideal of manhood is; what kind of man you long inexpressibly to be, and would thank the gods, with your whole soul, for being if you could."

"Who is to have a Statue? means, Whom shall we consecrate and set apart as one of our sacred men? Sacred; that all men may see him, be reminded of him, and, by new example added to old perpetual precept, be taught what is real worth in man. Whom do you wish us to resemble? Him you set on a high column, that all men, looking on it, may be continually apprised of the duty you expect from them." — THOMAS CARLYLE: *Latter-Day Pamphlets* (1850).

AT about three o'clock of the afternoon of September 3, 1658, the day of Worcester and of Dunbar, and as a great tempest was wearing itself to rest, Oliver Cromwell died. He died in London, in the palace of Whitehall; the palace of the great banqueting-hall through whose central window Charles I., a little less than ten years before, had walked forth to the scaffold. A few weeks later, "with a more than regal solemnity," the body of the great Lord Protector was carried to

---

[1] Oration delivered before the Beta of Illinois Chapter of the Phi Beta Kappa Society, at the University of Chicago, on Tuesday, June 17, 1902. This address was the natural sequence and complement of the paper, entitled "Lee at Appomattox" (*supra*, pp. 1–19), read before the American Antiquarian Society, at Worcester, Mass., on the 19th of the previous October. It was compressed in delivery, occupying one hour and thirty minutes.

Westminster Abbey, and there buried " amongst kings." Two years then elapsed ; and, on the twelfth anniversary of King Charles's execution, the remains of the usurper, having been previously disinterred by order of the newly restored king, were by a unanimous vote of the Convention Parliament hung at Tyburn. The trunk was then buried under the gallows, while Cromwell's head was set on a pole over the roof of Westminster Hall. Nearly two centuries of execration ensued, until, in the sixth generation, the earlier verdict was challenged, and the question at last asked : " Shall Cromwell have a Statue ? " Cromwell, the traitor, the usurper, the execrable murderer of the martyred Charles ! At first, and for long, the suggestion was looked upon almost as an impiety, and, as such, scornfully repelled. Not only did the old loyal king-worship of England recoil from the thought, but, indignantly appealing to the church, it declared that no such distinction could be granted so long as there remained in the prayer-book a form of supplication for " King Charles, the Martyr," and of " praise and thanksgiving for the wonderful deliverance of these kingdoms from the great rebellion, and all the other miseries and oppressions consequent thereon, under which they had so long groaned." None the less, the demand was insistent ; and at last, but only after two full centuries had elapsed and a third was well advanced, was the verdict of 1661 reversed. To-day the bronze effigy of Oliver Cromwell — massive in size, rugged in feature, characteristic in attitude — stands defiantly in the yard of that Westminster Hall, from a pole on the top of which, twelve-score years ago, the flesh crumbled from his skull.

In this dramatic reversal of an accepted verdict, — this complete revision of opinions once deemed settled and immutable, — there is, I submit, a lesson, — an academic lesson. The present occasion is essentially educational. The Phi Beta Kappa oration, as it is called, is the last, the crowning utterance of the college year, and very properly is expected to deal with some fitting theme in a kindred spirit. I propose to do so to-day; but in a fashion somewhat exceptional. The phases of moral and intellectual growth through which the English race has passed on the subject of Cromwell's statue afford, I submit, to the reflecting man an educational study of exceptional interest. In the first place, it was a growth of two centuries; in the second place, it marks the passage of a nation from an existence under the traditions of feudalism to one under the principles of self-government; finally, it illustrates the gradual development of that broad spirit of tolerance which, coming with time and study, measures the men and events of the past independently of the prejudices and passions which obscure and distort the immediate vision.

We, too, as well as the English, have had our " Great Rebellion." It came to a dramatic close thirty-seven years since; as theirs came to a close not less dramatic some seven times thirty-seven years since. We, also, as they in their day, formed our contemporaneous judgments and recorded our verdicts, assumed to be irreversible, of the men, the issues, and the events of the great conflict; and those verdicts and judgments, in our case as in theirs, will unquestionably be revised, modified, and in not a few cases wholly reversed. Better knowledge, calmer reflection, and a more judicial frame of mind come with the passage of the years; slowly passions subside, prejudices disappear, truth asserts itself. In England this process has been going on for close upon two centuries and a half; with what result, Cromwell's statue stands as proof. We live in another age and a different environment; and, as fifty years of Europe outmeasure in their growth a cycle of Cathay, so I hold one year of twentieth century America works far more progress in thought than seven years of Britain during the interval between its Great Rebellion and ours. We who took active part in the Civil War have not yet wholly vanished from the stage; the rear guard of the Grand Army, we linger. To-day is separated from the death of Lincoln by the same number of years only which separated "the Glorious Revolution of 1688" from the execution of Charles Stuart; yet to us is already given to look back on the events of which we were a part with the same perspective effects with which the Victorian Englishman looks back on the men and events of the Commonwealth.

I propose on this occasion to do so; and reverting to my text, — "Shall Cromwell have a Statue," — and reading that text in the gloss of Carlyle's *Latter-Day Pamphlet* utterance, I quote you Horace's familiar precept, —

> "Mutato nomine, de te
> Fabula narratur," —

and ask abruptly, "Shall Robert E. Lee have a Statue?" I propose also to offer to your consideration some reasons why he should, and, assuredly, will have one, if not now, then presently.

Shortly after Lee's death in October, 1870, leave

was asked in the United States Senate, by Mr. Mc-
Creery, of Kentucky, to introduce a joint resolution
providing for the return of the estate and mansion of
Arlington to the family of the deceased Confederate
Commander-in-chief. In view of the use which had
then already been made of Arlington as a military
cemetery, this proposal, involving, as it necessarily did,
a removal of the dead, naturally led to warm debate.
The proposition was one not to be considered. If a
defect in the title of the government existed, it must
in some way be cured; as, subsequently, it was cured.
But I call attention to the debate because Charles
Sumner, then a Senator from Massachusetts, participated in it, using the following language: "Eloquent
Senators have already characterized the proposition
and the traitor it seeks to commemorate. I am not
disposed to speak of General Lee. It is enough to
say he stands high in the catalogue of those who have
imbrued their hands in their country's blood. I hand
him over to the avenging pen of History." This was
when Lee had been just two months dead; but, three-
quarters of a century after the Protector's skull had
been removed from over the roof of Westminster Hall,
Pope wrote in similar spirit —

> " See Cromwell, damn'd to everlasting fame ; "

and, sixteen years later, — close upon a century after
Cromwell's disentombment at Westminster and re-
burial at Tyburn, — a period from the death of Lee
equal to that which will have elapsed in 1960, Gray
sang of the Stoke Pogis churchyard —

> " Some mute inglorious Milton here may rest,
> Some Cromwell guiltless of his country's blood."

And now, a century and a half later, Cromwell's

statue looms defiantly up in front of the Parliament House. When, therefore, an appeal is in such cases made to the "avenging pen of History," it is well to bear this instance in mind, while recalling perchance the aphorism of a greater than Pope, or Gray, or Sumner, — "and thus the whirligig of Time brings in his revenges."

Was, then, Robert E. Lee a "traitor," — was he also guilty of his "country's blood?" These questions I propose now to discuss. I am one of those who, in other days, was arrayed in the ranks which confronted Lee ; one of those whom Lee baffled and beat, but who, finally, baffled and beat Lee. As one thus formerly lined up against him, these questions I propose to discuss in the calmer and cooler, and altogether more reasonable light which comes to most men, when a whole generation of the human race lies buried between them and the issues and actors upon which they undertake to pass.

Was Robert E. Lee a traitor? Technically, I think he was indisputably a traitor to the United States ; for a traitor, as I understand it technically, is one guilty of the crime of treason ; or, as the Century Dictionary puts it, violating his allegiance to the chief authority of the State ; while treason against the United States is specifically defined in the Constitution as "levying war against them, or in adhering to their enemies, giving them aid and comfort." That Robert E. Lee did levy war against the United States can, I suppose, no more be denied than that he gave "aid and comfort" to its enemies ; and to the truth of the last proposition I hold myself, among others, to be a very competent witness. This technically; but, in history, there is treason and treason, as there are traitors and traitors. And, furthermore, if Robert E. Lee was a traitor, so also, and indisputably, were George Washington, Oliver Cromwell, John Hampden, and William of Orange. The list might be extended indefinitely ; but these will suffice. There can be no question that every one of those named violated his allegiance, and gave aid and comfort to the enemies of his sovereign. Washington furnishes a precedent at every point. A Virginian like Lee, he was also a British subject; he had fought under the British flag, as Lee had fought under that of the United States ; when, in 1776, Virginia seceded from the British Empire, he " went with his State," just as Lee went with it eighty-five years later ; subsequently Washington commanded armies in the field designated by those opposed to them as " rebels," and whose descendants now glorify them as " the rebels of '76," much as Lee later commanded, and at last surrendered, much larger armies, also designated " rebels " by those they confronted. Except in their outcome, the cases were, therefore, precisely alike ; and logic is logic. It consequently appears to follow, that, if Lee was a traitor, Washington was also. It is unnecessary to institute similar comparisons with Cromwell, Hampden, and William of Orange. No defence can in their cases be made. Technically, one and all, they undeniably were traitors.

But there are, as I have said, traitors and traitors, — Catilines, Arnolds, and Görgeis, as well as Cromwells, Hampdens, and Washingtons. To reach any satisfactory conclusion concerning a candidate for

" everlasting fame," — whether to deify or damn, — enroll him as saviour, as martyr, or as criminal, — it is, therefore, necessary still further to discriminate. The cause, the motive, the conduct must be passed in review. Did turpitude anywhere attach to the original taking of sides, or to subsequent act? Was the man a self-seeker? Did low or sordid motives impel him? Did he seek to aggrandize himself at his country's cost? Did he strike with a parricidal hand?

These are grave questions ; and, in the case of Lee, their consideration brings us at the threshold face to face with issues which have perplexed and divided the country since the day the United States became a country. They perplex and divide historians now. Legally, technically, — the moral and humanitarian aspects of the issue wholly apart, — which side had the best of the argument as to the rights and the wrongs of the case in the great debate which led up to the Civil War ? Before entering, however, on this well-worn — I might say, this threadbare — theme, as I find myself compelled in briefest way to do, there is one preliminary very essential to be gone through with, — a species of moral purgation. Bearing in mind Dr. Johnson's advice to Boswell on a certain memorable occasion, we should at least try to clear our minds of cant. Many years ago, but only shortly before his death, Richard Cobden said, in one of his truth-telling deliverances to his Rochdale constituents, — " I really believe I might be Prime Minister. If I would get up and say you are the greatest, the wisest, the best, the happiest people in the world, and keep on repeating that, I don't doubt but what I might be Prime

Minister. I have seen Prime Ministers made in my experience precisely by that process." The same great apostle of homely sense, on another occasion, bluntly remarked in a similar spirit to the House of Commons, — " We generally sympathize with everybody's rebels but our own." In both these respects I submit we Americans are true descendants from the Anglo-Saxon stock; and nowhere is this more unpleasantly apparent than in any discussion which may arise of the motives which actuated those of our countrymen who did not at the time see the issues involved in our Civil War as we saw them. Like those whom Cobden addressed, we like to glorify our ancestors and ourselves, and we do not particularly care to give ear to what we are pleased to term unpatriotic, and, at times, even treasonable talk. In other words, and in plain, unpalatable English, our minds are saturated with cant. Only in the case of others do we see things as they really are. Ceasing to be individually interested, we then at once become nothing unless critical. So, when it comes to rebellions, we, like Cobden's Englishmen, are wont almost invariably to sympathize with everybody's rebels but our own.

Our souls spontaneously go forth to Celt, Pole, Hungarian, Boer, and Hindoo; but when we are concerned, language quite fails us in which adequately to depict the moral turpitude which must actuate Confederate or Filipino who rises in resistance against what we are pleased really to consider, as well as call, the best and most beneficent government the world has yet been permitted to see, — Our Government! This, I submit, is cant, — pure cant; and at the threshold of discussion we had best free our minds of it, wholly, if we can; if not wholly, then in so far as we can. Philip the Second of Spain, when he directed his crusade in the name of God, Church, and Government against William of Orange, indulged in it in quite as good faith as we; and as for Charles " the Martyr " and the " sainted " Laud, for two centuries after Cromwell's head was stuck on a pole all England annually lamented in sackcloth and ashes the wrongs inflicted by sacrilegious hands on those most assuredly well-meaning rulers and men. All depends on the point of view; and, during our own Civil War, while we unceasingly denounced the wilful wickedness of those who bore parricidal arms against the one immaculate authority yet given the eye of man to look upon, the leading newspaper of the world was referring to us in perfect good faith " as an insensate and degenerate people." An English member of Parliament, speaking at the same time in equally good faith, declared that, throughout the length and breadth of Great Britain, public sentiment was almost unanimously on the side of " the Southerners," — as ours was on the side of the Boers, — because our " rebels " were " fighting against one of the most grinding, one of the most galling, one of the most irritating attempts to establish tyrannical government that ever disgraced the history of the world." [1]

Upon the correctness or otherwise of these judgments I do not care to pass. They certainly cannot be reconciled. The single point I make is that they were, when made, the expression of views honestly and sincerely entertained. We sympathize with Great Britain's rebels; Great Britain sympathized with our rebels.

[1] *Supra*, pp. 63, 75.

Our rebels in 1862, as theirs in 1900, thoroughly
believed they were resisting an iniquitous attempt to
deprive them of their rights, and to establish over
them a "grinding," a "galling," and an "irritating"
"tyrannical government." We in 1861, as Great
Britain in 1898, and Charles "the Martyr" and Philip
of Spain some centuries earlier, were fully convinced
that we were engaged in God's work while we trod
under foot the "rebel" and the "traitor." Presently,
as distance lends a more correct perspective, and things
are viewed in their true proportions, we will get perhaps to realize that our case furnishes no exception to
the general rule; and that we, too, like the English,
"generally sympathize with everybody's rebels but our
own." Justice may then be done.

Having entered this necessary, if somewhat hopeless
caveat, let us address ourselves to the question at issue.
I will state it again. Legally and technically, — not
morally, again let me say, and wholly irrespective of
humanitarian considerations, — to which side did the
weight of argument incline during the great debate
which culminated in our Civil War? The answer
necessarily turns on the abstract right of what we term
a Sovereign State to secede from the Union at such
time and for such cause as may seem to that State
proper and sufficient. The issue is settled now; irrev-
ocably and for all time decided: it was not settled
forty years ago, and the settlement since reached has
been the result not of reason, based on historical evidence, but of events and of force. To pass a fair
judgment on the line of conduct pursued by Lee in
1861, it is necessary to go back in thought and imagination, and see things, not as they now are, but as

they then were. If we do so, and accept the judgment of some of the more modern students and investigators of history, — either wholly unprejudiced or with a distinct Union bias, — it would seem as if the weight of argument falls into what I will term the Confederate scale. For instance, Professor Goldwin Smith, — an Englishman, a lifelong student of history, a friend and advocate of the Union during the Civil War, the author of one of the most compact and readable narratives of our national life, — Goldwin Smith has recently said: " Few who have looked into the history can doubt that the Union originally was, and was generally taken by the parties to it to be, a compact, dissoluble, perhaps, most of them would have said, at pleasure, dissoluble certainly on breach of the articles of Union." [1] To a like effect, but in terms even stronger, Mr. Henry Cabot Lodge, now a Senator from Massachusetts, has declared, not in a political utterance but in a work of historical character, — " When the Constitution was adopted by the votes of States at Philadelphia, and accepted by the votes of States in popular conventions, it is safe to say that there was not a man in the country, from Washington and Hamilton, on the one side, to George Clinton and George Mason, on the other, who regarded the new system as anything but an experiment entered upon by the States, and from which each and every State had the right peaceably to withdraw, a right which was very likely to be exercised." [2]

Here are two explicit statements of the legal and technical side of the argument made by authority to

---

[1] *Atlantic Monthly Magazine* (March, 1902), vol. lxxxix. p. 305.

[2] *Webster*, American Statesmen Series, p. 172.

which no exception can be taken, at least by those of the Union side. On them, and on them alone, the case for the abstract right of secession might be rested, and we could go on to the next stage of the discussion.

I am unwilling, however, so to do. The issue involved is still one of interest, and I am not disposed to leave it on the mere dictum of two authorities, however eminent. In the first place I do not altogether concur in their statement; in the next place, this discussion is a mere threshing of straw unless we get at the true inwardness of the situation. When it comes to subjects — political or moral — in which human beings are involved, metaphysics are scarcely less to be avoided than cant; alleged historical facts are apt to prove deceptive; and I confess to grave suspicions of logic. Old time theology, for instance, with its pitiless reasoning, led the world into very strange places and much bad company. In reaching a conclusion, therefore, in which a verdict is entered on the motives and actions of men, acting either individually or in masses, the moral, the sentimental, and the practical must be quite as much taken into account as the legal, the logical, and the material. This, in the present case, I propose presently to do; but, as I have said, on the facts even I am unable wholly to concur with Professor Smith and Mr. Lodge.

Mr. Lodge, for instance, cites Washington. But it so chances Washington put himself on record upon the point at issue, and his testimony is directly at variance with the views attributed to him by Mr. Webster's biographer. What are known in history as the Kentucky resolutions, drawn up by Thomas Jefferson, then Vice-President, were passed by the legislature of the State whose name they bear in November, 1798. In those Resolutions the view of the framers of the Constitution as to the original scope of that instrument accepted by Professor Smith and Mr. Lodge was first set forth. The principles acted upon by South Carolina on the 20th of December, 1860, were enunciated by Kentucky November 16, 1798. The dragon's teeth were then sown. Washington was at that time living in retirement at Mt. Vernon. When, a few weeks later, the character of those resolutions became known to him, he was deeply concerned, and wrote to Lafayette, — " The Constitution, according to their interpretation of it, would be a mere cipher; " and again, a few days later, he expressed himself still more strongly in a letter to Patrick Henry, — " Measures are systematically and pertinaciously pursued which must eventually dissolve the Union, or produce coercion." [1] Coercion Washington thus looked to as the remedy to which recourse could properly be had in case of any overt attempt at secession. But, so far as the framers of the Constitution were concerned, it seems to me clear that, acting as wise men of conflicting views naturally would act in a formative period during which many conflicting views prevailed, they did not care to incur the danger of a shipwreck of their entire scheme by undertaking to settle, distinctly and in advance, abstract questions, the discussion of which was fraught with danger.[2] In so far as they could,

[1] Sparks: *Writings of Washington*, vol. xi. pp. 378, 389.

[2] The discussion on this point has hitherto proved as inconclusive as interminable ; and it seems likely so to remain. (See *Proceedings of Massachusetts Historical Society*, New Series, vol. xvi. pp. 151–173, May 8, 1902.) From the days of Mr. Webster, and his answer to

they, with great practical shrewdness, left those questions to be settled, should they ever present themselves in concrete form, under the conditions which might then exist. The truth thus seems to be that the mass of those composing the Convention of 1787, working under the guidance of a few very able and exceedingly practical men, of constructive mind, builded a great deal better than they knew. The delegates met to harmonize trade differences; they ended by perfecting a scheme of political union that had broad consequences of which they little dreamed. If they had dreamed of them, the chances

Hayne, to the present time, it is all matter of inference and argument, and of surmise. Meanwhile, no one will deny that the framers of the Constitution were gifted with an entirely adequate power of expressing themselves, when they thought fit so to do. The defenders of the principle of nationality scrutinize the instrument in vain in search of any clause declaring the absolute sovereignty of the Nation and prohibiting the secession of a State, or the dissolution of the compact by a State; or, under certain conditions, permitting it to such number, or proportion, of States as were prescribed for original adoption. This could easily have been expressed, and would have obviated any question. It was not. On the other hand, the advocates of State Sovereignty, and defenders of the sovereign right of secession, make no pretence of finding in the Constitution any words expressly setting forth that right, or distinctly reserving the power to one State, or any number of States, of dissolving what they designate as "the compact." They have to reach their results through a process of elaborate argumentation. The silence of the framers is undeniable; the reason thereof is as obvious as the fact. They wisely refrained from any declaration which, while setting forth precisely the rights and obligations of the parties to the instrument, would inevitably involve its rejection. They thus intentionally left the question in doubt, to be decided by the course of events, and the process of what we now know as evolution. Such seems to be the only common-sense conclusion to be derived from a careful study of both the Constitution and the debates on its adoption. Both sides to the subsequent discussion had, and have, reason; neither, proof. Nor will proof ever be attainable.

are the fabric would never have been completed. That Madison, Hamilton and Jay were equally blind to consequences does not follow. They probably designed a nation. If they did, however, they were too wise to take the public fully into their confidence; and, to-day, " no impartial student of our constitutional history can doubt for a moment that each State ratified" the form of government submitted in " the firm belief that at.any time it could withdraw therefrom." [1] A Mr. Davie, a North Carolina delegate to the Philadelphia Convention of 1787, put the case very clearly in the course of a speech in favor of the adoption of the Constitution by his own State. " Every man of common sense knows that political power is *political right;* " [2] and, well assured that Virginia, Pennsylvania, or New England " could," at any time, " withdraw," — for who was to withstand them in so doing? — the men of that day representing those States were not disposed to scrutinize over closely the legal aspects of such withdrawal. Probably, however, the more farseeing — and, in the long run, they alone count — shared with Washington in the belief that in process of time, after the machine was once put in successful action, this withdrawal would not be unaccompanied by practical difficulty. And, after all is said and done, the legality of secession is somewhat of a metaphysical abstraction so long as the right of revolution is inalienable. As matter of fact it was to might and revolution the South appealed in 1861; and it was to coercion the government of the Union had recourse. So, with his supreme good sense and

---

[1] Donn Piatt: *George H. Thomas*, p. 88.
[2] Elliot: *Debates*, vol. iv. p. 238.

that political insight at once instinctive and unerring, in respect to which he stands almost alone, Washington foresaw this alternative in 1798.[1] He looked

[1] Washington seems, indeed, to have foreseen it from the commencement. Hardly was the independence of the country achieved before he began to direct his efforts toward the creation of a nation, with a central power adequate to a coercive policy if called for by the occasion. Thus, in March, 1783, he wrote to Nathanael Greene (Ford : *Writings of Washington*, vol. x. p. 203, note), " It remains only for the States to be wise, and to establish their independence on the basis of an inviolable, efficacious union, and a firm confederation." The following month he wrote in the same spirit to Tench Tilghman (*Ib.* vol. x. p. 238), "In a word, the Constitution of Congress must be competent to the *general purposes* of Government, and of such a nature as to bind us together. Otherwise we shall be like a rope of sand, and as easily broken." Finally, in the Circular Letter addressed to the Governors of all the States on disbanding the Army, June 8, 1783 (*Ib.* vol. x. p. 257), "There are four things which, I humbly conceive, are essential to the well-being, I may even venture to say, to the existence of the United States as an independent power. First, An indissoluble union of the States under one federal head." In language even stronger he, July 8, 1783, — only a month later, — wrote to Dr. William Gordon, the historian (*Ib.* vol. x. p. 276), " We are known by no other character among nations than as the United States. Massachusetts or Virginia is no better defined, nor any more thought of by Foreign Powers, than the County of Worcester in Massachusetts is by Virginia, or Gloucester County in Virginia is by Massachusetts (respectable as they are) ; and yet these counties with as much propriety might oppose themselves to the laws of the States in which they are, as an individual State can oppose itself to the Federal Government, by which it is, or ought to be bound."

With the passage of time, Washington's feelings on this subject seem to have grown stronger, and, March 10, 1787, he wrote to John Jay, " A thirst for power, and the bantling — I had liked to have said MONSTER — sovereignty, which have taken such fast hold of the States," etc. (William Jay: *Life of John Jay*, vol. i. p. 259.) A year earlier, August 1, 1786, he had written to Jay, "Experience has taught us, that men will not adopt and carry into execution measures the best calculated for their own good, without the intervention of a coercive power. I do not conceive we can exist long as a nation without having lodged somewhere a power, which will pervade the whole Union in as energetic a manner as the authority of the state governments extends over the several States." (Ford: *Writings of* upon the doctrine of secession as a heresy; but, none the less, it was a heresy indisputably then preached, and to which many, not in Virginia only, but in New England also, pinned their political faith. Even the Devil is proverbially entitled to his due.

So far, however, as the abstract question is of consequence, as the utterances of Professor Smith and Mr. Lodge conclusively show, the Secessionists of 1861 stand in history's court by no means without a case. In that case, moreover, they implicitly believed. From generation to generation they had grown up indoctrinated with the gospel, or heresy, of State Sovereignty, and it was as much part of their moral and intellectual being as was clanship of the Scotch highlanders. In so far they were right, as Governor John A. Andrew said of John Brown. Meanwhile, practically, as a common-sensed man, leading an every-day existence in a world of actualities, John Brown was not right; he was, on the contrary, altogether wrong, and richly merited the fate meted out to him. It was the same with the Secessionists. That, in 1861, they could really have had faith in the practicability — the real working efficacy — of that peaceable secession which they professed to ask for, and of which they never wearied of talking, I cannot believe. I find in the record no real evidence thereof.

Of the high-type Southron, as we sometimes designate him, I would speak in terms of sincere respect. I know him chiefly by hearsay, having come in per-

Washington, vol. xi. p. 53.) This, it will be observed, was within a few days less than seven months only before the passage by the Confederation Congress of the resolution of February 21, 1787, calling for the Convention which, during the ensuing summer, framed the present Constitution.

sonal contact only with individual representatives of
the class; but such means of observation as I have
had confirm what I recently heard said by a friend of
mine, once Governor of South Carolina, and, so far
as I know, the only man who ever gave the impossible
and indefensible plan of reconstruction attempted
after our Civil War a firm, fair, and intelligent trial.
He at least put forth an able and honest effort to
make effective a policy which never should have been
devised. Speaking from "much and varied experience," I recently heard Daniel H. Chamberlain say of
the "typical Southern gentleman" that he considered
him "a distinct and really noble growth of our American soil. For, if fortitude under good and under
evil fortune, if endurance without complaint of what
comes in the tide of human affairs, if a grim clinging to ideals once charming, if vigor and resiliency of
character and spirit under defeat and poverty and
distress, if a steady love of learning and letters when
libraries were lost in flames and the wreckage of war,
if self-restraint when the long delayed relief at last
came, — if, I say, all these qualities are parts of real
heroism, if these qualities can vivify and ennoble a
man or a people, then our own South may lay claim
to an honored place among the differing types of our
great common race." Such is the matured judgment
of the Massachusetts Governor of South Carolina
during the Congressional reconstruction period; and,
listening to it, I asked myself if it was descriptive of
a Southern fellow countryman, or a Jacobite Scotch
chieftain anterior to "the '45."

The Southern statesmen of the old slavery days —
the antediluvian period which preceded our mid-cen-

tury cataclysm — were the outcome and representatives of what has thus been described. As such they presented a curious admixture of qualities. Masterful in temper, clear of purpose, with a firm grasp on principle, a high sense of honor, and a moral perception developed on its peculiar lines, as in the case of Calhoun, to a quality of distinct hardness, they were yet essentially abstractionists. Political metaphysicians, they were not practical men. They did not see things as they really were. They thus, while discussing their " forty-bale theories " and the " patriarchal institution " in connection with States' rights and nullification, failed to realize that on the two essential features of their policy — slavery and secession — they were contending with the stars in their courses. The whole world was moving irresistibly in the direction of nationality and an ever increased recognition of the rights of man ; while they, on both of these vital issues, were proclaiming a crusade of reaction.

Moreover, what availed the views or intentions of the framers of the Constitution ? What mattered it in 1860 whether they, in 1787, contemplated a Nation or only a more compact federation of Sovereign States ? In spite of logic and historical precedent, and in sublime unconsciousness of metaphysics and abstractions, realities have an unpleasant way of asserting their existence. However it may have been in 1788, in 1860 a Nation had grown into existence. Its peaceful dismemberment was impossible. The complex system of tissues and ligaments, the growth of seventy years, could not be gently taken apart, without wound or hurt ; the separation, if separation there was to be, involved a tearing asunder, supplementing a liberal use of the knife. Their professions to the contrary notwithstanding, this the Southern leaders failed not to realize. In point of fact, therefore, believing fully in the abstract legality of secession, and the justice and sufficiency of the grounds on which they acted, their appeal was to the inalienable right of revolution, and to that might by which alone the right could be upheld. Let us put casuistry, metaphysics, and sentiment aside, and come to actualities. The secessionist recourse in 1861 was to the sword; and to the sword it was meant to have recourse.

I have thus far spoken only of the South as a whole. Much has been said and written on the subject of an alleged conspiracy, in those days, of Southern men and leaders against the Union ; of the designs and ultimate objects of the alleged conspirators; of acts of treachery on their part, and the part of their accomplices, towards the government, of which they were the sworn officials. Into this phase of the subject I do not propose to enter. That the leaders in Secession were men with large views, and that they had matured a comprehensive policy as the ultimate outcome of their movement, I entertain no doubt. They looked unquestionably to an easy military success, and the complete establishment of their Confederacy ; more remotely, there can be no question they contemplated a policy of extension, and the establishment along the shores of the Gulf of Mexico and in the Antilles of a great semi-tropical, slave-labor republic; finally, all my investigations have tended to satisfy me that they confidently anticipated an early disintegration of the Union, and the accession of the bulk of the Northern States to the Confederacy, New England only being sternly excluded therefrom — " sloughed off," as they expressed it. The capital of the new Confederacy was to be Washington ; African servitude, under reasonable limitations, was to be recognized throughout its limits ; agriculture was to be its ruling interest, with a tariff and foreign policy in strict accord therewith. " Secession is not intended to break up the present government, but to perpetuate it. We go out of the Union, not to destroy it, but for the purpose of getting further guarantees and security," — this was said in February, 1861 ; and this in 1900, — " And so we believe that, with the success of the South, the ' Union of our Fathers,' which the South was the principal factor in forming, and to which she was far more attached than the North, would have been restored and reëstablished ; that in this Union, the South would have been again the dominant people, the controlling power." Conceding the necessary premises of fact and law, — a somewhat considerable concession, but, perhaps, conceivable, — conceding these, I see in this position, then or now, nothing illogical, nothing provocative of severe criticism, certainly nothing treasonable. Acting on sufficient grounds, of which those thus acting were the sole judge, proceeding in a way indisputably legal and regular, it was proposed to reconstruct the Union in the light of experience, and on a new, and, as they considered, an improved basis, without New England. This cannot properly be termed a conspiracy ; it was a legitimate policy based on certain assumed data legal, moral, and economical. But it was in reality never for a moment believed that this programme could be peaceably and quietly carried into effect ; and the assent of New England to the arrangement was neither asked for, assumed, nor expected. New England was distinctly relegated to an outer void, — at once cold, dark, inhospitable.

As to participation of those who sympathized in these views and this policy in the councils of the government, so furthering schemes for its overthrow while sworn to its support, I hold it unnecessary to speak. Such were traitors. As such, had they met their deserts, they should, at the proper time, and on due process of law, have been arrested, tried, convicted, sentenced, and hanged. That in certain well-remembered instances this course was not pursued, is, to my mind, even yet much to be deplored. In such cases clemency is only another form of cant.

Having now discussed what have seemed to me the necessary preliminaries, I come to the particular cases of Virginia and Robert E. Lee. The two are closely interwoven, — for Virginia was always Virginia, and the Lees were, first, over and above all, Virginians. It was the Duke of Wellington who, on a certain memorable occasion, indignantly remarked in his delightful French-English, — "Mais avant tout je suis gentilhomme Anglais." So might have said the Lees of Virginia of themselves.

As respects Virginia, moreover, I am fain to say there was in the attitude of the State towards the Confederacy, and, indeed, in its bearing throughout the Civil War, something which appealed strongly, — something unselfish and chivalric, — worthy of Virginia's highest record. History will, I think, do justice to it. Virginia, it must be remembered, while a Slave State, was not a Cotton State. This was a distinction implying a difference. In Virginia the insti-

tution of slavery existed, and because of it she was
in close sympathy with her sister Slave States; but,
while in the Cotton States slavery had gradually assumed a purely material form, in Virginia it still
retained much of its patriarchal character. The
" Border " States, as they were called, and among them
Virginia especially, had, it is true, gained an evil name
as " slave-breeding ground; " but this was merely an
incident to a system in which, taken by and large, —
viewed in the rule and not in the exception, — the
being with African blood in his veins was not looked
upon as a mere transferable chattel, but practically,
and to a large extent, was attached to the house and
the soil. This fact had a direct bearing on the moral
issue; for slavery, one thing in Virginia, was quite
another in Louisiana. The Virginian pride was moreover proverbial. Indeed, I doubt if local feeling and
patriotism and devotion to the State ever anywhere
attained a fuller development than in the community
which dwelt in the region watered by the Potomac and
the James, of which Richmond was the political centre.
We of the North, especially we of New England, were
Yankees; but a Virginian was that, and nothing else.
I have heard of a New Englander, of a Green Moun-
tain boy, of a Rhode Islander, of a " Nutmeg," of a
" Blue-nose " even, but never of a Massachusettensian.
The word somehow does not lend itself to the mouth,
any more than the thought to the mind.

But Virginia was strongly attached by sentiment
as well as interest to the Union. The birthplace of
Washington, the mother of States as well as of Presidents, " The Old Dominion," as she was called, and
fondly loved to call herself, had never been affected by

the nullification heresies of South Carolina; and the long line of her eminent public men, though, in 1860, showing marked signs of a deteriorating standard, still retained a prominence in the national councils. If John B. Floyd was Secretary of War, Winfield Scott was at the head of the Army. Torn by conflicting feelings, Virginia, still clinging to the Nation, was unwilling to sever her connection with it because of the lawful election of an anti-slavery President, even by a distinctly sectional vote. For a time she even stayed the fast flooding tide of secession, bringing about a brief but important reaction. Those of us old enough to remember the drear and anxious winter which followed the election and preceded the inauguration of Lincoln, recall vividly the ray of bright hope which, in the midst of its deepest gloom, then came from Virginia. It was in early February. Up to that time the record was unbroken. Beginning with South Carolina on the 20th of December, State after State, meeting in convention, had with significant unanimity passed ordinances of secession. Each successive ordinance was felt to be the equivalent of a renewed declaration of war. The outlook was dark indeed , and, amid the fast gathering gloom, all eyes, all thoughts, turned to Virginia. She represented the Border States; her action it was felt would largely influence, and might control theirs. John Letcher was then Governor, — a States' Rights Democrat, of course, — but a Union man. By him the legislature of the State was called together in special session, and that legislature, in January, passed what was known as a convention bill. Practically Virginia was to vote on the question at issue. Events moved rapidly.

South Carolina had seceded on the 20th of December; Mississippi, on the 9th of January; Florida, on the 10th; Alabama, on the 11th; Georgia followed on the 19th; Louisiana on the 26th, with Texas on the 1st of February. The procession seemed unending; the record unbroken. Not without cause might the now thoroughly frightened friends of the Union have exclaimed with Macbeth —

> " What! will the line stretch out to the crack of doom?
> Another yet? A seventh?"

If at that juncture the Old Dominion had, by a decisive vote, followed in the steps of the Cotton States, it implied consequences which no man could fathom. It involved the possession of the national capitol, and the continuance of the Government. Maryland would inevitably follow the Virginian lead; the recently elected President had not yet been inaugurated; taken wholly by surprise, the North was divided in sentiment; the loyal spirit of the country was not aroused. It was thus an even question whether, on the 4th of March, the whole machinery of the *de facto* government would not be in the hands of the revolutionists. All depended on Virginia. This is now forgotten; none the less, it is history.

The Virginia election was held on the 4th of February, the news of the secession of Texas — seventh in the line — having been received on the 2d. Evidently, the action of Texas was carefully timed for effect. Though over forty years ago, I well remember that day — gray, overcast, wintry — which succeeded the Virginia election. Then living in Boston, a young man of twenty-five, I shared — as who did not? — in the common deep depression and intense anxiety. It was as if a verdict was to be that day announced in a case involving fortune, honor, life even. Too harassed for work, I remember abandoning my desk in the afternoon to seek relief in physical activity, for the ponds in the vicinity of Boston were ice-covered, and daily thronged with skaters. I was soon among the number gloomily seeking unfrequented spots. Suddenly I became aware of an unusual movement in the throng nearest the shore, where those fresh from the city arrived. The skaters seemed crowding to a common point; and a moment later they scattered again with cheers and gestures of relief. An arrival fresh from Boston had brought the first bulletin of yesterday's election. Virginia, speaking against secession, had emitted no uncertain sound. It was as if a weight had been taken off the mind of every one. The tide seemed turned at last. For myself, I remember my feelings were too deep to find expression in words or sound. Something stuck in my throat. I wanted to be by myself.

Nor did we overestimate the importance of the event. If it did not in the end mean reaction, it did mean time gained; and time then, as the result showed, was vital. William H. Seward, about to become Secretary of State, was then in the Senate, and no one was better advised as to the true posture of affairs, and the significance of events. His son now wrote : " The people of the District are looking anxiously for the result of the Virginia election. They fear that if Virginia resolves on secession, Maryland will follow ; and then Washington will be seized." On February 3, Seward himself wrote to his wife: " The election to-morrow probably determines whether all the Slave States will take the attitude of disunion. Everybody around me thinks that that will make the separation irretrievable, and involve us in flagrant civil war. Practically everybody will despair." A day or two later the news came "like a gleam of sunshine in a storm." The disunion movement was checked, perhaps would be checkmated. Well might Seward remark, with a sigh of profound relief: "At least the danger of conflict, here or elsewhere, before the 4th of March, has been averted. Time has been gained."[1] Time was gained; and the few weeks of precious time thus gained through the expiring effort of Union sentiment in Virginia involved the vital fact of the peaceful delivery, four weeks later, of the helm of state into the hands of Lincoln.

Thus, be it always remembered, Virginia did not take its place in the secession movement because of the election of an anti-slavery President. It did not raise its hand against the national government from mere love of any peculiar institution, or a wish to protect and to perpetuate it. It refused to be precipitated into a civil convulsion; and its refusal was of vital moment. The ground of Virginia's final action was of wholly another nature, and of a nature far more creditable. Virginia, as I have said, made State Sovereignty an article — a cardinal article — of its political creed. So, logically and consistently, it took the position that, though it might be unwise for a State to secede, a State which did secede could not, and should not be coerced.

To us now this position seems worse than illogical; it is impossible. So events proved it then. Yet, after

[1] *Seward at Washington*, vol. i. p. 502.

all, it is based on the great fundamental principle of the consent of the governed; and, in the days immediately preceding the war, something very like it was accepted as an article of correct political faith by men afterwards as strenuous in support of a Union reëstablished by force, as Charles Sumner, Abraham Lincoln, William H. Seward, Salmon P. Chase, and Horace Greeley. The difference was that, confronted by the overwhelming tide of events, Virginia adhered to it; they, in presence of that tide, tacitly abandoned it. In my judgment, they were right. But Virginia, though mistaken, more consistent, judged otherwise. As I have said, in shaping a practical outcome of human affairs logic is often as irreconcilable with the dictates of worldly wisdom as are metaphysics with common sense. So, now, the issue shifted. It became a question, not of slavery, or of the wisdom, or even the expediency, of secession, but of the right of the National Government to coerce a Sovereign State. This at the time was well understood. The extremists of the South, counting upon it, counted with absolute confidence; and openly proclaimed their reliance in debate. Florida, as the representatives of that State confessed on the floor of Congress, might in itself be of small account; but Florida, panoplied with sovereignty, was hemmed in and buttressed against assault by protecting sister States.

So, in his history, James F. Rhodes asserts that — " The four men who in the last resort made the decision that began the war were ex-Senator Chestnut, Lieutenant-Colonel Chisolm, Captain Lee, all three South Carolinians, and Roger A. Pryor, a Virginia secessionist, who, two days before, in a speech at the

Charleston hotel, had said, ' I will tell your governor
what will put Virginia in the Southern Confederacy
in less than an hour by Shrewsbury clock. Strike a
blow ! ' " [1] The blow was to be in reply to what was
accepted as the first overt effort at the national coercion of a Sovereign State, — the attempted relief of
Sumter. That attempt, — unavoidable even if long
deferred, the necessary and logical outcome of a situation which had become impossible of continuance,
— that attempt, construed into an effort at coercion,
swept Virginia from her Union moorings.

Thus, when the long-deferred hour of fateful decision came, the position of Virginia, be it in historical
justice said, however impetuous, mistaken, or ill-advised, was taken on no low or sordid or selfish grounds.
On the contrary, the logical assertion of a cardinal
article of accepted political faith, it was made gener-
ously, chivalrously, in a spirit almost altruistic ; for,
from the outset, it was manifest Virginia had nothing
to gain in that conflict of which she must perforce be
the battle-ground. True ! her leading men doubtless
believed that the struggle would soon be brought to a
triumphant close, — that Southern chivalry and fighting qualities would win a quick and easy victory over a
more materially minded, even if not craven, Northern
mob of fanatics and cobblers and pedlers, officered by
preachers ; but, however thus deceived and misled at
the outset, Virginia entered on the struggle others had
initiated, for their protection and in their behalf. She
thrust herself between them and the tempest they had
invoked. Technically it may have been treasonable ;
but her attitude was consistent, was bold, was chivalrous:

[1] Rhodes: *United States,* vol. iii. p. 349.

"An honourable murderer if you will ;
For nought did I in hate, but all in honour."

So much for Virginia; and now as to Robert E.
Lee.   More than once already, on occasions not unlike this, have I quoted Oliver Wendell Holmes's remark in answer to the query of an anxious mother as
to when a child's education ought to begin, — " About
250 years before it is born; " and it is a fact — somewhat necessitarian, doubtless, but still a fact — that
every man's life is largely moulded for him far back
in the ages.   We philosophize freely over fate and
free will, and one of the excellent commonplaces of
our educational system is to instil into the minds of
the children in our common schools the idea that every
man is the architect of his own life.   An admirable
theory to teach; but, happily for the race, true only
to a very limited extent.   Heredity is a tremendous
limiting fact.   Native force of character — individuality — doubtless has something to do with results;
but circumstances, ancestry, environment have much
more.   One man possibly in a hundred has in him the
inherent force to make his conditions largely for himself; but even he moves influenced at every step from
cradle to grave by ante-natal and birth conditions.
Take any man you please, — yourself, for instance;
now and again the changes of life give opportunity,
and the individual is equal to the occasion, — the
roads forking, consciously or instinctively he makes
his choice.   Under such circumstances, he usually
supposes that he does so as a free agent.   The world
so assumes, holding him responsible.   He is nothing
of the sort; or at best such only in a very limited
degree.   The other day one of our humorists took

occasion to philosophize on this topic, delivering what might not inaptly be termed an occasional discourse appropriate to the 22d of February. It was not only worth reading, but in humor and sentiment it was somewhat suggestive of the melancholy Jacques. " We are made, brick by brick, of influences, patiently built up around the framework of our born dispositions. It is the sole process of construction ; there is no other. Every man, woman, and child is an influence. Washington's disposition was born in him, he did not create it. It was the architect of his character ; his character was the architect of his achievements. It had a native affinity for all influences fine and great, and gave them hospitable welcome and permanent shelter. It had a native aversion for all influences mean and gross, and passed them on. It chose its ideals for him ; and out of its patiently gathered materials it built and shaped his golden character.

" And we give *him* the credit."

Three names of Virginians are impressed on the military records of our civil war, — indelibly impressed, — Winfield Scott, George Henry Thomas, and Robert Edward Lee ; the last, most deeply. Of the three, the first two stood by the flag ; the third went with his State. Each, when the time came, acted conscientiously, impelled by the purest sense of loyalty, honor, and obligation, taking that course which, under the circumstances and according to his lights, seemed to him right ; and each doubtless thought he acted as a free agent. To a degree each was a free agent ; to a much greater degree each was the child of anterior conditions, hereditary sequence, existing circumstances, — in a word, of human envi-

ronment, moral, material, intellectual. Scott, or
Thomas, or Lee, being as he was, and things being as
things were, could not decide otherwise than as he did
decide. Consider them in order ; Scott first : —

A Virginian by birth, early association, and marriage, Scott, at the breaking out of the Civil War,
had not lived in his native State for forty years. Not
a planter, he held no broad acres and owned no slaves.
Essentially a soldier, he was a citizen of the United
States ; and, for twenty years, had been the General
in command of its army. When, in April, 1861, Virginia passed its ordinance of secession, he was well
advanced in his seventy-fifth year, — an old man, he
was no longer equal to active service. The course he
would pursue was thus largely marked out for him in
advance ; a violent effort on his part could alone have
forced him out of his trodden path. When subjected
to the test, what he did was infinitely creditable to
him, and the obligation the cause of the Union lay
under to him during the critical period between December, 1860, and June, 1861, can scarcely be over-
stated ; but, none the less, in doing as he did, it cannot be denied he followed what was for him the line
of least resistance.

Of George Henry Thomas, no American, North or
South, — above all, no American who served in the
Civil War, — whether wearer of the blue or the gray,
— can speak, save with infinite respect, — always with
admiration, often with love. Than his, no record is
clearer from stain. Thomas also was a Virginian.
At the time of the breaking out of the Civil War, he
held the rank of Major in that regiment of cavalry of
which Lee, nine years his senior in age, was Colonel.

He never hesitated in his course. True to the flag from start to finish, William T. Sherman, then General of the Army, in the order announcing the death of his friend and classmate at the Academy, most properly said of him : " The very impersonation of honesty, integrity, and honor, he will stand to posterity as the *beau ideal* of the soldier and gentleman." More tersely, Thomas stands for character personified ; Washington himself not more so. And now having said this, let us come again to the choice of Hercules, — the parting of those terrible ways of 1861.

Like Scott and Lee, Thomas was a Virginian ; but, again, there are Virginians and Virginians. Thomas was not a Lee. When, in 1855, the Second United States cavalry was organized, Jefferson Davis being Secretary of War, Captain Thomas, as he then was and in his thirty-ninth year, was appointed its junior Major. Between that time and April, 1861, fifty-one officers are said to have borne commissions in that regiment, thirty-one of whom were from the South ; and of those thirty-one, no less than twenty-four entered the Confederate service, twelve of whom, among them Robert E. Lee, Albert Sidney Johnston, and John B. Hood, became General officers. The name of the Virginian, George H. Thomas, stands first of the faithful seven ; but, Union or Confederate, it is a record of great names, and fortunate is the people, great of necessity their destiny, which in the hour of exigency, on the one side or the other, naturally develops from the roster of a single regiment men of the ability, the disinterestedness, the capacity, and the character of Lee, Thomas, Johnston, and Hood. It is a record which inspires confidence as well as pride.

And now of the two men — Thomas and Lee. Though born in Virginia, General Thomas was not of a peculiarly Virginian descent. By ancestry, he was, on the father's side, Welsh; French, on that of the mother. He was not of the old Virginia stock. Born in the southeastern portion of the State, near the North Carolina line, we are told that his family, dwelling on a " goodly home property," was " well to do " and eminently "respectable;" but, it is added, there " were no cavaliers in the Thomas family, and not the remotest trace of the Pocahontas blood." When the war broke out, in 1861, Thomas had been twenty-one years a commissioned officer; and during those years he seems to have lived almost everywhere except in Virginia. It had been a life passed at military stations; his wife was from New York; his home was on the Hudson rather than on the Nottoway. In his native State he owned no property, land or chattels. Essentially a soldier, when the hour for choice came, the soldier dominated the Virginian. He stood by the flag.

Not so Lee; for to Lee I now come. Of him it might, and in justice must, be said, that he was more than of the essence, he was of the very quintessence of Virginia. In his case, the roots and fibres struck down and spread wide in the soil, making him of it a part. A son of the revolutionary " Light-Horse Harry," he had married a Custis. His children represented all there was of descent, blood, and tradition of the Old Dominion, made up as the Old Dominion was of tradition, blood, and descent. The holder of broad patrimonial acres, by birth and marriage he was a slave-owner, and a slave-owner of the patriarchal type, holding "slavery, as an institution, a moral and political evil." Every sentiment, every memory, every tie conceivable bound him to Virginia; and, when the choice was forced upon him, — had to be made, — sacrificing rank, career, the flag, he threw in his lot with Virginia. He did so with open eyes, and weighing the consequences. He at least indulged in no self-deception, wandered away from the path in no cloud of political metaphysics, nourished no delusion as to an early and easy triumph. "Secession," as he wrote to his son, "is nothing but revolution. The framers of our Constitution never exhausted so much labor, wisdom, and forbearance in its formation, and surrounded it with so many guards and securities, if it was intended to be broken by every member of the Confederacy at will. It is idle to talk of secession." But he also believed that his permanent allegiance was due to Virginia; that her secession, though revolutionary, bound all Virginians, and ended their connection with and duties to the national government. Thereafter, to remain in the United States army would be treason to Virginia. So, three days after Virginia passed its ordinance, he, being then at Arlington, resigned his commission, at the same time writing to his sister, the wife of a Union officer, — " We are now in a state of war which will yield to nothing. The whole South is in a state of revolution, into which Virginia, after a long struggle, has been drawn ; and, though I recognize no necessity for this state of things, and would have forborne and pleaded to the end for redress of grievances, real or supposed, yet in my own person I had to meet the question whether I should take part against my native

State. With all my devotion to the Union, and the feeling of loyalty and duty of an American citizen, I have not been able to make up my mind to raise my hand against my relatives, my children, my home. I have, therefore, resigned my commission in the army ; and, save in defence of my native State, I hope I may never be called upon to draw my sword." Two days before he had been unreservedly tendered, on behalf of President Lincoln, the command of the Union army then immediately to be put in the field in front of Washington, — the command shortly afterwards held by General McDowell.

So thought and spoke and wrote and acted Robert E. Lee in April, 1861. He has, for the decision thus reached, been termed by some a traitor, a deserter, almost an apostate, and consigned to the " avenging pen of History." I cannot so see it ; I am confident posterity will not so see it. The name and conditions being changed, those who uttered the words of censure, invoking " the avenging pen," did not so see it — have not seen it so. Let us appeal to the record. What otherwise did George Washington do under circumstances not dissimilar ? What would he have done under circumstances wholly similar ? Like Lee, Washington was a soldier; like Lee, he was a Virginian before he was a soldier. He had served under King George's flag; he had sworn allegiance to King George ; his ambition had been to hold the royal commission. Presently Virginia seceded from the British empire, — renounced its allegiance. What did Washington do ? He threw in his lot with his native province. Do you hold him then to have been a traitor, — to have been false to his colors ? Such is not your

verdict; such has not been the verdict of history.
He acted conscientiously, loyally, as a son of Virginia,
and according to his lights. Will you say that Lee
did otherwise ?

But men love to differentiate : and of drawing of
distinctions there is no end. The cases were dissimilar, it will be argued; at the time Virginia renounced its allegiance Washington did not hold the
King's commission, indeed he never held it. As a
soldier he was a provincial always, — he bore a Virginian commission. True! Let the distinction be
conceded ; then assume that the darling wish of his
younger heart had been granted to him, and that he
had received the King's commission, and held it in
1775 ; — what course would he then have pursued?
What course would you wish him to have pursued?
Do you not wish — do you not know — that, circum-
stanced as then he would have been, he would have
done exactly as Robert E. Lee did eighty-six years
later? He would first have resigned his commission ;
and then arrayed himself on the side of Virginia.
Would you have had him do otherwise? And so it
goes in this world. In such cases the usual form of
speech is : " Oh! that is different! Another case
altogether ! " Yes, it is different; it is another case.
For it makes a world of difference with a man who
argues thus, whether it is his ox that is gored or the
ox of the other man !

And here in preparing this address I must fairly
acknowledge having encountered an obstacle in my
path also. When considering the course of another,
it is always well to ask one's self the question, —
What would you yourself have done if similarly placed ?

Warmed by my argument, and the great precedents of Lee and of Washington, I did so here. I and mine were and are at least as much identified with Massachusetts as was Lee and his with Virginia; traditionally, historically, by blood and memory and name, we with the Puritan Commonwealth as they with the Old Dominion. What, I asked myself, would I have done had Massachusetts at any time arrayed itself against the common country, though without my sympathy and assent, even as Virginia arrayed itself against the Union without the sympathy and assent of Lee in 1861? The question gave me pause. And then I must confess to a sense of the humor of the situation coming over me, as I found it answered to my hand. The case had already arisen; the answer had been given; nor had it been given in any uncertain tone. The dark and disloyal days of the earlier years of the century just ended rose in memory, — the days of the Embargo, the *Leopard* and the *Chesapeake*, and of the Hartford Convention. The course then taken by those in political control in Massachusetts is recorded in history. It verged dangerously close on that pursued by Virginia and the South fifty years later: and the quarrel then was foreign; it was no domestic broil. One of my name, from whom I claim descent, was in those years prominent in public life. He accordingly was called upon to make the choice of Hercules, as later was Lee. He made his choice; and it was for the common country as against his section.[1] The result is matter of history.

[1] "I fully opened to [Josiah Quincy, then a member of Congress from Massachusetts] my motives for supporting the administration at this crisis [February 1, 1808], and my sense of the danger which a

Because he was a Union man, and held country higher
than State or party, John Quincy Adams was in 1808

spirit of opposition is bringing on the Union. I told him where that
opposition in case of war must in its nature end, — either in a *civil*
war, or in a dissolution of the Union, with the Atlantic States in
subserviency to Great Britain. That to resist this I was ready, if
necessary, to sacrifice everything I have in life, and even life itself."
Memoirs of J. Q. Adams, vol. i. p. 510.

" With regard to the project of a separate Northern Confederacy,
formed in the winter of 1803–4, in consequence of the Louisiana cession, it is not to me that you must apply for copies of the correspondence in which it was contained. To that and to every other project
of disunion, I have been constantly opposed. My principles do not
admit the right even of the people, still less of the legislature of any
one State in the Union, to secede at pleasure from the Union. No
provision is made for the exercise of this right, either by the Federal
or any of the State constitutions. The act of exercising it presup-
poses a departure from the principle of compact, and a resort to that
of force.

" If, in the exercise of their respective functions, the legislative,
executive, and judicial authorities of the Union on one side, and of
one or more States on the other, are brought into direct collision with
each other, the relations between the parties are no longer those of
constitutional right, but of independent force. Each party construes
the common compact for itself. The constructions are irreconcilable
together. There is no umpire between them, and the appeal is to
the sword, — the ultimate arbiter of right between independent States,
but not between the members of one body politic. I therefore hold
it as a principle, without exception, that, whenever the constituted
authorities of a State authorize resistance to any act of Congress, or
pronounce it unconstitutional, they do thereby declare themselves and
their State *quoad hoc* out of the pale of the Union. That there is no
supposable case, in which the *people* of a State might place themselves
in this attitude, by the primitive right of insurrection against oppression, I will not affirm ; but they have delegated no such power to their
legislatures or their judges : and if there be such a right, it is the
right of an individual to commit suicide, — the right of an inhabitant
of a populous city to set fire to his own dwelling-house. These are my
views." J. Q. Adams, December 30, 1828 : *Correspondence between
John Quincy Adams . . . and several citizens of Massachusetts concerning the charge of a design to dissolve the Union* [1829], pp. 32, 33 ;
Henry Adams : *New England Federalism*, pp. 57–8.

" Fellow-citizens, if there be on this side of the grave a subject of

driven from office, a successor to him in the United
States Senate was elected long before the expiration
of his term, and he himself was forced into what at
the time was regarded as an honorable exile. Nor
was the line of conduct then by him pursued — that
of unswerving loyalty to the Union — ever forgotten,
or wholly forgiven. He had put country above party;
and party leaders have long memories. Even so
broad-minded and clear-thinking a man as Theodore
Parker, when delivering a eulogy upon J. Q. Adams
forty years later, thus expressed himself of this act
of supreme self-sacrifice and loyalty to Nation rather
than to State: " To my mind, that is the worst act
of his public life; I cannot justify it. I wish I could
find some reasonable excuse for it. . . . However, it
must be confessed that this, though not the only instance of injustice, is the only case of servile compliance with the Executive to be found in the whole life
of the man. It was a grievous fault, but grievously
did he answer it; and if a long life of unfaltering resistance to every attempt at the assumption of power
is fit atonement, then the expiation was abundantly
made." [1]

deep and awful solemnity to you all, it is this. Here, in this first
resolution appended to the final report of the Hartford Convention, is
the last result of that project which had been fermenting in New
England at least from the spring of the year 1804 until January,
1815. Here it is in its nakedness before you. It is a recommendation to the legislatures of the five New England States to pass laws
for the protection of their citizens, in direct and open resistance
against existing acts of Congress, — against the supreme law of the
land. . . . To resist and defeat that system of measures has been the
greatest struggle of my life. It was that to which I have made
the greatest sacrifices, and for which I have received, in the support
and confidence of my country, the most ample rewards." Henry
Adams: *New England Federalism*, pp. 300, 301.

[1] *Works* (London, 1863), vol. iv. pp. 154, 156.

What more, or worse, on the other side, could be said of Lee?

Perhaps I should enter some plea in excuse of this diversion; but, for me, it may explain itself, or go unexplained. Confronted with the question, what would I have done in 1861 had positions been reversed, and Massachusetts taken the course then taken by Virginia, I found the answer already recorded. I would have gone with the Union, and against Massachusetts. None the less, I hold Massachusetts estopped in the case of Lee. " Let the galled jade wince, our withers are unwrung;" but, I submit, however it might be with me or mine, it does not lie in the mouths of the descendants of the New England Federalists of the first two decennials of the nineteenth century to invoke " the avenging pen of History " to record an adverse verdict in the case of any son of Virginia who threw in his lot with his State in 1861.

Thus much for the choice of Hercules. Pass on to what followed. Of Robert E. Lee as the commander of the Army of Northern Virginia, — at once the buckler and the sword of the Confederacy, — I shall say few words. I was in the ranks of those opposed to him. For years I was face to face with some fragment of the Army of Northern Virginia, and intent to do it harm; and during those years there was not a day when I would not have drawn a deep breath of relief and satisfaction at hearing of the death of Lee, even as I did draw it at hearing of the death of Jackson. But now, looking back through a perspective of nearly forty years, I glory in it, and in them as foes; they were worthy of the best of steel. I am proud now to say that I was their countryman. Whatever differences of opinion may exist as to the

course of Lee when he made his choice, of Lee as a
foe and the commander of an army but one opinion
can be entertained. Every inch a soldier, he was as
an opponent not less generous and humane than formidable, a type of highest martial character; cautious,
magnanimous, and bold, a very thunderbolt in war,
he was self-contained in victory, but greatest in defeat.
To that escutcheon attaches no stain.

I now come to what I have always regarded — shall
ever regard — as the most creditable episode in all
American history, — an episode without a blemish, —
imposing, dignified, simple, heroic. I refer to Appomattox. Two men met that day, representative
of American civilization, the whole world looking on.
The two were Grant and Lee — types each. Both
rose, and rose unconsciously, to the full height of the
occasion, — and than that occasion there has been none
greater. About it, and them, there was no theatrical
display, no self-consciousness, no effort at effect. A
great crisis was to be met; and they met that crisis as
great countrymen should. Consider the possibilities,
think for a moment of what that day might have been;
you will then see cause to thank God for much.

That month of April saw the close of exactly four
years of persistent strife, — a strife which the whole
civilized world had been watching intently. Democracy — the capacity of man in his present stage of
development for self-government — was believed to be
on trial. The wish the father to the thought, the
prophets of evil had been liberal in prediction. It so
chances that my attention has been specially drawn to
the European utterances of that time; and, read in
the clear light of subsequent history, I use words of

moderation when I say that they are now both inconceivable and ludicrous.[1] Staid journals, grave public
men, seemed to take what was little less than pleasure
in pronouncing that impossible of occurrence which
was destined soon to occur, and in committing themselves to readings of the book of fate in exact opposition to what the muse of history was wetting the
pen to record. Volumes of unmerited abuse and
false vaticination — and volumes hardly less amusing
now than instructive — could be garnered from the
columns of the London *Times*, — volumes in which
the spirit of contemptuous and patronizing dislike
sought expression in the profoundest ignorance of
facts, set down in bitterest words. Not only were
republican institutions and man's capacity for self-
government on trial, but the severest of sentences was
imposed in advance of the adverse verdict, assumed
to be inevitable. Then, suddenly, came the dramatic
climax at Appomattox, — dramatic, I say, not theatrical, — severe in its simple, sober, matter-of-fact
majesty. The world, I again assert, has seen nothing
like it; and the world, instinctively, was conscious
of the fact. I like to dwell on the familiar circumstances of the day, — on its momentous outcome, on its
far-reaching results. It affords one of the greatest
educational object-lessons to be found in history; and
the actors were worthy of the theatre, the auditory,
and the play.

A mighty tragedy was drawing to a close. The
breathless world was the audience. It was a bright,
balmy April Sunday in a quiet Virginia landscape,
with two veteran armies confronting each other; one,

[1] *Supra*, pp. 74, 75, 77, 262.

game to the death, completely in the grasp of the
other. The future was at stake. What might ensue?
What might not ensue? Would the strife end then
and there? Would it die in a death grapple, only
to reappear in that chronic form of a vanquished but
indomitable people writhing and struggling in the
grasp of an insatiate, but only nominal victor, — such
a struggle as all European authorities united in confidently predicting?

The answer depended on two men, — the captains
of the contending forces. Grant that day had Lee
at his mercy. He had but to close his hand, and his
opponent was crushed. Think what then might have
resulted had those two men been other than they were,
— had the one been stern and aggressive, the other
sullen and unyielding. Most fortunately for us, they
were what and who they were, — Grant and Lee.
More, I need not, could not say; this only let me add,
— a people has good right to be proud of the past and
self-confident of its future when on so great an occasion it naturally develops at the front men who meet
each other as those two met each other then. Of the
two, I know not to which to award the palm. Instinctively, unconsciously, they vied not unsuccessfully each
with the other, in dignity, magnanimity, simplicity.

> "Si fractus illabatur orbis
> Impavidum ferient ruinæ."

With a home no longer his, Lee then sheathed his
sword. With the silent dignity of his subsequent
life, after he thus accepted defeat, all are familiar.
He left behind him no querulous memoirs, no excul-
patory vindication, no controversial utterances. For
him, history might explain itself, — posterity formu-

late its own verdict. Surviving Appomattox but a
little more than five years, those years were not un-
marked by incidents very gratifying to American recollection; for we Americans do, I think, above all
things love magnanimity, and appreciate action at
once fearless and generous. We all remember how
by the grim mockery of fate — as if to test to the
uttermost American capacity for self-government —
Abraham Lincoln was snatched away at the moment
of crisis from the helm of state, and Andrew Johnson substituted for him. I think it no doubtful anti-
cipation of historical judgment to say that a more
unfortunate selection could not well have chanced.
In no single respect, it is safe to say, was Andrew
Johnson adapted for the peculiar duties which Booth's
pistol imposed upon him. One of Johnson's most
unhappy, most ill-considered convictions was that our
Civil War was a conventional old-time rebellion; that
rebellion was treason; that treason was a crime; and
that a crime was something for which punishment
should in due course of law be meted out. He, therefore, wanted, or thought he wanted, to have the scenes
of England's Convention Parliament and the Restoration of 1660 reënacted here, as a fitting sequel of our
great conflict. Most fortunately, the American people then gave evidence to Europe of a capacity for
self-restraint and self-government not traceable to
English parentage or precedents. No Cromwell's
head grinned from our Westminster Hall; no convicted traitor swung in chains; no shambles dripped
blood. None the less Andrew Johnson called for
"indictments," and one day demanded that of Lee.
Then out spoke Grant, General of the Army. Lee

he declared was his prisoner. He had surrendered to him, and in reliance on his word. He had received assurance that so long as he quietly remained at his home, and did not offend against the law, he should not be molested. He had done so ; and, so long as Grant held his commission, molested he should not be. Needless, as pleasant, to say, what Grant then grimly intimated did not take place. Lee was not molested ; nor did the General of the Army indignantly fling his commission at an accidental President's feet. That, if necessary, he would have done so, I take to be quite indubitable.

Of Lee's subsequent life, as head of Washington College, I have but one anecdote to offer. I believe it to be typical. A few months ago I received a letter from a retired army officer of high character from which I extract the following : " Lee was essentially a Virginian. His sword was Virginia's, and I fancy the State had higher claims upon him than had the Confederacy, just as he supposed it had than the United States. But, after the surrender, he stood firmly and unreservedly in favor of loyalty to the Nation. A gentleman told me this anecdote. As a boy he ran away from his Kentucky home, and served the last two years in the rebel ranks. After the war he resumed his studies under Lee's presidency ; and on one occasion delivered as a college exercise an oration, with eulogistic reference to the ' Lost Cause ' and what it meant. Later, General, then President, Lee sent for the student, and, after praising his composition and delivery, seriously warned him against holding or advancing such views, impressing strongly upon him the unity of the Nation, and urging him to devote himself loyally to maintain the integrity and the honor of the United States. The kindly paternal advice thus given was, I imagine, typical of his whole *post bellum* life." Let this one instance suffice. It illustrates all. Here was magnanimity, philosophy, true patriotism, — the pure American spirit. Accepting the situation loyally and in manly, silent fashion, — without self-consciousness or mental reservation, — he sought by precept, and yet more by a great example, to rebuild through constitutional action the shattered community, of which he was the most observed representative, in accordance with the new conditions by war and fate imposed upon it. Talk of traitors and of treason! The man who pursued that course and instilled that spirit had not, could not have had, in his whole being, one drop of traitor's blood or conceived a treacherous thought. His lights may have been wrong, — according to our ideas then and now they were wrong; but they were his lights, and, acting in full accordance with them, he was right.

But, to those thus speaking, it is sometimes replied, " Even tolerance may be carried too far, and is apt then to verge dangerously on what may be better described as moral indifference. It then, humanly speaking, assumes that there is no real right or real wrong in collective human action. But put yourself in his place, and to those of this way of thinking Philip II. and William of Orange, Charles I. and Cromwell, are much the same; the one is as good as the other, provided only he acted according to his lights. This will not do. Some moral test must be applied, — some standard of right and wrong.

" It is by the recognition and acceptance of these

that men prominent in history must be measured, and approved or condemned. To call it our Civil War is but a mere euphemistic way of referring to what was in fact a slaveholders' rebellion, conceived and put in action for no end but to perpetuate and extend a system of human servitude, a system the relic of barbarism, an insult to advancing humanity. To the furtherance of this rebellion, Lee lent himself. Right is right, and treason is treason; and as that which is morally wrong cannot be right, so treason cannot be other than a crime. Why, then, because of sentiment, or sympathy, or moral indifference, seek to confound the two? Charles Stuart and Cromwell could not both have been right. If Thomas was right, Lee was wrong."

To this I would reply, that we, who take another view, neither confound, nor seek to confound, right with wrong, or treason with loyalty. We accept the verdict of time; but, in so doing, we insist that the verdict shall be in accordance with the facts, and that each individual shall be judged on his own merits, and not stand acquitted or condemned in block. And, in the first place, Philip II. and William the Silent, Charles I. and Cromwell, were not much the same, nor, indeed, in any respect the same. Characteristics cannot thus be left out of the account; individuality will not be ignored. So long as men differ, in one we will continue to see those qualities we all seek to commemorate; in another, those we condemn. Philip II. was not an admirable character; William the Silent was. In the second place, the passage of the centuries works wonders, especially in the views men hold of the causes and incidents of civil strife. We

get at last to see that the right is never wholly on one
side; that in the grand result all the elements were
fused. Things then are seen with other eyes. Take,
for instance, one of the final contentions of Charles
Sumner, that, following old-world precedents, founded,
as he claimed, in reason and patriotism, the names
of battles of the war of the rebellion should be removed from the regimental colors of the national
army, and from the army register. He based it on the
ground that, from the republics of antiquity down to
our days, no civilized nation ever thought it wise or
patriotic to preserve in conspicuous and durable form
the mementos of victories won over fellow-citizens in
civil war. As the sympathizing orator said at the
time of Sumner's death, " Should the son of South
Carolina, when at some future day defending the Republic against some foreign foe, be reminded by an
inscription on the colors floating over him that under
this flag the gun was fired that killed his father at
Gettysburg ? " This assuredly has a plausible sound.
" His father; " yes, perhaps. Though even in the
immediately succeeding generation something might
well be said on the other side. Presumably, in such
case, the father was a brave, an honest, and a loyal
man, contending for what he believed to be right, —
for it, laying down his life. Gettysburg is a name
and a memory of which none there need ever feel
ashamed. As in most battles, there was a victor and
a vanquished ; but on that day the vanquished, as
well as the victor, fought a stout fight. If, in all recorded warfare, there is a deed of arms the name and
memory of which the descendants of those who participated therein should not wish to see obliterated

from any record, be it historian's page or battle-flag,
it was the advance of Pickett's Virginian division
across that wide valley of death in front of Cemetery
Ridge. I know in all recorded warfare of no finer,
no more sustained and deadly feat of arms. I have
stood on either battlefield, and, in scope and detail,
carefully compared the two ; and, challenging denial,
I affirm that the much vaunted charge of Napoleon's
guard at Waterloo, in fortitude, discipline, and deadly
energy will not bear comparison with that other. It
was boy's work beside it. There, brave men did all
that the bravest men could do. Why, then, should
the son of one of those who fell coming up the long
ascent, or over our works and in among our guns, feel
a sense of wrong because " Gettysburg " is inscribed
on the flag of the battery, a gun of which he now may
serve? On the contrary, I should suppose he would
there see that name only.

But, supposing it otherwise in the case of the son,
— the wound being in such case yet fresh and green,
— how will it be when a sufficient time has elapsed
to afford the needed perspective? Let us suppose a
grandson six generations removed. What Englishman, be he Cavalier or Roundhead by descent, did
his ancestor charge with Rupert or Cromwell, did
he fall while riding with levelled point in the grim
wall of advancing Ironsides, or go hopelessly down
in death beneath their thundering hoofs, — what de-
scendant of any Englishman who there met his end,
but with pride would read the name of Naseby on his
regimental flag ? What Frenchman would consent to
the erasure of Ivry or Moncontour ? Thus, in all these
matters, time is the great magician. It both mellows

and transforms. The Englishman of to-day does not apply to Cromwell the standard of loyalty or treason, of right and wrong, applied after the Restoration; nor again does the twentieth century confirm the nineteenth's verdicts. Even slavery we may come to regard as a phase, pardonable as passing, in the evolution of a race.

I hold it will certainly be so with our Civil War. The year 1965 will look upon its causes, its incidents, and its men with different eyes from those with which we see them now, — eyes wholly different from those with which we saw forty years ago. They — for we by that time will have rejoined the generation to which we belonged — will recognize the somewhat essential fact, indubitably true, that all the honest conviction, all the loyalty, all the patriotic devotion and self-sacrifice were not then, any more than all the courage, on the victor's side. True! the moral right, the spirit of nationality, the sacred cause of humanity even, were on our side; but, among those opposed, and who in the end went down, were men not less sincere, not less devoted, not less truly patriotic according to their lights, than he who among us was first in all those qualities, — men of whom it was and is a cause of pride and confidence to say, " They, too, were countrymen! "

Typical of those men — most typical — was Lee. He represented, individualized, all that was highest and best in the Southern mind and the Confederate cause, — the loyalty to state, the keen sense of honor and personal obligation, the slightly archaic, the almost patriarchal, love of dependent, family, and home. As I have more than once said, he was a Virginian of the Virginians. He represents a type which is gone,

— hardly less extinct than that of the great English nobleman of the feudal times, or the ideal head of the Scotch clan of a later period; but just so long as men admire courage, devotion, patriotism, the high sense of duty and personal honor, — all, in a word, which go to make up what we know as Character, — just so long will that type of man be held in affectionate, reverential memory. They have in them all the elements of the heroic. As Carlyle wrote more than half a century ago, so now — "Whom do you wish to resemble? Him you set on a high column. Who is to have a statue? means, Whom shall we consecrate and set apart as one of our sacred men? Sacred; that all men may see him, be reminded of him, and, by new example added to old perpetual precept, be taught what is real worth in man. Show me the man you honor; I know by that symptom, better than by any other, what kind of man you yourself are. For you show me there what your ideal of manhood is; what kind of man you long inexpressibly to be, and would thank the gods, with your whole soul, for being if you could."

It is all a question of time; and the time is, probably, not quite yet. The wounds of the great war are not altogether healed, its personal memories are still fresh, its passions not wholly allayed. It would, indeed, be cause for special wonder if they were. But, I am as convinced as an unillumined man can be of anything future, that when such time does come, a justice, not done now, will be done to those descendants of Washington, of Jefferson, of Rutledge, and of Lee who stood opposed to us in a succeeding generation. That the national spirit is now supreme and the nation cemented, I hold to be unquestionable.

That property in man has vanished from the civilized world is due to our Civil War. The two are worth the great price then paid for them. But, wrong in respect to these as he may have been, and as he was proved by events to be, the Confederate had many great and generous qualities; he also was brave, chivalrous, self-sacrificing, sincere, and patriotic. So I look forward with confidence to the time when he, too, will be represented in our national Pantheon. Then the query will be answered here, as the query in regard to Cromwell's statue, put sixty years ago, has recently been answered in England. The bronze effigy of Robert E. Lee, mounted on his charger and with the insignia of his Confederate rank, will from its pedestal in the nation's capital gaze across the Potomac at his old home at Arlington, even as that of Cromwell dominates the yard of Westminster upon which his skull once looked down. When that time comes, Lee's monument will be educational, — it will typify the historical appreciation of all that goes to make up the loftiest type of character, military and civic, exemplified in an opponent, once dreaded but ever respected; and, above all, it will symbolize and commemorate that loyal acceptance of the consequences of defeat, and the patient upbuilding of a people under new conditions by constitutional means, which I hold to be the greatest educational lesson America has yet taught to a once skeptical but now silenced world.

INDEX

ADAMS, C. F., American Minister at London, protests against the construction of the *Alabama*, 49; presents demand for reparation, 80, 81; on Russell's proposal of a joint commission, 87; on reaction of English policy, 87, 90; interview with Clarendon, 88; with Forster, 89; with Oliphant, 90; on recognition of Southern belligerency, 92, 97; on rejection of the Johnson-Clarendon Convention, 103; on Motley, 139; on the indirect claims, 192.

Adams, J. Q., on State sovereignty, 414–416 n.; personal effect of his views, 415.

Alabama, keel laid, 39; purpose patent, 45; preparation of equipment, 46; evasion, 50; responsibility for the evasion, 50 n.; equipped, 50; purified of evasion, 51; ravages, 60; received in British ports, 62; destruction, 78; Great Britain disclaims responsibility, 80; status, 197. *See also* Alabama claims.

Alabama claims, Great Britain refuses to consider, 80, 81; Great Britain neglects a favorable opportunity to settle, 82-87; Derby favors a settlement, 91; Sumner on greatness of the controversy, 95; and British withdrawal from America, 104, 147, 156, 159, 162, 177, 209, 210, 241; retroactive effect on English belligerency proclamation, 115, 207, 209, 211; Fish on basis of settlement, 125, 162; influence of Franco-Prussian War,

130, 133, 135; Grant's message of 1870 on, 134; British comment, 134; Grant's proposals, 161; Great Britain ready to negotiate, 163, 177. *See also* Indirect claims, Johnson-Clarendon Convention, Treaty of Washington.

Alexander II. of Russia, assassination, 258.

Alexander, E. P., Confederate general, retentive memory, 9; consultation with Lee after Sailor's Creek, 10, 20, 22; advises dispersion of Lee's army, 11, 22-24; account of Lee at Appomattox, 20-30.

Alexandra trial, 60.

American Historical Association, tabooes political discussions, 274; political duty, 275, 282, 293, 299, 303, 336-338; purpose, 275.

Americans, English opinion during the Civil War, 35, 61–66, 74-78, 267; change in English opinion of, 261–264, 266-273; insight into English feelings, 264; wealth and masterfulness, 266, 269, 272; transmutation of national character, 271, 272. *See also* United States.

Annexation, Grant's policy, 109, 113. *See also* Canada, Imperialism, Manifest Destiny.

Appomattox, Confederate army blocked at, 10, 21; condition of Confederate army at, 22, 29; temporary Confederate success, 26; Custer's demands, 27; the apple tree, 28; meeting of Lee and Grant, 28; importance of the episode, 418-420. *See also* Lee, R. E.